FIRE

ON THE

TRACK

FIRE
ON THE
TRACK

Betty Robinson and the Triumph
of the Early Olympic Women

ROSEANNE MONTILLO

CROWN
NEW YORK

10\17

Copyright © 2017 by Roseanne Montillo

Published in the United States by Crown, an imprint of the Crown
Publishing Group, a division of Penguin Random House LLC, New
York.
crownpublishing.com

CROWN is a registered trademark and the Crown colophon is a
trademark of Penguin Random House LLC.

Library of Congress Cataloging-in-Publication Data is available upon
request.

ISBN 978-1-101-90615-6
Ebook ISBN 978-1-101-90617-0

Printed in the United States of America

Book design by Ellen Cipriano
Jacket design by Elena Giavaldi and Alane Gianetti
Jacket photograph by ullstein bild/Getty Images

10 9 8 7 6 5 4 3 2 1

First Edition

*To the forgotten athletes of
the early Olympics*

CONTENTS

FIRE
ON THE
TRACK

PROLOGUE

W hen Lee Newland spied the plane hovering just above his head that afternoon, he was surprised by how low it was flying. He had heard the growling of its propeller growing steadily louder somewhere behind him, then had looked up to see the glint of a cherry red biplane gaining altitude close to Riverdale's gritty factories. It was Sunday, June 28, 1931, and just as he'd been doing every Sunday and every other day of the week for the past several months, Newland had been driving his truck through the town, as his job entailed.

It was not a day of rest for him, or for anyone else. Working hard, if one had a job, was a matter of course—even on weekends. The country was in the midst of a depression, and though most experts already had a hankering for dating its beginning to the infamous "Black Thursday" and "Black Tuesday," October 24 and 29, 1929, when the stock market had crashed, people had been feeling the pinch of a slumping economy for several years. It was a challenging time for the nation as a whole: 1931 was the second warmest year in all of Chicago, in all of the Midwest; the heat wave that summer killed nearly eight hundred people, though it was only a prelude of the one to come in 1936, when almost five thousand people succumbed to the hot spell. And President Herbert Hoover's plans for stabilizing the national economy were proving inefficient. At the time Newland found himself in his truck that Sunday, nearly a quarter of the country's adult population was unemployed, and many of those who worked did so at a reduced schedule. In many towns the situation was even more dire, with nearly 50 percent of their residents out of work, particularly the unskilled workers.

Newland was one such unskilled worker, and he was painfully aware of his deficiencies. For most of the last decade, he had held a decent job in one of the many brick factories along the banks of the Calumet River, the pay he earned allowing him to own a home, his truck, and some pride. But the company had gone bankrupt, his job had disappeared, his house had been repossessed, and all that remained of his former life was his truck, the payments recurring every month—even though the contraption was virtually run to the ground.

A tall and naturally husky man in his late thirties, Newland had of late been working for the local funeral parlor, locating bodies that had been left abandoned around the city's streets and collecting the corpses of those who had died alone. The job was as unsavory and disquieting as it sounded and had earned him the unfortunate local nickname "body chaser." There was no particular method or talent to what he did, only sheer luck. He stepped into his truck and drove along the ugly sprawl of boarded-up buildings and clusters of uninhabited homes, often finding nothing but a stray dog or two hiding under heaving porches or, in the winter, homeless families huddling over charcoal braziers. If that was the case, he ventured farther afield, searching for the bodies of those who might have gone out of their way to make their death a private ordeal.

People died alone all the time. In the past few weeks the heat had reduced the members of the community by several dozen, the thermostat inching up to well over 100 degrees Fahrenheit and rendering the air a soupy mess that clutched at one's throat. And if the weather didn't kill somebody, the collapsing economy surely could. Those who were already poor tightened their belts even further as their poverty deepened, though their daily lives didn't change a great deal. The crash came more as a surprise for the wealthy, those who had gone to bed rich one night and woken up paupers. Hustling for work was not in their nature; nor was pleading for food at the corner of a local store, waiting in long bread lines, or scavenging through refuse bins for the next meal to feed their children. They did not know what to make of their new status, and to many of them, death often seemed a more dignified option than poverty.

That's when Newland found them. They would wash up along the edge of the Calumet River, where the stench and scum of the waters rose with the heat; or facedown in weed-choked yards where children had once played and women had hung their sheets out to dry; or flat at the bottom of an abandoned brownstone, clutching an old photograph or some other personal item in their cold hands.

NEWLAND HAD BEEN driving for several hours that Sunday when he noticed the plane, just a quick flash in the sky leaving a thin trail of smoke behind it, like the long string from a kite. Powered by a standard OX5 motor, it was a Waco 10 biplane, a bright red and very popular model in the area, neither too difficult to fly nor tremendously advanced in its design. It whirled back and forth, its acrobatics not unlike those in a show Newland had seen once in a barn field near Chicago.

He stopped the truck in the middle of the road and watched the plane. It rose slowly at first, then more swiftly as it reached an altitude he figured was as good as six hundred feet, when suddenly, as it turned left, it seemed to stall in midair.

He saw the nose-dive and first thought it some kind of fancy maneuver by a pilot feeling too secure in his abilities. He then realized that the plane was in some sort of trouble and wondered if the weather was to blame. It had rained for the past four days, strong thunderstorms accompanied by lightning flashes streaking through the sky and breaking the night slumber. Perhaps the airplane had been hit by lightning, but when Newland scanned the horizon for further thunderbolts he might have missed, he saw none.

The plane plummeted and disappeared, crashing somewhere in the acreage nearby. Newland pressed on his truck's accelerator and sped toward the grounds. He would be making a stop by the funeral parlor later, after all.

THE PLANE HAD landed in a soggy parcel of land belonging to the Whiting Corporation, between 159th Street and Cicero Avenue in the village of Harvey, some twenty miles from Chicago. Newland waded through the underbrush and reached the spot just as another man, Peter Adamaski, who had witnessed the accident from his porch, rushed toward the wreckage. There was a curl of smoke billowing from the plane's rear, but no flames were visible. It had not exploded, most likely because it had landed with its nose deep into the wet terrain, blunting the impact and embedding itself several feet into the soil. Inside the shambles were wedged two youths: a young woman still buckled into the front seat, and the boy who had been the pilot sitting in the rear open cockpit.

The girl wore goggles and a small leather helmet the likes of which, reports would later detail, Amelia Earhart had worn on her flight across the Atlantic. She was outfitted in a silky ensemble that was now soaked in blood and that to the rescuers did not look appropriate for flying. Both of the boy's legs were twisted at an unusual angle, his right ankle appearing to have taken the brunt of the collision, shreds of bones protruding grotesquely from the flesh. Yet the boy was still alive, his chest heaving up and down. The girl, on the other hand, who had suffered at the very least a broken leg, judging by the bone poking out, appeared to be dead.

Neither of the rescuers recognized the two victims, which was unusual; most everybody in this general area knew everybody else. The men removed them from the plane and carefully placed them on the wet ground, inspecting them before Adamaski rushed the boy to his Model T and quickly drove him to the nearby Ingalls Memorial Hospital. Newland lifted the girl in his arms and hurried to his truck, where he deposited her in the bed and drove to the funeral home to collect payment.

There the parlor's director searched through the girl's clothing, intent on identifying her. Even after the accident, she was still pretty, a girl of average height with shoulder-length chestnut hair and in remarkably excellent shape. She had the faint look of a movie star, though he couldn't place which one. But as he began to prepare his instruments, he detected something peculiar. He leaned his ear closer to the girl's lips and realized that she was slowly taking faint breaths in and out. They were tiny gasps indeed, yet—without question—she was still breathing.

PART ONE

AMSTERDAM, 1928

CHAPTER ONE

ON TRACK

Early 1928 had been one of the coldest winters Charles Price could remember. He felt a gust of wind blow against his neck as he stood on the platform waiting for the train, then huddled deeper into his heavy coat. He looked up toward a gray sky heavy with clouds, removed his wire-rimmed glasses, and wiped away the snowflakes that had rested on his lenses. He assumed the wind was coming from the west and, looking up once again, further guessed that the flurries would soon turn into a more substantial snowfall. A science man, he delighted in gathering such details from his surroundings. He was eager to get home, even though a stack of papers on his desk was awaiting him. Correcting his students' assignments could wait, but he preferred to deal with them right away. He was a disciplined man, never giving precedence to leisure when a task awaited him.

At thirty-seven, Price shared his home with his wife, Ethel, a few years younger than he, and his three children: Jane was now twelve; Raymond, eight; and baby Harry was still in diapers, at barely a year old. Their house, just one stop away from Thornton Township High

School in Harvey, Illinois, where he taught biology, was a modest one-story brick structure at the end of a bland, dimly lit lane a few blocks north of Main Street, where the spindly trees wouldn't reach their maturity for decades to come. He knew the house he had purchased was small, but it nonetheless thrilled him that he owned it, as much as it thrilled him that he owned the latest-model radio he had seen advertised in the local newspaper, *The Pointer*—a splurge, but one that he had desired since the gadget hit the market. The radio afforded him intervals of respite and entertainment that he could not get anywhere else.

As he tightened his coat, he hovered at the edge of the platform, where he finally heard the whistle of the train as it rattled over the elevated rails. From his vantage point on the platform, Price looked up toward Broadway Avenue, where the main doors of the high school were located. It had become the largest school serving the Riverdale, Harvey, and Dolton areas, as well as the other smaller communities nearby. A history buff, he had learned when he started teaching that the school dated to 1892, when it had been a mere schoolroom located in the basement of the First Methodist Church. Back then, only twenty-two students had crowded the single room, though three years later the number had already grown to seventy-five.

Price liked his job. He was a graduate of the University of Illinois, where he had earned a bachelor of science degree and also pursued his interest in sports. Now he taught biology and was one of the coaches of the boys' track team. He noticed several of his students crossing the sodden front lawn of the main building and heading toward the train station. He presumed they were continuing their conversations about the snow that had recently fallen, canceling the latest football game, or about the play that would take place in the auditorium two weeks from Sunday. He knew the topics well; they had made up the bulk of the students' chats in homeroom that morning. Most were not in a hurry, despite the inclement weather, but walked in small groups at the leisurely pace young people always tended to adopt. That is, all but one. A lone girl caught his attention.

Betty Robinson had broken away from the rest and was running to catch the incoming Illinois Central commuter train—the same one for which Price stood waiting on the platform. He turned to his left, from which the train was now fast approaching, and then back toward his student. Quickly calculating the speed at which both were traveling, he knew Betty would never make it; it was a simple matter of time versus speed.

She was one of his biology students and in his homeroom, too; he knew her to be a good pupil and enormously popular with both her teachers and her peers. The previous November he had seen her perform in one of the school plays, a production his family had thoroughly delighted in. Betty's hazel eyes, which the audience had been able to glimpse even from their seats, had shone from the stage and had captivated his wife, as had her short bobbed hair, an odd shade that was neither bright blond nor the color of hay.

He watched, mesmerized, as Betty filled her lungs with the cold air and lunged toward the station. There was nothing particularly sophisticated about her running; she was obviously untrained. With big long strides, arms aflutter and hair buoyed by the wind, a book bag slung over one shoulder and papers in hand, she appeared as if she were running to catch a runaway dog or a wayward child. But her ungainliness amused him, and he admired her determination. Being a coach, he appreciated her efforts, regardless of their seeming futility. She was still some distance away when the train stopped in front of him and its doors opened; he walked inside, finding a seat near the window.

He removed a newspaper from his pocket and settled in for the short ride home. There was no need to remove his coat or to make himself too comfortable. He was about to deposit his briefcase on the empty spot next to him when a stack of books landed on the seat.

He recognized them: they included the required biology text he assigned to his classes. He looked up to see Betty Robinson, shaking snow off herself before sitting down. She unbuttoned the top of her jacket, flashing him a confident grin that would eventually earn her the nickname of "smiling Betty."

Price was stunned. Having mentally estimated her running speed against the train, he'd never thought it possible that she would reach it on time; he should have removed the stopwatch from his briefcase and timed her.

He asked her if she liked to run. She shrugged her shoulders and said she did, although no more than anything else she enjoyed. She was also a reader; she liked to care for her nephews and enjoyed the company of her cousins. Most especially, though, she enjoyed dancing and performing in school plays, she said, her face brightening as she spoke of those activities.

The train whistled as it slowly made its way to the next stop, snow coming down a little more heavily. But she *did* like running, Price insisted. Betty casually told him that she liked to run up and down her neighborhood with her friends and across her family's and neighbors' backyards during the late afternoons, when the sun slowly dipped behind the clotheslines and the grass was cool against her feet. She ran during the church picnics her parents brought her to, winning almost as many ribbons for those races as she did for her cakes. She also ran at her father's Masonic meetings, with the same results.

Had she ever been timed? Price asked. Had anyone ever used a stopwatch to see how fast she could run? Betty seemed a little taken aback by this and said no one had ever shown any interest in doing that.

The train slowed as it approached Price's stop. When it pulled into the station, its doors opened and he got up. Before leaving, he turned back to Betty and made her a proposition that would change the course of her days: Would she mind meeting him tomorrow afternoon in the first-floor corridor of their high school? He wanted to time her, to see how fast she could *really* run.

BETTY CONSIDERED HIS request; she liked Mr. Price, with his quiet, awkward manners and the thoughtfulness he brought to even the most boring lessons he taught. So she agreed, and the doors closed behind him. She watched him walk over the elevated platform into the waning light, still unsure of what the conversation had been about or why it had mattered so much to him that she'd come for a run tomorrow.

CHAPTER TWO

A NEW ARRIVAL

Elizabeth "Betty" Robinson was born on August 23, 1911, in Riverdale, Illinois, to Harry and Elizabeth Robinson. Harry had arrived in the United States in the late months of 1888 from his native village in Ireland, where he had spent his free hours between dawn and dusk practicing his own athletic interests, including sprinting up and down the country lanes, all the while dreaming of ways to cross the Atlantic. People had watched as the years went by and the exercises strengthened him, so that by the time he had managed to leave his country, the tall young man, who stood over six feet, had distinguished himself by his powerful legs.

After disembarking in the United States, Harry remained in New York for a few short months before making his way to the Midwest, where he met his future wife, Elizabeth Wilson, a young woman born in Goderich, Ontario, Canada. Lizzie and her two sisters, Debora and Fannie, had been born to parents who had also emigrated from Ireland. Just months after Lizzie's birth, the Wilsons moved to Chicago, where nearly two decades later she married Harry Robinson. Lizzie was a very opinionated woman who'd gone to work in a candy factory and who, unlike her fellow workers, did not know how to bite her tongue or hide her thoughts when in the presence of a man. Perhaps it was this innate straightforwardness that initially appealed to Harry. He had no idea that the willful girl would eventually drive him mad and would, in her later years, develop a peculiar fondness for watching wrestling on television.

Just days after their marriage, the two moved to Nebraska, where in 1899 their first daughter, Jeannette "Jean" Robinson, was born. Not two years after Jean's birth, the restless feeling Harry had always suffered from reared its head again, prompting him to relocate the family back to Illinois. Chicago and its surrounding towns were providing favorable opportunities for recently arrived immigrants and business-minded men like himself. By 1901, thousands had flocked to the Windy City, but it was one of its suburbs that appealed most to Harry, an up-and-coming community in need of a new infusion of blood: Riverdale.

The Calumet River to the north and 138th Street to the south bordered the town. It was only seventeen miles south of Chicago, a mere extension of it—far enough away to be called a village—yet close enough for residents to be able to find work in the city's factories or shop in its fine stores. The village worked very hard to develop a separate identity from its larger neighbor, so much so that an article went so far as to state, "There is no desire on the part of Riverdale settlers to be part of Chicago. Indeed, it would cause quite a stir if anything like that should come up."

By 1878, an abundance of lumberyards had grown along the Calumet, what is now the Indiana River, replenishing the area with additional employment. It wasn't long before settlers discovered that the clay in the area made for excellent bricks, and soon large brickyards such as Purlington & Company and Pather Brickyards sprang up and dotted the landscape. With that discovery eventually came an influx of Canadian, French, British, and Irish workers who made Riverdale their home, the Robinsons included.

For Harry, this was the place where he wanted his family to settle. He witnessed the industrial efficiency of a small town on the move, with factories planting roots there and bringing with them not only prosperity but also a sense of optimism as everyone rushed headlong into the new century.

By 1901, a second daughter, Evelyn, was born. Though a son had not appeared, as Harry had always wished, he and his wife now believed that her childbearing years were over—until 1911. It was on a steamy August day in 1911 that Betty Robinson made her debut, during one of the hottest spells the town had ever felt. This precocious child with hazel eyes and blond hair (which would eventually darken to a more chestnut hue) quickly became the apple of the family's eyes.

Harry was a happy man. By the time he had gained employment at the Riverdale Bank, which had opened in 1917, little more than a thousand inhabitants populated Riverdale. During the years spanning the 1850s to the 1890s, railroad construction had provided employment to countless immigrants and was also a vital link between the village and Illinois's larger communities. In the last half of the nineteenth century, streetcar companies such as the Chicago Surface Lines lengthened their service from Michigan Avenue to Riverdale's 138th Street and Leydan Avenue. Some six years later, Riverdale was connected to Roseland by the Red Line Company. And in 1918, the Acme Steel Company relocated to Riverdale, purchasing large swaths of land along the river and adding to the fleet of factories and brickyards on its banks. Though the steel plant did not add much physical charm to the landscape, the fact that it employed nearly twelve hundred people made up for its unsightliness.

Right away, Harry became a part of the town's establishment, ingraining himself so deeply in the bank's daily operations that by 1928 he had become its president. His employees respected him, though occasionally they regarded him as rigid. They would respect him more only a year or two down the line, when the bank, just like other banks across the country, teetered on the verge of bankruptcy, yet he continued to employ them. But in 1928, he had no vision of a darker future looming ahead, nor could he be bothered to think about it.

As he settled into middle age, his hair, a thick mop into which he smeared a daily dab of pomade, began to sprout gray at the temples. He sported a sweeping black mustache that he kept neatly trimmed and curled at the ends. He had become a prominent member of the town, moving about its streets in double-breasted, dark-tailored suits over pressed white shirts, a sign of success. Another mark of his achievements was buying a large, three-story brownstone for his ever-expanding extended family. It was located at 3 East 138th Street, then a quiet, respectable leafy street inhabited by other families raising young children of their own.

On the first floor lived Evelyn and her family. Prior to World War I, Evelyn had married a local boy, Frank Mills. Frank, who had been drafted, returned from the war with a reminder of his time abroad that didn't fully disclose itself until 1930, when he died of complications from mustard gas exposure. He never saw his daughters, Betty and Patricia, grow up into young ladies, or his son, Jack, follow his footsteps into the army.

Jean occupied the third floor with her own family. She had married James "Jim" Rochfort, a man of Irish ancestry (a fact that pleased Harry enormously), and from that union a boy was born, James Jr. Jim had also served in World War I, his own memento of the ordeal being a Distinguished Service Cross, of which he never spoke. During his time abroad he had also developed gloomy moods and a certain reticence that set him apart from the rest of the family, and whatever ghosts still plagued him he tried to keep at bay with solitary backyard games of basketball or baseball, which Betty Robinson often watched while leaning against the window of her bedroom on the second floor she shared with her parents.

It was with Jean and Jim that Betty had formed a unique alliance.

Her mother and Evelyn were two of a kind, sharing similar characteristics: both were loud, stubborn, always wanting to get their way. Two peas in a pod, relatives said—a pod neither Betty nor Jean could penetrate. It was Jean and her family, happily more than dutifully, who attended most of Betty's school and afternoon performances, and it was to them she related her adventures, her musical achievements, the small tokens of flowers and candies boys handed to her. It was to Jean and Jim that she took her fretful thoughts when she lost the lead part in a school play and to them that she spoke when a boy she had taken a liking to seemed to prefer her cousin, a much homelier and less charming girl. And in time it would be Jean and Jim—Jim in particular—she would rely on once her running career took flight.

Because Betty's father worked long hours and was involved in the church activities and his various clubs, he was rarely home, and when he was, he retired to his comfortable chair to read. Whereas Jim, a stoic younger man, was always available and listened intently to Betty regardless of the triviality of her words, even when they involved boys, a subject he knew she could not speak of with her strict Irish Catholic parents. For Jim, religion did not matter as much, particularly after his return from the war. Betty appreciated that, for she had never felt the same religious devotion that the rest of her family did.

Her sisters were already married by the time Betty started elementary school, and her father, a pillar of the community who—unlike others in the area—had money to spare, delighted in splurging on his youngest child. He was also a little more lenient in his parenting skills, a fact Betty soon learned to take full advantage of.

Betty was schooled at the Bowen Grammar School at 137th and State Streets, a one-room schoolhouse where many of the children who attended were related to one another. After her school day ended, she was allowed to join a sewing club, become involved in a children's theater group, and enroll in ballet lessons, and she was free to partake in whatever other activities she desired. Newspaper photographs of her as a child taken at various recitals show a pretty, smiling young girl in a blush-colored tutu and ballet slippers, a large bejeweled tiara atop her head and her hands folded before her, striking poses for the camera.

She also learned to play the guitar, and a photograph of her in *The Pointer* features her as part of the 1920 school band, wearing a checkered dress cut high at the waist while draping an arm over her cousin Evelyn Palmer, who played the piano. Theodore Hedtke, her bandmate, the tenor sax player, stands apart, and Theodore Reich is on the drums and xylophone. Her friend Betty Wike strikes a pose while holding a guitar, and Oliver Schwab shows off his hands on the violin.

By 1925, Betty had moved from the printed page and taken over the airwaves. Bowen School pupils were offered the opportunity to give broadcast performances from WLS (the Sears-Roebuck station) in Chicago, and "Miss Robinson," *The Pointer* noted, "gave the solo titled 'Buttercups and Daisies.' "

She also played the piano, the natural outcome being regular recitals. During the summer she attended Miss Naomi Grant's classes at the A.O.U.W. Hall, where each Monday night the pupils displayed their talents to the Riverdale community. Of particular interest was June 29, 1925, when she played two solos. The paper gushed over her with the headlines "A Perfect Little Lady" and "Revel of the Wood Nymphs."

What *The Pointer* didn't tell its readers, or preferred to keep at bay, perhaps thinking it inappropriate for such a gentle little girl, was that Betty, aside from all her singing, dancing, and recitations, also handled a rifle with the ease of a hunter, a skill her father had taught her early on. It was not unusual for Betty, at five or six, to arm herself with a shotgun and aim it masterfully at a target propped up against a stump in the woods behind her home—wearing the same pink tights and fluffy ballet slippers she had donned hours earlier at a dance recital. She always shot at her mark carefully, yet she never displayed a moment of hesitation. In fact, it was a skill she practiced and carried with her throughout her life.

By 1928, sixteen-year-old Betty had grown to be a slight girl of five feet, six inches tall, not quite 120 pounds, with those bewitching hazel eyes and light chestnut hair that she kept bobbed short in the fashion of the latest starlets. Her grades were straight A's, and her social calendar was full to the brim: Theater Club, sewing classes, Latin Club, Glee Club, and the Girls' Club of the Oak Hospital Party Committee, of which she was the chair. Those activities alone would have made her a popular student at Thornton Township. That she resembled a Hollywood ingenue also lent her a certain allure. Her bright personality, sociable demeanor, and genuine interest in other people further solidified her stellar reputation.

CHAPTER THREE

A NEW PAIR OF SHOES

Thornton Township High School, a large brick building flanked by oak trees, reveled in the reputation of its boys' football team, baseball team, and track team, as well as its other various male sporting clubs. Like most high schools in the country, it had few athletic activities for the girls. It did not even have a track team for them, though the young women had been requesting one for years and the coaches had been offering their support.

Betty arrived to meet Coach Price in the first-floor corridor minutes after the last bell of the day sounded. She was punctual as always, a trait her father had instilled in her from a very young age. Right away Price introduced her to Bob Williams, a student whose help he had enlisted to time her.

Robert "Bob" Williams was a senior and a member of the track team. A tall, handsome boy with a haphazard flop of sandy hair falling across his forehead and large dark eyes, he had, according to the 1928 yearbook, fixed his ambition on becoming "the coach's right hand man." In following that aspiration, he had quickly assented to Coach Price's request for help and now, clad in his track uniform, was holding a stopwatch in his hand. Bob was acquainted with Betty from afar and had attended several of her plays. Those were always popular not only in school but also in the community, weepy romances concocted by the theater teacher, which all the girls clamored to take part in, while the boys were often conned into participating to earn extra credit. (Luckily for Bob, his grades were always very good.) He smiled at her as he looked down at her shoes: she was wearing not track shoes but simple scuffed white tennis shoes. He was not surprised; track shoes were ugly, and she struck him as the kind of girl who paid attention to such things.

Betty followed Coach Price toward one end of the corridor, while Bob moved to the other. Prior to Betty's arrival, Coach Price had measured out 50 yards, nearly the length of the entire corridor, and placed markers at each end. The corridor was otherwise empty, but Betty heard voices just beyond it as the after-school bustle of the afternoon's activities got under way. She was grateful that today she wasn't missing any social engagements, though tomorrow she was required to attend Latin Club. She did not know what she would have done if Coach Price had asked her to meet him tomorrow; she never missed her club's commitments.

Betty had not run in any official races and knew nothing of the rudimentaries of track and field. Feeling apprehensive, she asked Coach Price what to do. For the moment, he told her, she was simply to bend one knee, crouch down, take a deep breath, and at the sound of his whistle run toward Bob as fast as she could. He was interested in her speed more than her form or technique. That would come later.

Betty did as told, crouching, breathing, and setting off—waging war against the watch until she reached Bob, sweat pouring down her forehead, her lungs expanding with the effort. It was extremely hot in the corridor, as humid as it was when she was running by the lakeside during the summer holidays with her family. At the other end, Coach Price held his thumb firmly on the stopwatch.

He then asked Betty to return to her starting position and repeat the run. She walked back toward him, crouched down once again, and awaited the blow of the whistle before racing toward Bob. Catching her breath, she reached him seconds later and wiped her face with a towel he handed her. When she looked back at Coach Price, he was staring down at the stopwatch in disbelief.

Price had clocked her at 6.2 seconds in the 50-yard dash. It was an astonishing time, and he knew it. Betty, ripe with untapped potential, had just run the length of the corridor barely a tenth of a second shy of the US indoor record. Remarkably, she had no sense of what she had just accomplished. Coach Price immediately told her he'd like to coach her, as well as allow her to train with the boys' team. The two of them could also run together after her classes. She agreed, said she would like that. All she needed now, he told her, was an appropriate pair of track shoes.

CHAPTER FOUR

THE DEBUT

Betty felt impeded by her new shoes, unaccustomed to their tight grip. The pair she'd purchased in Chicago's Loop district, with Bob's help, molded snugly around her feet, the tightly drawn strips emphasizing the curves of her toes. She tried to wiggle her toes, but they wouldn't budge. The black shoes were a far cry from the ballet slippers hanging on a hook behind her bedroom door. They were hard, unyielding, could be heard from afar, whereas the ballet shoes left no echo. There was a rhythm to the track shoes as they beat over the cinder tracks—a rhythm that some likened to heartbeats.

Although she still didn't know precisely what she was training for, she had started a daily workout regime, Coach Price awaiting her as the last bell of the day rang. When she was not running with the boys, she was back in the corridor, going through a series of drills, runs, and jumps. Coach Price doled out his directions quietly and sparingly, following each set of exercises with a nod of his head that indicated that she should repeat them.

Betty soon realized that running after a nephew and running toward a finish line were two very different things. She also learned that there were many details that most amateur runners never paid attention to until they started working with a coach, and that running on spiked shoes was not the only obstacle. She learned that sprinters use the balls of their feet first, landing on their toes, while keeping their bodies either totally upright when reaching maximum velocity or leaning forward when running against the wind. A runner had to appear relaxed, and even when entirely exhausted and agitated, she had to try to keep her facial muscles calm. Would-be athletes also learned that different race distances made different demands on the body, that the muscles required a certain amount of oxygen to work properly, and that the mind was just as important as the body: the two needed to work in unison to excel in a proper race.

As Coach Price knew, Betty could develop the leg muscles so crucial for a runner only by performing a variety of strength-training exercises that included jogging at various speeds, hopping from leg to leg and atop boxes, and leaping over hurdles of various heights. Acceptable running starts were practiced over and over again, and in the process her posture, angle of the elbows, and position of the trunk in relation to the rest of the body were adjusted. While all of this strengthened her body and improved endurance, it also increased her mental stamina. It was hard work, but the hours went by quickly.

COACH PRICE POSSESSED an innate talent and a reputation for spotting athletic strength, though it seemed odd to those he came in contact with that he was privy to such insights; he did not look the part of a recruiter. Even in his youth, his bland appearance had conveyed nothing extraordinary. That did not change as he aged. In a faculty yearbook photograph taken a year or so before 1928, Coach Price came across as a bespectacled, sallow-eyed educator fighting a receding hairline and the inevitable decline of middle age. In person, that was the case as well. Still, people were drawn to the quietness of his character, to that unidentifiable quality that allowed them to share their secrets without prying into his (which they didn't believe he had).

And that was how Price wanted it, as there were areas of his life few people knew about and that he fought hard to keep to himself. For example, he did not want people to know about the property he owned, or that he had a lot more money on hand than others did. He also had a weakness for women, a quirk that few were aware of; nor did people need to learn that he had fathered several children while involved in a handful of previous relationships, or that his two oldest children, who lived with him in Harvey, had not been born to his wife (though she had agreed to take them in) but were the products of short-term relationships that had ended badly. Even fewer would understand why he would go on to marry four times and have numerous affairs as an aging man, earning him a complex romantic reputation that would accompany him until his death. Nonetheless, he had an undeniable aptitude for discovering athletic abilities. And he did not coach merely to express the devotion he felt toward his students or to find the next star athlete, or because he was content to stand in the background. He did it (mostly) to satisfy his own unfulfilled youthful desires. He had been a college runner and had coveted an athletic career of his own, a dream that had never materialized.

He had been hired to teach the students not only the technicalities of a race or of becoming an athlete but also the art of it, for although it was completed in a manner of seconds, even the 100 meters was an art form. He also taught them about the lonely intimacy one had to develop with a track, an aspect of racing a runner had to get used to, as he had. There was an affinity between an athlete and a field, he often told his students. It was to the track that an athlete brought his or her disappointments. It was there that a runner learned to work with the elements: with the wind, which could provide refreshing coolness on a hot summer's day or hinder one's speed on a blustery afternoon; with the rain, beating down against one's skin or muddying the track; with the sun, scorching hot in the summer, yet rejuvenating throughout the rest of the year.

Parents in Riverdale, Harvey, and the surrounding towns took their boys to Coach Price for advice on how to fortify their natural talent and succeed as athletes. It was the finish line that interested them most, how quickly they could cross it. But for Coach Price, their talent, if there was any at all, appeared well before they broke through a ribbon. There were things he noticed firsthand: Were there any visible glitches that needed to be adjusted? How were their form and posture? How far forward did an athlete lean? Was his trunk consistently that erect during a run, or did he have to work hard at making it appear so? When did an athlete begin decelerating, how far before the finish line? And, most important, did the athlete have to think about all of this, or did it come naturally?

A true athlete possesses various qualities and characteristics that differentiate him or her from a casual runner, including personal dietary likes and dislikes and their sleeping patterns. Yet, though most coaches believed that real runners were born with a natural instinct, Coach Price knew that there was much that he could teach them. Usually, by the time he was done with an athlete for the season, the techniques had become second nature. It took a lot of effort to make those kids look and act effortlessly.

Girls, on the other hand, were never taken to Coach Price; instead, parents enrolled them in the county's finest sewing classes, as it seemed irrational to them that their daughters might want to participate in track and field. Those who did want to participate in competitive running were discouraged, as it was considered too masculine. Even the *American Physical Education Review*, which most teachers like Coach Price read, in 1913 had reported that "for girls there should be little competitive track and field work." But a well-trained woman, Coach Price knew, could race down a track as well and as fast as a man.

.   .   .

IN EARLY MARCH 1928, just two weeks after he began training with Betty, Coach Price was paging through *The Pointer* when he spotted an advertisement for a track meet sponsored by the Institute Banking Society. It was an amateur competition held in one of Chicago's amphitheaters, and, without Betty knowing it, he added her name to the list of participants and paid her entrance fee.

Although it was premature to register her in a competition, he wanted to see how she compared with other women athletes. From the start, his aim had been to increase her speed quickly and help her participate in as many meets as possible, working until she reached the one he wanted most: the Olympic tryouts in Newark, New Jersey, in July.

This was not the usual tactic a coach used when training an athlete. If a coach was faced with the prospect of working with an athlete who showed promise and had a whole season ahead of him or her, training began slowly, emphasizing a basic workout routine that helped develop good technique and endurance. As the season progressed, so would the training, the bulk of it stressing high-speed sprinting. It was the job of a good coach to make sure the athlete warmed up properly before every practice, to reduce the likelihood of injuries. Coaches also always advised short sessions of light jogging, leg extensions, and leg lifts, as well as back extensions and lunges. Each exercise had to be done correctly, step-by-step, as it could otherwise cause injuries.

But Coach Price behaved differently with Betty; given their limited time, there was greater urgency to his instructions. And though she immersed herself in learning the elementals, he pushed her to run at her fastest speed right away. How was she to know what her body could tolerate if she did not push herself? There was no time to waste.

Betty was unaware of it, but at the meet she would be running against the seemingly invincible Helen Filkey, the twenty-year-old undisputed superstar of the sport. A tall girl with fine porcelain skin and a bouncy dark bob akin to that of a Hollywood actress she adored, Helen had taken the track-and-field scene by storm. For the last three years, she had won the Amateur Athletic Union (AAU) National Championships and the 60-yard hurdles, not to mention setting world records in the 70- and 100-yard dashes.

THE NIGHT OF March 30, 1928, the Institute Banking Society meet was crowded with attendees wanting to see if Helen could maintain those records. The boisterous fans had gathered hours earlier, and as Betty ran laps around the corridor, getting to know her new track shoes, she could hear the crowd's earsplitting cheers. Bob had tagged along and now explained how the shoes should feel on her feet; the difference of the fit in the toes compared to the heels; what to do in case of discomfort; how to dig in her spikes at the starting line.

One thing Betty could tell for certain: the shoes were ugly. Black and sturdy, they certainly commanded attention. The first track shoes were actually quite heavy and hot on the foot, very similar to a man's dress shoe, with six sharp half-inch spikes embedded in the sole. The shoe was originally made of tough cowhide, although over the years it evolved into leather. It was ugly, most athletes agreed, though their most pressing concern was its burdensomeness.

Only a decade or so earlier, the German cobbler Adolf Dassler, an amateur runner himself, had begun experimenting with various materials to see if he could devise a softer shoe that could gain better traction on the track. Track shoes had to not only possess strength and flexibility, he determined, but be light enough to catapult an athlete forward, giving him or her an edge over opponents. He tinkered with rubber, then designed different shapes geared toward various events athletes took part in, though in essence they were all the same basic design: narrow at the tip, with sharp spikes inserted toward the front to assist in gaining speed as the runner went over the cinders. Those protrusions, pointy like claws, were usually made of metal and screwed tightly to the bottom of the shoes. Dassler's improvements were such that they revolutionized not only the way sprinters prepared for a race but also how they ran.

Adolf Dassler and his brother Rudolf started a company they first named Addis, though family conflicts eventually caused a rift between the brothers and each went his separate way. Adolf's Addis in time evolved into Adidas, while Rudi went on to build his own sportswear company, known worldwide as Puma.

THE CROWD ROSE to its feet as the runners entered the auditorium, cheering so loudly the floors vibrated with applause as each of the competitors' names was called. Betty took her place at the starting line and looked for Bob and Coach Price, who stood at the periphery, watching quietly. She turned and smiled toward Helen, noticing the hard, fierce look on her face, the set of her jaw as she scanned the crowd, determined. Betty settled at the starting line, awaiting the command, trying to remember all that she'd learned in the past few weeks.

The most important element of a race is achieving maximum speed right off the line. A strong push from a powerful takeoff would propel her through the rest of the race at top velocity. Coach Price, like others, advocated this wisdom of a strong push and a quick start. He had trained Betty to relax and stretch out her limbs before standing up on the balls of her feet, before her toes touched the ground. She then had to lean slightly forward with her hands an inch or so behind the starting line.

Betty felt a flutter in her stomach as she crouched down in her lane, staring forward along the track, awaiting the starter's signal. She ran through the mental checklist: Her arms formed a ninety-degree angle, pulled back and turned upward. She'd been cautioned to relax her hands and to do the same with the muscles of her jaw and her face. She looked ahead, bent forward slightly, and concentrated on her arms. Her legs felt tight and ready to explode as she excitedly waited for the gun to go off.

The auditorium was so hot and loud—with thousands of spectators chanting Helen's name—that Betty could barely think. She saw the official grasp the pistol, curl his finger around the trigger, then lift it up to the sky and pop it.

The voices became louder as the runners dashed off down the track. Betty felt her breath catching in her chest, the muscles in her legs burning with effort, the breeze kicked up by the other competitors hitting her face like a gust of wind during an early-morning heat. The race was quick and dizzying; suddenly it was over before she even had time to think about it too much.

As expected, Helen broke the ribbon. She took the lead right away and did not let up until she crossed the finish line, clipping off two-fifths of a second from the previous best run and tying the world indoor record for the 60-yard dash. The noise in the auditorium was overwhelming; fans and reporters barreled down the bleachers and crowded around her.

Bob and Coach Price stepped off their benches and reached Betty, who stood at the sidelines watching the commotion, pleased with her second-place finish. It was odd, but it seemed to her that they were the only ones who had noticed her placement, that she had nearly overcome the champion at the last moment, when, having made a push for the finish line, she had sidled up next to Helen and forced her to work even harder for her win. For a split second, Betty had imagined overtaking her and been disappointed when she hadn't.

But Betty was mistaken. Helen had become aware of Betty running next to her; the newcomer had forced her to dash down the track faster than ever before. In fact, the idea that Betty, running her first official race, had finished second was not something that Helen could easily disregard. Meanwhile, officials of the Illinois Women's Athletic Club (IWAC) had also noted Betty nipping at Helen's heels, eager and awash with potential. They had observed Betty's drive, the look in her eyes that told them she had the requisite hunger to be the first. So even though she had not won the coveted blue ribbon, the IWAC rewarded Betty with an invitation to join their club and to train under its banner. She quickly accepted.

CHAPTER FIVE

OFF TO THE RACES

Membership in the IWAC offered Betty far more than the opportunity to train in their facilities. She was given a freedom that other girls of her age did not enjoy. On Mondays, Wednesdays, and Fridays, when her school day ended, rather than heading to Coach Price, she boarded the I.C. train on 137th Street from Riverdale and took a forty-five-minute ride to Chicago's Randolph Station.

The city's chaotic streets greeted her, an array of congestion, a multitude of acrid smells, people of every sort, and an abundance of criminals (or so the papers had visitors believe). In the early 1830s, much in the same vein as Betty was doing in 1928, a young man named John Wentworth, from Dartmouth College, had made his way to Chicago, and the cosmopolitan atmosphere of its people had struck him as odd. In a letter home to his family he'd written: "People from almost every creed and almost every opinion . . . Jews, Christians, Protestants, Catholics, and infidels . . . Calvinists and Armenians . . . nearly every language was represented. . . . Some were quite learned and some were ignorant." And for the first time in her life, Betty, too, was being confronted by a combination of creeds and races.

When she did not take the city bus to the IWAC, she walked across the river and up Michigan Avenue, leaning against the rails and watching the wide sweep of the waters below her or staring at the buildings mushrooming behind her. She marveled at this opportunity given to her, reveled in her solitary pursuits, and was thrilled by her sudden independence. It invigorated her that her mother was home, her father was working at the bank, and neither of them could keep a watch on her. That her sisters were in their apartments, enveloped in their domestic duties, while her friends were confined by their school responsibilities and she was free to ride the train, roam the streets to the IWAC, spend the afternoon with persons unknown to her family and friends, and then return home in the dark. It was the evenings that produced the most enthusiasm, the times she left the IWAC late and came across heavily rouged women and elegant men entering places of grandeur or ill repute, cabarets and movie theaters. (Especially the movie theaters, for by the end of the decade, Chicago had nearly enough movie seats to accommodate every one of the city's inhabitants, should they all have wanted to attend a movie at the same time.)

The city's mystique rubbed off on her, thrilling her, while this newfound adulthood also provoked an increased measure of arrogance that her schoolmates soon became aware of, an untapped self-confidence. In that respect, Betty was like many of the young modern women of her time, showing signs of empowerment that worried most men.

Having earned the right to vote, women now were fighting for equality in other areas of their lives as well. Many had moved into the workplace (though household duties still awaited them after a long day on the job). They no longer settled for marriages that did not satisfy them, and unprecedented numbers sought divorces. Sexually, the modern woman was becoming increasingly aware that she was free to choose her partner. In the age of the flapper, women now sheared their hair, shortening it with the same eagerness that they shortened their hemlines. They drank in public and smoked if they desired. Where and when would this end? Next, critics feared, young women would be trespassing into the man's domain not only at work but even in sports, where they were already making strides.

By the time Betty walked into the IWAC, women were not just breaking all kinds of barriers—they were setting records. Glenna Collett Vare, who had learned to play golf at the age of fourteen, had been dominating the American women's golf scene throughout the 1920s. In 1922, her skills had earned her the first of six US championships. Vare was also a proficient swimmer, but Gertrude Ederle surpassed her. In 1926, Ederle, an American competitive swimmer and bronze medalist in the 100-meter freestyle in the 1924 Olympics, became the first woman to swim the English Channel; she did it in fourteen hours and twenty-one minutes, besting the male record by nearly two hours and earning the nickname "Queen of the Waves."

Betty was aware of all this, felt lucky to have become a part of this group, and intended to reap the benefits of these new circumstances. Perhaps it was not by mere chance that track and field had come into her life now, at the cusp of this new women's movement, this next step of radical change, as some of her teachers deemed it.

"THIS BEAUTIFUL 17 story, newly erected building, a monument to Chicago's largest Women's Club, rises majestically in plain sight of all those travelling on Michigan Boulevard," *The Chicago Tribune* wrote. And it was majestic. When Betty arrived at the IWAC for the first time, the seventeen-floor Italian Renaissance–style building, with its arched windows and low cornices, drew her eyes upward. On the first two floors, specialty shops had been opened, including a small bakery, its sweet buttery smells wafting out. Continuing upward, the third to ninth floors were occupied by offices, whose employees strutted in and out of its doors always in a hurry. The men wore dark suits and neatly pressed white shirts, their oxfords polished and brief-cases in hand. Betty watched the women wobble on tall heels, their blue or brown midcalf-length pleated skirts accentuated by frilly silk blouses. They kept their hair in place with shiny bobby pins, stray wisps tucked behind their ears with well-manicured nails.

From the tenth to the seventeenth floors, the IWAC held court; the tenth to the fifteenth were reserved for music and singing classes. Betty sometimes heard the instrumental notes through the walls, even as far up as the top two floors, where many of the athletes were engaged in athletic pursuits, while others were finishing up their workouts and changing out of their uniforms.

Betty usually rode the elevator to the sixteenth floor and checked in with a guard at the desk. Then she headed for a small room in the back used as a changing area, where she exchanged her skirt and blouse for shorts and a jersey emblazoned with the IWAC logo, before heading to the short track to practice.

The facilities were shared with coaches from DePaul University, who assisted the IWAC with their track program. Betty and the other athletes often went to them for advice. They also used their time there to view other sprinters and learn the jargon of the sport, along with witnessing proper athletic form. She learned, for example, that when she accelerated from a still position to a quick-moving one, it was re-ferred to as a change in velocity and not speed, though the monikers frequently referred to the same thing. When such tidbits were shared, Betty and the other athletes would gather around the coaches, scrib-bling feverishly in tiny notebooks they kept stashed in their pockets.

If they wanted to be taken seriously in track and field, they reck-oned, they had to study the sport much like they studied their subjects in school, with the same curiosity and respect they reserved for al-gebra, history, and the English language, those coaches advised. The older students, who were studying physical education at the local uni-versities, especially thirsted for the kind of knowledge that books did not share, information that they were unable to gain elsewhere and that they wished to someday impart to others.

Betty also learned that her runs with Coach Price had been not a fluke but something deeper; that, just as he had told her, there was talent within her that needed to be explored. She looked forward to another competition, working hard to become aware of her body, from the natural lean of her back, to which she had never paid attention before, to which leg was innately stronger than the other and whether or not she had a tendency to impulsively look sideways or forward. She worked tirelessly, remaining at the IWAC for hours, well into the evening, running up and down its track until her feet hurt, often until they bled. When the afternoon darkened into evening, only then would she shower, wrap her toes in tape, and scramble back to Riverdale.

ON JUNE 2, 1928, she made her first public appearance under the auspices of the IWAC at Soldier Field, at the Central AAU Meet.

Soldier Field had its beginnings in 1919, when the firm of Holabird and Roche was commissioned to design the stadium, which opened in October 1924 under the name of Municipal Grant Park Stadium. In 1925, it was renamed Soldier Field, thanks to the efforts of Chicago Gold Star mothers to commemorate soldiers fallen in combat. Able to hold more than 100,000 attendees, by 1928 it had already hosted several celebrated large-scale events, including the famed 1927 Jack Dempsey–Gene Tunney heavyweight boxing match. The Central AAU Meet, however, was not one of the noted episodes for which the field would become renowned; it wasn't even well attended.

The local papers allotted only an inch of space to the meet, and officials feared that such lackluster advertisement wouldn't draw much of a crowd. That evening, a stiff wind blew into the stadium. Though the few spectators did not mind it, it was bad news for the competitors: referees, in gauging the wind's direction with a handkerchief, warned the athletes that any new record set by them would not likely be confirmed due to the climatic conditions. Not every official cared much about wind direction, even though all of them knew that a breeze blowing against athletes' backs gave them what was considered an unfair push. Prior to official wind gauges, which would not be in use until 1936, when introduced in Berlin, wind direction was determined in a more haphazard manner, generally with the aid of a handkerchief.

But wind indeed had a profound effect on athletes. Usually, as an athlete accelerated, her body leaned forward by small degrees until she reached her maximum velocity, and then a process of slowing down began, the posture adjusting to it. Spectators would notice a more pronounced lean when sprinters ran against the resistance of a strong headwind. This forward lean allowed them to balance against the wind, though their velocity wasn't reduced. (A tailwind, naturally, had the opposite effect, pushing the athlete forward.) That was the situation the athletes found themselves in that particular evening in Soldier Field.

Betty waited impatiently on the sidelines. She had been training since the end of March and suspected she could beat her competitors, even those who had been running for years. Her stride had lengthened, her timing was improving, she was developing greater muscular strength, and her confidence was growing in proportion to her equally growing ego. Her mind told her that she could do this, and she listened to that inner voice, as she did to Coach Price's words. As they trained, Price kept her abreast on whose records she was breaking, whose timing she was sinking, whose speed she was beating or nearing—so that each time she dashed down the corridor of her school or the street near her house, she felt she was running with an invisible opponent, against whom she was always victorious.

In developing a strategy, an athlete still had to take into account things that were often beyond her control: nerves had a way

of surfacing at the most random times; and—although architectur-
ally similar—not all tracks were created the same way, so an unseen
crinkle in the pattern could be detrimental during a race. As much
as she had learned, a competitor could be having a much better day.

In the stands, excited as no one else, sat Betty's brother-in-law
Jim Rochfort. As the races were about to begin, he listened to the
spectators sitting behind him: the DeVry family, who were obvious
fans of Helen Filkey. They cheered loudly, unafraid of making fools
of themselves. Jim often turned to look at them, smiling at the young
William DeVry, who smirked as he suggested that Helen could win
the competition with her hands tied behind her and running backward. (A few years later, Jim would understand the passion behind
William's comment. The boy would go on to marry Helen and build
an empire as the chairman of the board of directors of the DeVry
Technical Institute.)

INSIDE THE STADIUM, the din of the crowd resonated wildly as the
official's fingers curled around the trigger. Her own skills with a gun
gave Betty a distinct advantage, as she knew the official's maneuvers:
the moment when he took the pistol in his hand, the initial intake
of air into his lungs, the small twitchy movements he would make
before the gun went off, and the instant he would pull the trigger.

She felt her muscles come alive as she dashed down the track, the
auditorium pulsating wildly as time seemed to stop altogether yet simultaneously blast forward faster than she could ever have imagined.
The atmosphere in the building was rambunctious, not the quiet still-
ness of a crowd that appreciated her ballet performances. In its stead
was an entity alive with energy, pushing her ahead as she broke the
ribbon.

She ran her race in twelve seconds, and to everyone watching
it seemed that she had hardly broken a sweat. But the fact that her

timing was four-tenths of a second better than the official record wouldn't matter, for, as the referees had suspected, the wind blowing through the stadium had helped her achieve it.

Studies performed decades later would show that a tailwind of 2 meters per second during a 100-meter race would have improved her time by only one-tenth of a second. But at the time, there was no gadget to provide such a sophisticated measurement. Betty didn't much care why she had won or that her record would not be documented. Even if the wind had indeed pushed her forward, she reasoned, she would have won. What mattered to her was that she had beaten Helen Filkey.

As she stood at the podium to receive her first-place ribbon, she went over the precise moment when she had decided to beat Helen; she didn't have the wildest notion where it had come from, that conscious decision to leave her competition behind and go for the win. Right off the starting line, she'd sensed she was already ahead of her opponent. She had decided to let her guard down a little but then had recalled Coach Price telling her that some kind of a record was on the line, which had spurred her onward with renewed vigor until she reached the end.

BY BEATING HELEN, Betty had become a serious contender for the Olympic team. Her win also caught the attention of the *Evening American*, which immediately decided to sponsor her way to the Olympic trials in Newark, New Jersey, set for July 4. She would now join a group of young competitive athletes whose talents had carried them to the Garden State and on whose shoulders the United States' inaugural women's track-and-field team would be built.

CHAPTER SIX

OFF TO THE GAMES

The first modern Olympic Games took place in 1896 in Athens, where twenty-two countries and more than 250 athletes participated in fifty-three events. None of the participants was a woman. The man known for reviving the Games was Baron Pierre de Coubertin, a French aristocrat who envisioned a rebirth of the classical Greek ideal of exposing perfect young athletes to the rigors of physical contests.

Although in time it would be accepted that the modern Games were due to Coubertin's efforts, the reality was that international athletic festivals had already been taking place in Europe (and occasionally in North America) well before he became involved. The English physician William Penny Brookes and the Greek merchant and philanthropist Evangelis Zappas were essential early advocates. While Coubertin was aware of their attempts to bring the Games back into the limelight, he never gave them credit for providing him with the models for the Olympics he eventually created.

Coubertin brought to the Games his own visions, ideas, and

biases, particularly regarding female athletes. And though he did not discount the idea that women were capable of great things, he did not think those skills extended to sports. But some people begged to disagree with him.

THE FIRST WOMEN to officially participate in the modern Olympic Games did so in Paris in 1900, where nineteen competed in tennis and golf. In 1904, archery made its Olympic appearance in St. Louis, though it was added only as an exhibition sport. Although those athletes made it look as though women were taking strides toward inclusion, nothing could have been further from the truth. They were all upper-class ladies who most of the time studied, read poetry, and led lives of leisure. They pursued sports not for their competitive benefits or health advantages, but simply for their social perks.

Only competitive swimming, which was added to the 1912 Games in Stockholm, seemed to add a layer of respectability and seriousness. But as increasing numbers of women entered the Games, their male counterparts and most of the International Olympic Committee (IOC) members wondered: What was to become of their beloved and esteemed male-only games?

THE FIRST FEMALE track-and-field athletes owe their admittance to the daring Frenchwoman Alice Milliat. Born in Nantes in 1884, Milliat had earned her living as a translator, though her real passion was rowing. She heartily believed that physical education could contribute to a person's character, regardless of gender. Sport, she felt, "develops personalities, gives confidence and courage, and generates a resourceful spirit." She believed this to be especially important for a woman, whose primary tasks—society insisted—were to procreate and to stand by her husband's side as he rose to professional heights.

Milliat became a sports administrator, and along the way was at the forefront of several demonstrations. Crucially, in 1912, she organized Femina Sport, a Parisian sports club that morphed into the Fédération des Sociétés Féminines Sportives de France, or French Federation of Women's Sporting Clubs. It was through the French Federation that she lobbied the IOC and the International Association of Athletics Federations (IAAF) to allow women's track and field to be officially included in the Olympic competitions. She argued that although tennis and golf, and even archery and swimming, had already made their debuts, it was high time that track and field be included.

Officials insisted that track and field was classically a men's sport and that female athletes would develop physical traits that would render them unattractive and possibly foster lesbian tendencies or—worse—turn them into men. The sports practiced by the female Olympians at the time added prestige to the games. Track and field, on the other hand, was something that anyone could take part in, including those who had no economic advantages.

But Milliat felt that class segregation had no place in Olympic competition. The IOC should open the games either to everyone or to no one at all. Therefore, after the IOC's repeated refusal, the only solution was to have an Olympiad geared exclusively toward global female athletes. During those games, women would be free to compete against one another regardless of social status, in as many events as they qualified for, and without adhering to all of the IOC rules. To this end, Milliat formed the Fédération Sportive Féminine Internationale (FSFI).

In 1921, Monaco hosted the inaugural Women's Olympics. The event was a success, but it paled in comparison to the one held in Paris the following year, where eleven events were scheduled. Opening day in Monaco welcomed participants from England, Ireland, France, and several other European countries, as well as the United States. More than twenty thousand spectators turned out to watch, attracting the attention of the IOC. In 1923, at one of its meetings, the question posed by Milliat was once again placed on the agenda. The committee's response to what it referred to as the "Feminine Question" was blunt: "They can do whatever they want, as long as it is not in public."

Despite the Women's Olympics' early successes, the IOC still refused to allow women equal entrance. That only spurred Milliat to go further with her own games, and in 1926, the Women's Olympics were held in Gothenburg, Sweden. That was the biggest spectacle yet, as Milliat had invited more countries to send the best athletes they had. The opening ceremonies included fireworks, choirs, parades, and a flight of white doves. The Swedish royal family attended, providing much-needed worldwide publicity. Milliat hoped that the IOC would take note of those prominent guests. "People are interested in the Women's Olympics," she said. "During the last games in Gothenburg, all foreign diplomats spent a night traveling from Stockholm to watch the athletic events. Is that not proof itself?"

The Women's Olympics' popularity was beginning to grate on the IOC. While the women's games had once been presumed to be merely a passing fad on the part of women who could not come to terms with their place in society, it was now becoming a public and direct challenge.

More irritating to the IOC was that Milliat insisted on using the same name: Olympics. How were people supposed to know the difference? Which one was the true Olympics? What worried them was the fact that Milliat had appropriated a name, a competition, and a vision that was theirs. "The Commission expressed concerns about the title 'Olympic' that this organization of the games appropriated itself and will take measures asking the FSFI's help so that this title, which belongs to the IOC, be exclusively reserved to the games organized by the IOC every first year of each Olympiad," the IOC concluded at a meeting in November 1925.

But Milliat had never intended for women to stand apart from the rest of the competitors. She yearned for them to gain the opportunities they deserved, to be seen not as intruding in a male-dominated arena but as equals. By building and transforming the Women's Olympics into a marquee event that was popular, distinguished, and respected—featuring disciplined athletes whose concentrated efforts had allowed them to reach the pinnacle of their careers—she had achieved her goal.

After a barrage of IOC meetings in late 1926, an agreement was reached: the IOC would add track and field to the roster of women's events starting with the 1928 Olympics, but it would retain the sole title of Olympic Games. If Milliat wished to continue with her female-only games, she would have to change the name to the Women's World Games. (All of this occurred nearly two years after Pierre de Coubertin, the strongest opponent to women's participation in track and field, had retired from the IOC.) That was how, by 1928, the first group of female Olympic track-and-field athletes were approved to attend the games. Now all they had to do was qualify.

NOT A GUST of air entered the room; the suffocating heat seemed to exert its full power from floor to ceiling, stifling them. The window of Betty's cramped hotel room opened to the sounds of the city, the smells of the street below drifting inside. Voices from outside leapt into the room, while dogs barked in the distance and the occasional flash of unfulfilled lightning pierced the night sky. Betty took a breath of humid air and smelled the stench of uncollected garbage from the sidewalk, wafting heavily in the early night air.

On learning that she would be traveling to New Jersey and New York for the Olympic trials, she had been overtaken by a sense of disorientation. She had never ventured far from home, save for Stone Lake in northern Indiana, where her family rented a cabin every summer and spent a few months indulging in swimming, fishing, and catapulting down the side of a hill sloping into the water. She strolled along the paths, taking nearly an hour to round the lake, stooping to catch the turtles that lounged among the lily pads or gather wildflowers and scour for the small berries that she liked. This was certainly different, she thought as she looked out of her hotel window, the haze of the hot evening enveloping the buildings. She sensed that a grand adventure was about to begin.

New York was unlike Riverdale in every respect. The bristling sidewalks were a revelation, where a sea of humanity hurried over the sticky pavements, fanning themselves with newspapers as they rushed in every direction, so purposeful in their manners. She was curious about their lives and the places they were heading; none of them was aware of her pursuits and her desires, as lost in the crowd as anyone else. She loved the frenzy in the air, the invisible hum of the city that enlivened her body.

She had been told that this year's Olympics would be in Amsterdam, a place she could barely locate on a map. The Games had been awarded to Amsterdam thanks in part to the doings of Baron Frederik van Tuyll, the president of the Netherlands Olympic Committee, who in 1919, during an IOC meeting in Lausanne to decide where the Seventh Olympiads should take place, had made a bid for the 1924 Games, even though other cities, including Lyons and Rome, were already on the short list. The athletes did not know about the political finagling, and what mattered to Betty most was that they were the first Olympics where women would be allowed to participate in track and field. They were making history, being swept along in a dramatic change in women's athletics, and she was a part of it.

Elizabeth Waterman, the IWAC's athletic director, had accompanied the Chicago contingent on the overnight train journey to Newark. She had dragged a large valise with her, hoisting it up into the train's alcove while wearing a tweed dress that induced heavy sweating. She had seemed as excited about the trip as her athletes were, slouching forward in her seat as the concrete city rolled by, soon giving way to the pastoral landscape as the train headed east.

As Betty settled into her own plush seat, she felt ready to break the routine she had become accustomed to since March. Her training had intensified following her win at Soldier Field, and now, with her school year behind her, she was free to concentrate solely on her athletic endeavors. Racing had revealed to her a desire for winning she had never known she possessed, despite her years of dancing. Both disciplines required hard work, but they were of course different in many ways. The movements of ballet were fluid. They told a story, beautiful and at times tragic; languid and full of whimsy, the routines took time to appreciate, to develop as a character and a tale. But running was unlike that. Betty often had no time to think at all; a race ended almost as soon as it began. There was no fluidity to it; it was hurried and fast, as fast as a bullet from one of her guns. It was a test of strength and endurance rewarded only seconds later. And Betty liked that.

THE IOC HAD previously agreed to add ten disciplines to the women's track-and-field events, but by the time the 1928 Olympic tryouts rolled around, only five were officially on the roster: the 100-meter dash, the 800 meters, the high jump, the discus, and the 4-by-100-meter relay. This significantly narrowed the pool of athletes who'd been training.

Helen Filkey and Nellie Todd, a runner Betty did not know very well, were also representing the IWAC and had taken the train together. Helen and Nellie had become friendly—though not friends—in the past few months. Each knew she had a shot at making the team and was intent on proving she deserved it. They brought different strengths to her respective specialties: Helen had the chance of gaining a spot not only in the 100 meters but also in the 4-by-100-meter relay. Unfortunately for Nellie, who was the world record holder in the broad jump, that event was not going to be included in Newark or Amsterdam. She could potentially qualify only in the

800 meters, a race few American women took part in, and she was neither familiar with nor prepared for it. Betty, on the other hand, would run in the 100-meter qualifiers, as well as the 4-by-100-meter relay.

The three saw one another as impediments to their own dreams—and they had not only one another to beat but everyone else, too. As potential members of the first US women's track-and-field team, they were collectively working to appear as a united front. But Betty realized the truth: though they were fighting together to take their place alongside the men, each performed as an individual, and what mattered most to them was how they each came out in the end.

They spoke of their chances as they unpacked their clothes in their sticky hotel room, sweating with excitement in the unbearable heat. Although Betty appeared perfectly calm, the other two were apprehensive about the meets ahead. For them, this was to be the culmination of months and years of hard work, and everything would come down to seconds and inches. They were awed and slightly uneasy about the prospect of being there, their anxiety settling in their bellies like stones at the bottom of a river. Helen and Nellie spent a restless night tossing and turning in their beds, trying to wipe away the sweat that soaked their sheets. Betty, on the other hand, slept deeply.

AS JULY 4 dawned, the thermometer had already reached 90 degrees Fahrenheit and was predicted to climb even higher throughout the rest of the day. A warm yellow sun heralded the upcoming meets, which would be held at the Newark Schools Stadium, where seating for more than fifteen thousand spectators was available, making it one of the largest auditoriums in the area. Officials had expected a reasonable turnout, but by the start of the tryouts only some four thousand spectators had shown up—and even they looked ready to bolt. It was a perfect storm brought on by various conditions, officials assured anxious coaches, who were trying to determine why so few had attended. Held on a national holiday, the trials were interfering with earlier plans; barbecues, excursions to the beach, and visits with families were long-held traditions broken only by few important events—track and field not being one of them.

The weather had also colluded to bring about a lack of attendees. Who would want to spend hours watching young women go through drills in the heat of the afternoon when the cool waters of the Atlantic beckoned at the Jersey shore? Few people were enthusiastic about women's track and field, and those who showed up to root for their favorites wore light clothing and floppy beach hats, holding jugs of water to refresh themselves, the ice cubes in the bottles melting as quickly as the ice cream they licked.

By midafternoon, the stadium had nearly emptied; what had been tolerable earlier in the day soon became unbearable, and though a severe thunderstorm brought momentary relief as it swept over Newark and drenched the remaining contestants, it ultimately only caused further discomfort.

A local reporter hired to cover the events blamed neither the heat nor the thunderstorm for the lack of spectators but was more pragmatic about it. "Only about 1,500 people witnessed the contests at the stadium, which was a disappointment to the sponsors," wrote Len Elliott in the *Newark Evening News* on Thursday, July 5, 1928. "Newark is a great athletic town until it comes to track contests. The town doesn't give a tinker's heck for the Track and Field racket and maybe someday that fact may sink into the dear old A.A.U. and inspire that organization to try its championship meet in Scranton or Dobbs Ferry."

The officials worried that the young athletes would wilt beneath the punishing sun. Doctors had been brought to the stadium to deal with the eventuality of one of the athletes becoming ill in such extreme temperatures. They watched for exhaustion brought on by too much sweating as well as minor signs of heat cramps, perhaps involving the calf muscles. But they were most fearful of the violent signs of heatstroke. Several younger children had been enlisted to go onto the infield to hand out water, dousing the athletes like flowers in pots.

There was tension in the air as the long afternoon meets drew on. Although Helen was the superstar of the sport and Betty's own name was on the rise, it was not the Chicago athletes that the reporters had come to write about. Instead, it was the members of the Northern California Athletic Club who provided entertainment—in particular its star, Elta Cartwright, a twenty-year-old college student from Humboldt State College known as "Cinder-Elta."

Born on December 21, 1907, in California, Elta, the fourth of five daughters, always credited her mother for her astounding running abilities. When she was in high school, track meets were very popular, and Elta won them in dramatic fashion. She graduated in 1925, the same year the AAU National Championships were held in Pasadena. There she captured first place in the 50-yard dash and second place in the 100-yard dash, followed by the 50-yard-dash title in 1926 and 1927 along with second and third places in several other meets throughout 1926 and 1927.

By the time she reached Newark, Elta had grown into a tall, slim girl with dark hair who favored a round bowl haircut—an unsophisticated girl, some ventured to say, though on the track she was all lean perfection. Betty waited her turn and watched Elta—her biggest obstacle to qualifying—move from one event to the next. Some papers had even gone so far as to declare Elta victorious, even though the race had not yet taken place.

Yet Betty felt none of the anticipatory anxiety the others seemed to feel. Perhaps her age allowed her to swagger into Newark as she did. Younger than most of the competitors and certainly the least experienced, if she were to make it to Amsterdam, the Olympics would be only her fourth official competition. She did not have the baggage the others brought to the trials, namely, the expectations of coaches, fans, families, and, most especially, themselves. She did not have years of training that had led her to this moment, nor the terrible sting of recalling defeat suffered at other races. She came with a practically clean slate, which, she believed, would give her a distinct advantage. She also arrived in Newark wanting to prove that she not only belonged in the same class as the other athletes, despite her inexpertness, but was someone the others should watch out for.

The athletes warmed up lightly, not wanting to raise their temperature too much. They had already run laps, jogging up and down the darkened corridors of the hotel in the morning as the smell of bacon and coffee lingered. Still, not all seemed bothered by New Jersey's temperatures: the California contingent, apparently in its element, was hardly breaking a sweat.

THE CALIFORNIAN ANNE Vrana and Betty whizzed through the second and third semifinal heats; Elta won the fourth in 12.4 seconds. Sixteen-year-old Jean Shiley, who, along with Betty, was one of the youngest competitors, qualified as a high jumper. Jean was still a student at Haverford Township High School, and not a stranger to hard work. She was born in Harrisburg, Pennsylvania, in November 1911; the family soon relocated to pastoral Havertown, nearly twenty-six miles west of Philadelphia. Jean was a tomboy and always had ample open space surrounding her and enabling her and her siblings to run for miles.

Luckily for her, Haverford Township High School had no qualms about offering the same activities for girls that it did for boys. She competed in track and field and tennis, as well as basketball and hockey. Basketball, in particular, suited her well. Her tall, lean body—she stood over five feet, nine inches—came in handy with the jumping required, and her strong legs made running that much easier. It was that experience that ushered her into being an Olympian.

During one of Jean's basketball games, Dora Laurie, who wrote for a Philadelphia newspaper, spotted her. A former high jumper herself, Dora understood that Jean possessed untapped potential that went beyond basketball. She followed her into the locker room after one of her games and asked her if she had ever thought of being a track-and-field Olympian. Jean hadn't, but the idea intrigued her.

Jean's athletic promise was further solidified when Dora introduced her to Coach Lawson Robertson. Lawson, who would go on to coach the 1928 men's Olympic team, was at the time teaching at the University of Pennsylvania. He was known as a tough, hard-to-please man who hardly ever coached women. The meeting took place in Lawson's office, Dora and Jean sitting across the coach's desk as he spoke little and smiled even less, unnerving Jean, who fidgeted in her hard-backed chair. She spoke slowly about the sports she played, detailed the games she had taken part in. He only nodded. Finally he instructed her to move to the track field, where he put her through strenuous drills. Dora stood by the sidelines, watching. Lawson took out a stopwatch and timed Jean as she sprinted, jumped, and tumbled. He was quiet throughout and spoke only after she was finished, when he agreed to coach her.

Jean's relatives were not happy with what they considered her "masculine" bent and abilities. The place for a woman, her father believed, was in the home, behind a stove. All that jumping, running, hurdling, sweating, and playing was unbecoming, and he did not support her activities, let alone her desires and her ambitions to become an Olympian. In fact, he never attended any of her meets—not that she cared. She became defiant, and the more she was told not to run, the more inclined she was to do it.

WHEN ALL WAS said and done, on the evening of July 4, 1928, the members of the Northern California Athletic Club came away victorious. "Yesterday afternoon Newark got its first taste of what it means to be invaded by a California Track and Field outfit. For on the turf of the Newark Schools Stadium the girl athletes of the Northern California Athletic Club made a Roman Holiday out of what we thought was an American Holiday," the *Newark Evening News* reported. "These athletes of the N.C.A.C. . . . made a ridiculous show of what competition the East and Middle West could give them. . . . The total was more than three times the total of their nearest rival."

That evening, officials from the AAU had the difficult task of choosing thirteen athletes to represent the country. Not surprisingly, Betty, Elta, and Jean were among them. Although Betty had been picked by a few oddsmakers to win the 100 meters, given the numbers she had arrived with, Elta reached the finish line more than a foot ahead of Betty at 12.4 seconds, just a tenth of a second behind the world record. Elta also won the 50 yards and the running broad jump. Betty finished second and watched, disappointed, as Elta and her friends celebrated her win.

FORMER TRACK STAR Mel Sheppard was forty-four years old when he was appointed coach to the first all-female track-and-field team heading to the Olympics. He was a reserved man with dark, thinning hair and pointy ears that stuck out; few of his charges realized that, just like them, in his youth he had accomplished much to advance the sport, breaking long-standing records and winning titles in the AAU half-mile division in 1906, 1908, 1911, and 1912, earning the nickname "Peerless Mel" along the way. In 1910, he had broken Lon Myers's 1,000-yard record, which had stood unbroken for nearly thirty years.

Although he now worked as a personnel director for New York's John Wanamaker store, he often thought back to those years, particularly to 1908, when he had seen himself on the cusp of achieving all of his goals: passing the physical examination for the entrance into the police department and attending the London Olympic Games.

His police exam had been scheduled for just days prior to his departure for London, which had struck him as a good omen. He was in top physical condition thanks to his strict regimen, which he prided in detailing to examining doctors. So it came as a shock when doctors discovered an enlarged heart, which immediately disqualified him from entering the force. He never forgot how hard he had pled his case or how it felt to watch one of his two dreams evaporate so quickly.

Perhaps fueled by this exclusion, he dedicated the rest of his energies toward the Olympics, where he had displayed no signs of the heart condition the doctors had discovered, quickly and easily winning the 1,500 meters and defeating the British favorite and world record holder, H. A. Wilson. It was a feat few (including his own coach, Mike Murphy) believed could be repeated on the following day in the 800 meters. But he proved them all wrong, winning again and setting a world record of 1 minute, 52.8 seconds.

He had run as much to set records as to prove that his doctors had been wrong in their diagnosis, still assuming that there had been some kind of mistake. His training was brutal, but he never suffered chest pains or felt at a loss for air. He would have seen indications of the disease during those training sessions, which always followed the same pattern, interspersing long runs with exhausting bouts of exercise throughout the day. Even his coach had demanded a reexamination, for anyone who ran that much surely did not suffer from any heart conditions. (He had no way of knowing in 1908, of course, that he would die at the age of fifty-eight from what the coroner determined was a severe bout of indigestion, though many of his peers thought it more likely to have been due to heart problems.)

How strange, he thought that hot day in Newark in July. Having been forced to abandon his police officer dream and long since given up on his own career as an amateur runner, he'd now be coaching the first female track-and-field team bound for the Olympics.

.   .   .

ALTHOUGH BETTY WAS thrilled to have made the team, the reality was that she had expected a lot better of herself and was disappointed with her second-place finish. While traveling to Newark, she had rehearsed so long and so well that she had imagined emerging as the winner. She had gone so far as to feel the sweat trickling down her back and soreness from the blisters forming on her toes—small prices to pay for the glory that would have been hers when she crossed the finish line first. It was not only her burgeoning self-confidence but a sense of entitlement bestowed upon her by her newly discovered talent and the advantages of her early life: she simply could not, would not lose.

But she had come to learn the harsh truth. She was merely one of the many contenders vying for a spot to the Olympics, and she was not necessarily the best. In Riverdale she had been anointed the new queen of the track, capable of beating any opponent, but in Newark she had ended her run a shade lower than expected, disappointing not only herself but also her supporters from Riverdale.

She penned a letter to the *Evening American* in the hope of explaining. It was both full of feeble excuses and laced with a touch of humility that she had not expressed before. "I am sorry I did not do as well as everyone expected me to do," she wrote, "but I tried my best. We had to run the 100 meters three times inside an hour, which, I think, tried all of us quite a bit. We had a terribly warm day for the meet, which made it hard for those who were not used to such weather." She knew that her words, however true, sounded pitiful. "I am going to train hard and I think I will be able to work up to my record time again because the time for the final was slow compared to what I have done," she continued, humbly adding, "I promise you I will train harder than ever to win in the Olympics because I know now what it is to have keen competition and to be beaten."

On July 6, the *Evening American* replied by taking out a full-page ad to congratulate her on her accomplishments; it did not comment on her second-place finish or on the fact that Elta Cartwright had turned out to be the breakthrough athlete of the trials. The paper wrote nothing of her apology. It simply wished her good luck in Amsterdam.

AWAY FROM THE glare of flashbulbs from the few newspaper reporters in Newark, as the athletes celebrated their victories and induction into the inaugural team, an awkward young woman sat on a bench and took note of all that was happening around her. She stood up, wrapped a towel around her neck, and began a slow walk around the track, feeling the black cinders beneath her feet as she allowed the realization of what had just happened to sink in: having come a fraction too short, she had lost her bid to qualify for the team, edged out by Mary Washburn. It was a soul-crushing defeat that galled her.

The afternoon was growing darker, the sun having disappeared long before, though the stickiness of the day lingered on. Sweat collected around her neck and armpits as she inhaled a lungful of humid air. After the meets, she had changed from her running gear into her regular warm-up garb of long sweatpants and a wrinkled sweatshirt, and, after spending several days in Newark, found herself exhausted and ready to go home.

In the distance a bevy of photographers snapped pictures, and she was grateful they had not come to talk to her. She kept things too much to herself, people often said. She was now very relieved for this little bit of solitude that was afforded to her; only this time it came at a great price. It was hard to settle in to the idea that she would not be going to Amsterdam.

STELLA WALSH HAD come to Newark from Cleveland, Ohio. She had been born Stanisława Walasiewicz in Poland, in April 1911, although most people she met didn't know that. Unlike the wider immigrant community, she did not pepper her speech with a scattering of Polish words; she avoided any references to her upbringing, her native land, her family, her friends, or her boyfriends, particularly when prodded with questions. This pursuit of anonymity was aided by her lack of a foreign accent, which allowed her to fully assimilate into her new culture.

When she was two years old, she and her parents, Julian and Victoria, had left Poland for Cleveland, settling into the Slavic part of town, where other Polish families had already found a home. She could not recall that transatlantic voyage, but as a child she'd heard her parents speak of it with disgust, which in turn made her think of it with repulsion. During her early years she had lived under her given name of Stanisława, but as she grew older and adapted to her new country, she became aware that her name begged the questions that she liked to avoid. So she adopted a new moniker that was easier on the tongue, learning that few people wondered about a name like Stella Walsh. But her name was not the only thing that she changed or the only thing that she actively chose to keep to herself.

Stella was tall, with broad shoulders, and she stood on powerful and very muscular legs. People often described her as "sturdy," a description she did not like very much. She had taken to running as a very young girl; it was a skill that had been passed down to her, she thought, honed by hours spent sprinting against her mother and even her grandfather.

She had always known that there was nothing particularly delicate about her, and her teammates always reminded her of that, appraising her indiscreetly like a pack of hyenas. She was taunted by claims that she lacked the natural graces and feminine attributes to attract anyone of the opposite sex. In the changing rooms, rumors floated that several athletes had seen a peek of a five-o'clock shadow growing on her face. Even her neighbors back in Cleveland spoke of her peculiarities, her intense need for privacy meaning very little to them. But she shook off the rumors.

. . .

NOW, AS SHE observed the winning girls leave the track bound for the hotel, from where they would await their departure for Amsterdam, her anger grew further. They were perfect in every sense, reporters agreed; something that she would never be. Still, she swallowed her disappointment and vowed to return again. The 1932 games were not that far away, and she would make the most of these years. Next time, she would not be denied.

CHAPTER SEVEN

THE SS PRESIDENT ROOSEVELT

S tella Walsh returned to Cleveland on July 6, while the Olympic-bound athletes settled comfortably into the Prince George Hotel in Manhattan to await their embarkation. The sprawling old institution delighted Betty, as she continued to soak in all that New York provided. She walked the crowded streets, a feathered hat shielding her from the hot sun, looking up at the skyscrapers with a giddy dizziness, feeling the heat coming off the asphalt and through her shoes.

New York was then a sea of excitement, not so much because it was the site of the Olympians' departure for Amsterdam but because a parade was about to be held to honor the first female airplane pilot to cross the Atlantic. Although Amelia Earhart had been a passenger on the *Friendship* and not a pilot, her participation in the endeavor signified great strides for women, and her accomplishments needed to be recognized. A parade down the Canyon of Heroes was about to take place, and Betty thought it marvelous that she should find herself in New York during such a time—especially as she was embarking on her own pioneering journey. She recognized her own contributions to the sport, and the fact that female track athletes had never been allowed to participate before, while acknowledging that many people still disputed women's participation in the sport. It seemed absurd to her and her fellow athletes that such arguments were still taking place.

ON JULY 11, 1928, Betty and her mother hailed a taxicab bound for the port of Manhattan, where nearly three hundred of her team members, along with their families, coaches, and well-wishers, had gathered at Pier 86 to board the SS *President Roosevelt*, a comfortable ocean liner outfitted for the athletes. On its side, AMERICAN OLYMPIC TEAMS was painted in large white letters, thrilling the athletes as they crossed the plank walkway leading to the ship. The departure was a grand affair, streamers and balloons lending a jovial mood as music rippled through the air.

General Douglas MacArthur stood at the end of the gangway, awaiting his platoon. He took stock of the athletes coming on board from every corner of the country, excited and eager to represent the United States. In addition to the officials, coaches, family members, newspaper reporters, and assorted guests, the *Roosevelt* was transporting the greatest assemblage of US athletes the country had ever seen. MacArthur asserted that the athletes were in such "superb condition for the great test that Americans can rest serene and assured," and those gathered around him could not help but be enthralled by the words coming from his mouth.

At forty-eight, MacArthur was perfect for leading the team, as throughout his career he had been a great supporter of male athleticism. After a wartime career in the US Army and three years as superintendent of West Point Military Academy, followed by further service in the US Army, Army Chief of Staff General Charles P. Summerall had placed him on "detached service," granting him permission to accept the post of American Olympic Committee (AOC) president, believing that it would bring "favorable publicity to the

Army." For MacArthur, it was simply a different way of serving his country, his disciplined demeanor akin to what he showed to his army recruits.

MacArthur was aware that there was no love lost between the NCAA, the AAU, and the AOC. But he was not interested in becoming involved in their squabble. Rather, he "needed something to engage his attention and arouse his enthusiasm." He intended to bring his military style to this mission, with strictly enforced rules and regulations he employed with his soldiers, plus curfews for the female athletes and the younger ones on board. The athletes just didn't know it yet.

SS PRESIDENT ROOSEVELT had started life as *Peninsula State*, built for the United States Shipping Board by the New York Shipbuilding Corporation of Camden, New Jersey, in 1921 and 1922. Its first transatlantic service for United States Lines began in 1922, when it was renamed *President Pierce*. In August 1922, it was rebaptized *President Roosevelt*, a name it would keep until it was drafted by the US Navy in World War II.

The athletes did not know it at first, but the ship they were boarding had, in January 1926, been involved in the rescue of the crew of the British cargo ship SS *Antinoe*, which had floundered in the Atlantic. Although the historical details piqued everyone's interest, what the Olympic team delighted in most was the fact that the *Roosevelt* was carrying them to Europe, on what many felt was the grandest vacation imaginable. Having grown up on farms, in tiny midwestern towns, or on inner-city streets, most of them had barely traveled in their lives prior to competing in their respective sport, and thus this was on the whole a new and enjoyable experience.

Although it was a well-equipped ship, the *Roosevelt* was not fitted with all the training facilities the athletes required, though efforts had been made to turn it into a vessel worthy of Olympians: on the promenade, a 160-yard linoleum running track had been laid out, along with wrestling mats; and on the sundeck, a boxing ring and rowing machines had been installed so the athletes could keep up with their training and conditioning regimens. And the athletes were everywhere: stretching on the floor; power-walking or jogging on the deck; laughing on stationary equipment while biking or rowing. It was not the most conducive environment for maintaining athletic form, however, and rather than consistently exercising, most of them spent their time socializing and eating—so much so that many of them soon found themselves several pounds heavier than their ideal competing weights.

Some of the equipment had also been placed in very confined spaces, where many of the athletes tried to use it at the same time. "It was easier for runners," admitted Nick Carter, a southern California athlete scheduled to run in the 1,500 meters. Comparing the runners' troubles to those of the swimmers, though, he said they had their own problems: "The object was to do as much as you could to keep in shape by walking or jogging around the boat. Having so many people in such a small space with all of them having the same idea in mind, it was pretty crowded. That was hard to do to keep in condition, every-body was exercising, jogging, walking. It doesn't seem like there was ever a minute that there wasn't somebody running around that ship."

Traveling with Betty was fourteen-year-old Eleanor Holm, who, along with Betty, was one of the youngest competitors. She had been born in Brooklyn in December 1913 and taken her first strokes in the waters of a public pool not far from her family's summer cottage in Long Beach, New York. Eleanor was fond of MacArthur—and he, in turn, had a soft spot for the youngest members of his team, whom he liked to call his "little children." Though he had taken the position with the intention of running the team like a military platoon, he guided some of those junior members with a kinder hand.

Betty shared a cabin with Catherine Maguire and Delores "Dee" Boeckmann. Catherine, a lovely girl and a 1925 graduate of Pacific

High School in Pacific, Missouri, had been born and raised on a farm. One of six children, she had enjoyed hurdling over fences, an activity she later acknowledged had helped her to succeed at the Olympics. Shy but curious, she permitted herself very few confidences with her roommates, and they, in turn, did not encourage them.

But it was Dee whom Betty found the most fascinating. At twenty-three, Dee was one of the oldest and most experienced female athletes on the ship. Lately she had been working as a physical education teacher at the Loreto Academy in St. Louis, though what she wanted most was an Olympic gold medal. She gained a spot on the team by finishing second in the 800 meters, a standing she sought to better in Amsterdam. She'd been running since she was a little girl, and back in 1920, when she had been barely sixteen, she had held ten of the track-and-field records of the Amateur Athletic Union (AAU).

Dee was born in St. Louis, Missouri, to German and Irish parents and held two passports, one printed as Boeckmann and the other as Beckman, leaving her free to use whichever she deemed most appropriate in any given circumstance. But she always tried to de-emphasize her German heritage and often suggested that other runners of similar background do the same.

A tall, beautiful, dark-haired, dark-eyed girl, Dee had a fondness for the tiny four-leaf clovers that represented half of her heritage, collecting them with abandon and even sporting them on her clothes when she had the chance to show them off. Dee, at nearly five foot ten, managed to do almost everything better than a boy, including running, her father always said. He had also introduced her to official meets, signing her up for every race he could find. In 1927, with her father watching, of course, she had broken the world record for the indoor 50-yard dash, which she ran in 6.1 seconds, and during her Olympic training, she had set a new record for the 800 yards at 2 minutes, 31 seconds.

In Dee, Betty saw the embodiment of someone she could become: a strong, self-confident, self-reliant woman pursuing her goals. She had met such women in Chicago, brimming with confidence as they headed off to work. But here was Dee, not only working and being independent but excelling at a sport many considered masculine.

Betty had been mulling over such matters lately. Her seventeenth birthday was nearly upon her, as was her senior year of high school, which would begin soon after her return from Amsterdam. Then what? She had discussed the possibility of attending the nearby college in Harvey with her sister and Jim but was unsure about what to study. Her mother did not think dancing and theater viable means of making a living—but Betty neither agreed nor disagreed with her. Traveling by train to Chicago, she had gained the opportunity to view the world at large, a world where women worked beyond the confines of their homes; where they dressed up and headed to offices with purpose; where jovial meetings punctuated their evenings with friends, stops at the cinema, or drinks at a bar.

And now, in Dee, she saw even more possibilities: a woman who was making her mark in athletics, who had breached that masculine world and created a life of her own. It was that kind of woman Betty admired, the kind many feared and others held in awe. It thrilled her to think about becoming one of them.

THE *PRESIDENT ROOSEVELT* weighed 13,869 tons and had been traversing the Atlantic for six years. It was a comfortable (if not luxurious) ship, and the athletes took a liking to it right away, enjoying the sun as it shone upon the deck, watching other ships passing by. As the engines sputtered and the ship was nosed out of the harbor by tugboats, it was met halfway by the US warship *Rotterdam*, coming into the canal from the opposite direction, the band on its promenade playing "The Star-Spangled Banner" as it passed the Olympians. Betty had often viewed barges floating down the Calumet River, small vessels drifting through its waters on their way to and from the city. The *Roosevelt* was on a different scale. Her entire high school could have fit into the ballroom, Riverdale and Harvey combined onto its deck. The magnitude and the sheer power of the ship were breathtaking.

And Betty loved it all: the rocking of the ship as it listed in the choppy seas; the plentiful, free lunches and dinners offered every day; the liquor that was available only to first-class passengers (but that was shared and smuggled by everybody who wanted it); and the movies, dances, balls, and casino nights held as the afternoon faded into evening. The athletes often gathered on the parapet to view the sun burning over the horizon and to watch and gawk at the swimming team as they tried to keep up with their training.

In the makeshift pool the ship officials had built, the American swimmer Johnny Weissmuller often harnessed himself with a long rope to one side of the gangplank, lest he be thrown overboard when the ship listed. At six feet, three inches tall, with powerful legs and well-defined muscles, he was a favorite among the women as they looked on appreciatively while he paraded in his uniform. He had perfected what the experts called his "six-beat crawl stroke," which produced his speed while in the water. The style called "for six beats of the legs for every two arm strokes, with absolute synchronization of feet and arms." His prodigious strokes had already propelled him to great heights, the first of which had occurred in 1921, at age seventeen, when he had broken the first of many world records.

Born Peter Johann Weißmuller on June 2, 1904, in Freidorf, then a part of the Austro-Hungarian Empire, he had moved to the United States at a young age but left school before finishing the eighth grade. His first introduction to a swimming pool came when he was nine, when he took his first dip in a public pool in Chicago, to which his family had relocated from western Pennsylvania. Thereafter, he enjoyed long swims in the cold, icy waters of Lake Michigan, which few ever attempted. Several years later, at the age of fifteen, he came to the attention of Bill Bachrach, then a coach for the Illinois Athletic Club.

In 1923, while participating in the AAU National Championships, he made a splash by winning the 50, 100, 220, and 500 yards, along with competing in the 150-yard backstroke, from which he shaved 6.8 seconds from the world record. That was but a preview of what was to come at the 1924 Olympics, where he won three gold medals—in the 100, 400, and 800 meters. Expectations were high that he would be rewarded with another gold in Amsterdam. (Weissmuller would go on to parlay his successful athletic career into a profitable stint in Hollywood, where he starred in twelve *Tarzan* movies. Later in life, he would be remembered not for his gold medals but for the stunts he performed while swinging from tree to tree clad only in a loincloth.)

A tall, attractive, and fast swimmer, Weissmuller soon developed a reputation not only for breaking records but also for the attention he received from women who watched his races. Betty often stood with the rest of the team, Dee included, and looked on as he took a dip in the useless pool before hurrying to the dance halls, where lessons in the fox-trot, the Charleston, and the Lindy Hop were in session.

Most of the training workouts in the pool (or anywhere else) were short, and the only places the athletes seemed to linger were at meals, where they tried most things, and their faces just beamed as they overindulged with abandon. That gorging—the endless plates of eggs and bowls of cereal for breakfast, the steaks and potatoes for lunch followed by larger quantities for dinner—stunned Betty, who watched her fellow Olympians shovel in as much as they could, as if they had never had enough to eat. She had never suffered the pangs of hunger, did not feel the need to conserve, never had to, and the sight of her fellow athletes doing so often embarrassed her.

Stewart Heldor, the ship's chef, chided the athletes publicly for eating all the ice cream on board, which had been deemed sufficient for the round-trip, in less than a week. They liked it at breakfast in addition to the bountiful fare the ship provided. But there would be no more ice cream bars until Amsterdam, where he could replenish his supplies, Heldor eventually had to tell the disgruntled passengers.

It was not an optimal environment for world-class athletes who needed to keep their weight down and their muscles well conditioned. The journey was languorous and did not seem conducive to such strain; the sea was calm in the early days, calm enough to fill the athletes with a sense of well-being.

AS THE NINE-DAY journey reached its end, twenty-six-year-old Bud Houser was chosen as the team's captain and given the honor of carrying the flag at the opening and closing ceremonies. He was a senior member of the team; he had won a gold medal in the shot put and discus at the Paris Games. Weissmuller would carry the sign with the country's name emblazoned on it, and MacArthur would follow them.

AS THE *ROOSEVELT* crossed the Atlantic, reports began to trickle in that Amsterdam officials had been unable to finish the track fields. MacArthur scoffed at the idea. "On the battlefield, never believe reports of a disaster," he told the coaches. "Leave it to the Dutch engineering genius to provide a proper field for the games."

Undeterred by reports chronicling the Dutch lack of preparations, MacArthur concentrated on the task at hand. He gathered the trainers for daily updates, encouraging them to have the best team the United States could churn out and repeatedly urging the athletes not to pay any attention to the gossip. Reporters were allowed to attend those meetings, and one correspondent griped that they "had about them the same chilling spiritual temperature as a bank directors' meeting."

As they neared land, the training intensified. The weather still cooperated; a clear sky and tranquil sea lulled the ship forward. The swimmers continued to harness themselves and take a few minutes of exercise in the pool, and the divers, who could not dive into the pool, used springboards to land on mats laid out on the concourse. The boxers practiced with the wrestlers, the runners ran the length of the ship, and the equestrians used treadmills to keep limber, their sessions followed by vigorous rubdowns of alcohol liniment to prevent pain and joint stiffness. Seagulls screeched overhead as docked ships were sighted on the horizon.

THE ATHLETES AWOKE early on Friday, July 20, to a half-darkened sky. They soon learned that they would drop anchor momentarily, finally catching a glimpse of a land they had seen only in books or their imagination. A tugboat led them slowly up a canal toward Amsterdam's sprawling cityscape. They made their way through wide lonely wetlands dotted by vibrant patches of land where tulips and neat rows of vegetables grew. Windmills rotated in the distance, a pasty sky their backdrop.

Newspaper reporters traveling with the Olympians later described the tiny canals bursting out from the larger ones like a network of spiderwebs, marveling at the cleverness of the Dutch in growing a multitude of flowers and vegetables together. The reporters knew they would have opportunities to tour this Venice of the North beyond the Olympic grounds. There were museums to explore and canals upon which to row and spend breaks soaking in the sun, if it ever showed up. There were flower markets with native tulips taking center stage, and unexpected candy and chocolate shops that offered untold delights.

AT TWO O'CLOCK, the ship docked in Amsterdam. Stepping onto a foreign land for the first time evoked intense feelings of wonder in the athletes, though the coaches and trainers had no time for such reflection. They immediately left to inspect the field, hoping the reports that had come in during the journey had been mistaken.

Alas, the conditions within the stadium could hardly have been any worse. Usually, track quality depends on how well the cinders (small bits of black material) are mounted on the ground; if not done properly, heat causes them to become loose and break away, while rain can turn the track into muck. The plan for the track in Amsterdam had been to construct "two straight lines some 60 meters each, an arch at either end with extremities extended to form a complete circuit." But upon arrival the Americans realized that the Amsterdam officials' plan had not materialized, and the track they had built, or what remained of it, was not only half finished but mostly underwater.

It was all a matter of architecture and soil quality. The Games had been designed to take place around a brand-new stadium meant to hold more than fifty thousand spectators, its track taking center stage. The swimming pool was constructed next to the stadium, equipped for an audience of just fifteen hundred. In addition, just outside the main arena was the gymnasium for the fencing, boxing, and other competitions.

The grounds were soft, almost springy. New technology had to be implemented so that the buildings would not sink into the soil, as the rest of the city was doing. The track-and-field arena had been built in such a fashion that it had not occurred to officials that this would pose a problem for the athletes, though it soon became apparent that it would—particularly as rain poured down in the weeks prior to the opening ceremonies.

Lawson Robertson, the men's track-and-field coach, surveyed the conditions and observed that a miracle would be needed to make it adequate in time for the July 29 opening ceremony. There was a softness to the track, obvious the moment the runners stepped on it. An immediate casualty was James Quinn of the New York Athletic Club, who sprained his ankle.

The coaches all agreed that the conditions were shameful. Each coach, of course, had his own peculiarities and superstitions—but they all seemed to agree on what made a great track. It had to possess three equal layers of stratification: a base of either stone or what they called clinkers, which were a derivative of coal. That layer had to be leveled off particularly well and evenly. Above that was an overlap consisting of coarse cinders; and above that, the final layer and top sheet was made of cinders mixed with either clay or coal ashes. That fine mixture was then rolled out smoothly. But in Amsterdam, it appeared that the process had gone awry.

Aside from the track, Robertson was unimpressed with the physical conditions of his own athletes: they had grown lethargic and slow on the *Roosevelt*. With little to do besides making a pretense of training, they had eagerly awaited lunch, followed by the largest dinners any of them had ever been served.

The British newspapers, which had gotten hold of the menus on the *Roosevelt* and noticed the less-than-ideal physical condition of the Americans, enjoyed poking fun at the athletes and contrasting the food spreads on the *Roosevelt* with those on the British ship. While the Americans had indulged in biscuits and gravy, fried chicken, pancakes with syrup, pies, cookies, liquor (though not officially sanctioned), and chocolate, their British counterparts had satiated themselves with tea, an abundance of salads, chicken or beef, and steamed vegetables. The results showed. On landing, the British looked lean and ready to take on the world, while the Americans were pounds away from their ideal weight.

The *Evening Standard* mockingly wrote, "A good cargo of ice cream may perhaps act as ballast for the man whose business it is to put the shot. But it must be a heavy burden to carry in a sprint or long-distance race."

For their training, members of the American team had to spend most of their time back on the *Roosevelt*, berthed in the Coenhaven. As Nick Carter, scheduled to run in the 1,500 meters, explained, "The places to work out were like running in a plowed field."

The Netherlands Olympic Committee was aware of the issues with the track but begged everyone to be patient. On July 21, criticism reached such a height that Olympic officials, responding to protests, announced that the track would be reworked and completed within a day or two. They agreed that the engineer, who'd been in charge of constructing it, was not at fault. The blame lay with the country's geographical location and the site of the Olympic stadium itself. Officials were left scrambling and, not surprisingly, it took workers longer than anticipated; they finished the resurfacing only three days prior to the opening ceremonies.

The track field was not the only construction to suffer problems. The swimming pool, which had been built in similarly swampy terrain and without the use of pilings to stabilize its foundations, had sunk nearly six inches on one side by the time the opening ceremonies rolled around.

There was only one saving grace, the Americans thought: They were not the only ones having trouble running on the sodden Dutch track; the track was claiming victims from everywhere.

ASIDE FROM THE physical conditions, the American Olympic Committee was irritated by another source: the female athletes, particularly the swimmers. As they were having an issue finding a place to train, the women sensed an opportunity to leave Amsterdam for a few days and, unknown to anyone, traveled to Paris for a shopping expedition. Their behavior raised alarm with the committee members, who later learned from coaches that the athletes would continue their training in the French capital, though provisions had not been made for them to do so. There was an uproar among the American officials over the women's decision, fueled by newspaper reports declaring that they had left because "the team, considering itself unbeatable, anyhow, decided it might as well have a side trip now as at the close of the games, when time was short."

The shopping expedition did nothing to put the female athletes in a better light. Though the women participating in the Paris trip were from the swim team, the fallout was felt by every female Olympian, fortifying the stereotype already in place: when the time for training and hard work rolled around, if given the opportunity, women would rather go shopping.

ON SATURDAY, JULY 28, at 11:15, the athletes were treated to a hearty buffet lunch on the ship's hurricane deck; they all gorged on the offerings, despite their nerves. At 1:00 they formed long lines to board motorboats and then buses that led them to the stadium for the opening ceremony. Her Royal Highness Queen Wilhelmina had initially agreed to attend, but then suddenly declined. The royal consort, Prince Henry, took her place. Members of the IOC and the Netherlands Olympic Committee greeted him and his two companions with ceremonial gestures that included more than a thousand vocalists heralding his entrance, singing the national anthem, "Het Wilhelmus."

The gray sky provided a somber beginning to the games, but at least the rain had finally stopped falling. Athletes donned an array of colors to offset the ashen afternoon: the Belgian delegation wore pink, the South Africans were vivid in their rosy tints, the Americans were in white and blue, the Italians were in military green. The Greeks led the procession per tradition, the rest of the countries entering in alphabetical order (according to the Dutch alphabet).

They emerged from the concrete tunnel into a confusion of light, noise, and cheers—a virtual assault on the senses—as the applause from the stands reverberated in their ears. Athletes from forty-six nations paraded proudly around the large track-and-field stadium to the cheers of more than forty thousand spectators. The athletes found the track's surface soggy and mushy, and those who'd be running on it later feared they would be slowed down by the conditions. The US contingent was third from the last. Tradition held that when passing the Royal Box the flag bearer should salute the prince by dipping his country's flag horizontally, at about chest height. Bud Houser had spoken to MacArthur earlier, so he knew what to do, and he watched as most of the countries' flag bearers paid homage. The Americans hadn't dipped their flag since the 1908 Games in London, and he wasn't about to begin now. Houser passed the prince, stared at everyone in the box, and kept the American flag flying high above his head. He thought it looked majestic, waving in the late-afternoon breeze.

He heard the jeers and boos that followed, but he didn't care; he knew that MacArthur and everyone on the team supported him. European reporters were shocked by what many considered a typical sign of America's disrespect. The US papers, on the other hand, praised Houser's moxie and his spirit and patriotism. The slight was quickly forgotten as the Games began.

THE REST OF the athletes, wearing patriotic uniforms with a red-white-and-blue stripe down one side, the USA logo affixed above their hearts, and another red-white-and-blue stripe across their blouses, stared at the gold-beaded officials in the Royal Box in their gold-beaded uniforms, unaware as to who they were. Soon enough, they realized that they included the prince, along with various IOC members.

The athletes were startled by the day; by the thousands giving them a thunderous standing ovation in the stadium; and by the shouts of the more than seventy-five thousand individuals standing outside who had not been able to gain access but still wanted to be a part of such an event. The outsiders yelled and screamed the athletes' names as they crowded around the entrance. There were flags waving in the spectators' hands, and music filled the arena.

The Dutch Royal Military Band and the Band of Royal Marines, as well as twelve hundred white-robed vocalists from choir groups gathered from across the country, provided the music. The meets in which Betty had taken part in Chicago, much less back in Riverdale, were not remotely comparable to this. Some of the athletes wept openly as they marched around the track, taking in the glorious sight of spectators on their feet, waving flags and shouting with glee. Following dozens of formal speeches by the IOC members and Amsterdam's officials, the sound of bugles and gunshots officially declared the Ninth Olympic Games opened.

ON THE FOLLOWING day—a Sunday—the competitions finally began. The rain was blinding at times, though it often petered out to a drizzle that felt like pins on the athletes' skin. Many complained that the muck-soaked track felt heavy beneath their feet (yet it did not prevent Stanford University's Robert King from winning the gold medal in the high jump or Paavo Nurmi from securing the last of the nine medals of his career). Four Americans in the 100 meters and 800 meters, as well as two Americans in the 400-meter hurdles, advanced to the preliminaries.

On Monday, the women made their Olympic debut in several preliminary meets. The excitement was palpable, but despite the boundaries they were breaking, the attention of the world remained on the men's teams, particularly because their fortunes had turned.

The Associated Press claimed that the United States had "experienced one of the worst series of track and field setbacks it has ever known." Such setbacks began in the 400-meter hurdles, when the British marquess David George Brownlow Cecil, known as Lord Burghley, who had been third in the semifinal heat, beat the Americans Morgan Taylor and Frank Cuhel. More bad luck followed in the 100 meters, where Henry Russell and Claude Bracey were quickly eliminated in the semifinal, leaving a lone American, Frank Wykoff, in fourth place. And so it continued. *The New York Times* echoed what was on the minds everyone: "What's the matter with the American team?"

Coach Mel Sheppard watched from the sidelines, worry lines crossing his forehead. When asked how he felt the women would ultimately fare in their first Olympic showing, he said, "It is difficult to predict what definite results may be expected from the American Women's Track and Field team. Because of extremely poor training facilities, the women athletes haven't had any really satisfying work-outs, and have found it difficult to perform to the best of their ability." Then he added what everybody else was thinking: "Nor did we expect to find that the training field allowed to the best athletes from all corners of the globe was a mere sandbox."

A handful of the women sat in the benches, fearing what was to come on Tuesday, during their own meets, hoping the same question *The New York Times* had posed would not be asked about them: "What's the matter with the American team?"

CHAPTER EIGHT

QUEEN OF THE TRACK

E ach morning since arriving in Amsterdam, the athletes had awoken to a drencher. It was no different on the morning of July 31, the rain coming down unwaveringly. The dismal, cheerless weather that had greeted them since landing in Europe seemed to match the athletes' performances. Louis Nixdorff wrote in his diary, "There have been so many upsets on the track team that it is getting contagious." He joined the chorus and blamed the losses on the soggy conditions of the field: "It seems as though the stadium track is not suitable for our runners. It is slow and rather heavy, and the foreigners are more used to it than we are." Another enduring issue was the excess of food, in which the athletes continued to indulge.

Most of the women woke up frazzled, their nerves raw. They had witnessed the trouble on the track and experienced problems themselves in the preliminaries. In the 100 meters, three of the four American women failed to qualify for the final. Anne Vrana was quickly eliminated in the first round, finishing third in the preliminary heat. Elta Cartwright, who had been ill throughout the ocean journey, and Mary Washburn did not even advance to the semifinal, but wound up in only fourth and fifth place, respectively, during the following heat. Only Betty Robinson advanced, making her the sole 100-meters representative of the United States.

While awaiting her starting moment, Betty sat in the locker room treating her feet, as did all of the runners, their soles having become bothersome due to the repeated impact. There were massages to impart to sore and aching toes, last-minute blisters to lance, toenails to care for that had become blackened and were about to fall out. Some even soaked their feet in a brine solution concocted by themselves or their coaches. It was an ugly business (hardly anybody's definition of ladylike), but such attention was essential for any serious runner.

As Betty readied to enter the stadium and was about to put on her running shoes, she realized that she had packed two left ones when she had departed the *Roosevelt* that morning. She owned two pairs of track shoes, both of which had served her well up until that point, but in the fervor of the occasion she had grabbed two lefties. It was odd that she would have made such a careless mistake; she had awakened refreshed and unperturbed, unlike most of the other competitors. That was why she thought it bizarre that such a monumental mistake should have happened to her. Still, two left shoes. Looking down at her feet, she could not make sense of it. And now it was too late to go back to the ship to retrieve the correct one.

She looked at the clock, then walked barefoot to peer into the stadium, where the crowd was roaring. At any moment she would be called to take her place at the starting line. There would be no delays at the Olympics, particularly none due to missing shoes. She debated running barefoot, but officials would not allow that. Besides, the track was in such deplorable condition, she knew it would ruin her feet.

One of the coaches noticed her dejection and, upon discovering Betty's predicament, he frantically sent a member of the staff to the *Roosevelt* to retrieve her shoe. To Betty's surprised relief, minutes later, the man returned to the changing area, right shoe in hand. After thanking him profusely and quickly changing, she stepped onto the track—just moments before the official's call—looked up at a sky that promised rain, and smelled the humid air.

Having scarcely any time to warm up, on the track she met the Canadians Fanny "Bobbie" Rosenfeld and Myrtle Cook, who were loosened up and ready to flank her. Myrtle appeared heated and wore red shorts and a white silky blouse that barely covered her small figure. She was nervous and fidgety, her breaths coming out in short, uneven bursts. The official called the athletes to the starting line, where they took their places in their respective lanes. Even the crowd seemed to sense their anxiety, so it came as no surprise when Myrtle's apparent apprehension triggered a false start, prompting an admonition from the official. From the sidelines, Myrtle's coach instructed her to collect herself, but being subjected to such scrutiny, of course, did little to ease her mind.

The starter called the athletes to their places again, repeated the "set" command, and Betty and the others returned to their starting position, fixing their eyes ahead. As the official raised his gun, Myrtle once more made an early break for it. She was immediately disqualified, as regulations dictated.

The official waved Myrtle off the track, and for a moment she did not seem to understand what had happened. Eventually, crestfallen, she was led off the track in tears by her teammates, seemingly unaware of where she was or what had just occurred. The pressure of so many spectators was having a horrible effect on the runners, for the same fate befell Leni Schmidt, a robust twenty-one-year-old blond German who had won her semifinal the previous day. She also made two false starts, but, unlike the teary Myrtle Cook, Leni was dragged off the track screaming and shaking her fists at the official.

Four runners remained, and if Betty was flustered, she did not show it. Appraising the situation, she knew that Fanny Rosenfeld would be hard to beat; Fanny had already edged her out in the early heats, winning her own preliminary semifinal race at 12.4 seconds, but Betty had won her qualifying run in precisely the same time. Erna Steinberg did not seem much of a menace. The second of the German competitors, Erna was even younger and less experienced than Betty. Knowing that her biggest competitor was Fanny at her right, Betty strategized that if she could manage to always be aware of her position and keep Fanny in her line of vision, she would be fine.

She inhaled deeply several times, then exhaled slowly, very slowly, as Coach Price had taught her. Deep breathing relaxed her, and a relaxed athlete had a better chance for a fast takeoff. What was important, she had been told, was a good, clean start.

Anxious to begin, the runners planted their feet into position again. Betty heard "set," raised her hips, and shifted her weight toward her hands. Her coaches had trained her to form a 90-degree angle with her forward knee, which she did, while focusing her eyes way down the track. She began to count her breaths again, relaxing, relaxing.

At the crack of the starter's pistol, the athletes leapt off the starting line like coiled springs. Fanny Rosenfeld took the lead early on, but halfway down the lane Betty caught up with her. As they neared the finish line, they were practically in step with each other, matching strides. They raced in seeming tandem for seconds and were practically neck and neck as they broke the tape, pandemonium ringing in their ears.

Betty's skin tingled when she felt the tape break, sweat trickling down her face as she came to a screeching halt next to Fanny. There was great chaos as the officials hesitated to call the winner—the Canadians were celebrating Fanny's presumed victory, but Betty's teammates were celebrating Betty's, their faces beaming. For some reason, Betty assumed she had come in second, even as her teammates rushed forward and she found herself cocooned within their embrace. The crowd was on its feet, their cheers deafening, streamers falling down in a mass, white and heavy as a Chicago snowstorm.

Only when the scores went up did she realize what had happened:

she had won the first Olympic gold medal to be awarded to a woman in track and field.

IT WAS A win the Americans needed. The men's attempts had brought uniform failure (which delighted the international crowd), and Betty's gold came at a crucial time, just as the nation's hopes needed to be rekindled. She "flew down the stretch, surprising all the Americans," Knute Rockne, the famed Notre Dame coach, later wrote. "Both feet were off the ground and her arms raised in triumph when she broke the tape." He may have been embellishing the truth, given that the final was close and disputed; regardless, such embellishments were about to make the international press.

While the American fans celebrated and Betty tried to absorb the chaos around her, a middle-aged man sat in the crowd, marking her speed in his little notebook. Frank Hill, a Chicago native, was currently the men's coach at Northwestern University in Evanston, Illinois, having arrived there following a long stint at Naval Station Great Lakes; there he had quickly developed a reputation for being one of the leading coaches in the country—and also one of the toughest. He believed that athletes, regardless of their gender, should not be coddled into thinking that they were the best or always would be. Now Betty interested him, in the way all strong or promising athletes interested him. He had no plans to try to meet her but suspected that their paths would cross one day, as he tucked his notebook into his breast pocket and walked out of the arena.

"WHAT CHARLES PADDOCK, who holds more sprint records than any other man who ever ran, could not do; what Jackson Scholz, the St. Louis Sprinter, who won the 100 meters in the games four years ago, could not do; and what Lloyd Hahn, the Boston Flyer, could not do, slim Elizabeth Robinson, 15 years old [sic] Chicago girl . . . has done," declared one of the many US newspapers. It continued, "The American boys who were so easily outrun by pretty much all the rest of the world ought to buy Elizabeth a big box of candy."

The Associated Press echoed the praise: "Where the American men had been failing dismally, Miss Robinson, the only Yankee to reach the women's sprint final, ran a beautiful race to beat two Canadians and a German rival. . . . Bobbed hair flying to the breezes, the Chicago girl sped down the straight-away flashing a great closing spirit to best the Canadian favorite, Fanny Rosenfeld, by two feet."

Her victory was described with a flourish, though most reporters stretched the truth by a wide margin (at least two feet). Betty's finish hadn't been as clear and clean through the ribbon as they described. At first glance, she and Fanny seemed to have crossed the finish line at virtually the same time. They were so close together that the Canadians continued to celebrate, even after the official had given the final word: Betty was awarded the gold with a running time of 12.2 seconds—a new record—while Fanny got the silver at 12.3 seconds.

General MacArthur, in the stands to support the women athletes, watched as Betty "soared almost out of control" with "that sparkling combination of speed and grace which might have rivaled even Artemis herself on the height of Olympus."

A long article in the *Evening American* congratulated not only Betty but also itself for spotting and sponsoring her talent: "We take our hats off to this youngster, who competed in a strange country, against tried, veteran athletes. At a time when she should have weakened and faltered, she showed a stout, fighting heart and triumphed. It requires gameness to accomplish what she did and we say that she has gameness. Not only has she brought honor to Chicago with her victory, but her feat gives America the distinction of scoring the first triumph in a women's track event in the history of the Olympic Games. This is the first year in which the fair sex have been given recognition, and Elizabeth Robinson has shown the way."

In many respects, Betty typified the ideal American Olympic

princess, the press announced: a dainty young woman with athletic skills, beauty, excellent grades, good manners, and a friendly attitude—a great role model for other young women (not to mention the fantasy of thousands of young men). Most important, however, she was an Olympic gold medalist—and the fastest woman in the world.

AS BETTY CELEBRATED her win, Dee prepared for her race. It was a daunting challenge: the 800 meters. But she felt ready. On Wednesday, August 1, the athletes again awakened to rain that petered out to a dribble, before the gray gloom brought in a thick coat of humidity. Nonetheless, great throngs of people watched the race, one that had already been much maligned due to the strain it supposedly placed on its athletes. Reporters were wagering that few would be able to handle such a distance and wanted to see who would be the first to collapse, with newspapermen snickering and laughing in clear view and earshot of the female athletes who had come to support their teammates.

Betty and the vast majority of the women's team now stood on the sidelines, nearly jumping off their seats as they watched Dee and her competitors take their places. Following a large breakfast on the *Roosevelt*, the athletes had boarded their buses for the stadium. Dee was already sweating, complaining of the air's denseness before she even changed into her gear. Although she was accustomed to it, she disliked running in the humidity; it felt as if a great weight were pressing on her chest.

The mercury continued to climb to make this the hottest day of the entire Olympic Games. As they prepared for the run, the athletes swallowed great amounts of water, their shirts already clinging to their skin. After the starter pistol went off, those athletes who were unaccustomed to running the 800 meters very quickly showed signs of exhaustion.

The lead runners reached the final lap and crossed the finish line, but spectators did not pay attention to the winner or to the other two who had medaled as much as they did to what happened next. A few of the athletes collapsed with fatigue before reaching the finish line; others began to cry. Papers detailed how the exhausted runners had gracelessly rushed to the end, some of them removing their shoes as quickly as possible in order to clean the blood oozing out of their blistered feet, while a few vomited by the sidelines.

Reporters used the ordeal to bolster the notion that women should not be allowed to compete in track and field. *The Times* of London wrote: "The half dozen prostrated and obviously distressed forms lying in the grass at the side of the track after the race may not warrant a complete condemnation of the girl athletic championship, but it certainly suggests unpleasant possibilities."

Knute Rockne of Notre Dame also chimed in: "The half mile race for women was a terrible event. . . . If running the half mile for women is an athletic 'event,' they ought to include a six-day dance contest between couples. One is as ridiculous as the other."

The Chicago Tribune's judgment was harsher: "I have in front of me the picture of the half-mile for women in the Olympic Games at Amsterdam and of the eight girls who finished six of them fainted exhausted—a pitiful spectacle and a reproach to anyone who had any-thing to do with putting on a race of this kind."

Among those viewing the event was Dr. Fr. M. Messerli, who had been working with female athletes for several years. In a report he wrote after the race, he stated, "When reaching the winning post, two Canadians and one Japanese competitors [*sic*] collapsed on the lawn, the public and the journalists believed them to be in a state of exhaustion. I was judging this particular event and on the spot at the time, I can therefore certify that there was nothing wrong with them, they burst into tears betraying their disappointment at having lost the race, a very feminine trait!"

Betty witnessed the entire event. Although she had won a gold medal in the inaugural track–and–field event, she was not in a position to judge whether or not women should be allowed to participate in the 800 meters. She had never raced longer distances, and her training had commenced only months earlier, leaving her still unaware of what a body potentially could or could not sustain.

Nonetheless, as the new queen of the track, she was asked her opinion of the 800 meters. She answered, to the detriment of her fellow athletes. "I believe that the 220-yard dash is long enough for any girl to run. Any distance beyond that taxes the strength of a girl, even though some of them might be built 'like an ox,' as they sometimes say. Some of the scenes at the finish of various 800-meter races recently have been actually distressing. Imagine girls falling down before they hit the finish line or collapsing when the race is over! The laws of nature never provided a girl with the physical equipment to withstand the grueling pace of such a grind. . . . I do not profess to be an expert on heart and nerve reaction to the longer distances, but common sense will tell you that they must be quite severe."

It was not the answer the women athletes, particularly her teammates, expected to hear or appreciated. Those women had been running for years, and to them reports of Amsterdam's 800 meters felt grossly exaggerated. The chastising comments made by a young woman who'd won by only a fraction of a second seemed to them not only ignorant but offensive.

After the Olympics those athletes had to endure a barrage of snide and unsavory articles, including one in *The New York Times*. "When the race was tried at Amsterdam in 1928," it said, "the gals dropped in swooning heaps as if riddled by machine-gun fire." Newspapers from all corners of the globe emphasized the so-called shocking spectacle of the finish. Wythe Williams could not contain his flair for the dramatic: "The final of the women's 800-meter run plainly demonstrated that even this distance makes too great a call on feminine strength. At the finish six of the nine runners were completely exhausted and fell headlong on the ground. Several had to be carried off the track. The little American girl, Miss Florence MacDonald, who made a gallant try but was outclassed, was in a half faint for several minutes, while even the sturdy Miss Hitomi of Japan, who finished second, needed attention before she was able to leave the field."

COUNT HENRI DE BAILLET-LATOUR, who had succeeded Coubertin as president of the IOC, partially agreeing with those who believed that such races were too strenuous for women, thereafter suggested that perhaps "aesthetic events"—that is, sports with a perceived feminine bent, such as gymnastics and tennis—would be more appropriate.

The critics and educators who'd been arguing the harm that such "laborious" sports caused to women's bodies used the 800 meters to advocate the elimination of all women's sports from future Olympics. Although such dramatic motions didn't succeed, the event was removed from the Games and would not be reinstated until 1960. In its stead, the IAAF instituted the 100-meter hurdles, which was less maligned.

Though the race was criticized internationally and widely regarded as disastrous for the women, the men's 800 was never scrutinized or questioned, despite the fact that the male runners had suffered a similar fate. Only the St. Louis *Globe-Democrat* picked up on the discrepancy. "Thursday afternoon at the finish line of the 800 meter run, two men fell to the track completely exhausted. One man was carried to his training quarters helpless. Another was laid out upon the grass and stimulants used to bring him back to life," its article read. "All that officials said was that the race was a good one; that 'Breitreux was gone; that Range ran a good race'; yet no one condemned the race as being a detriment to the good of mankind, to the welfare of the runners."

Later studies would prove that women are not only capable of running such distances but actually excel in longer ones, as their bodies are much more capable of doing so than men's. Women, by their physical nature, are born with a larger supply of fat on their limbs, nearly 10 percent more than their "equally trained men." While training, fat is used as fuel, allowing women to run more efficiently and for longer periods, reaching the end of their races with their gas tanks only half empty. But in 1928, the so-called experts did not yet know what women were capable of achieving. And neither did Betty.

CHAPTER NINE

A NEW BABE IN TOWN

"An American girl helped to restore the prestige of the Olympic Team today and again brought the Stars and Stripes fluttering to the central flagstaff," an American newspaper wrote. "Elizabeth Robinson, to the surprise of herself, team officials, and the crowd generally, won the 100-meter dash."

The papers devoted numerous pages to the athletes, Betty's tale and triumphs in particular dominating sports pages across the country. In fact, her victory stole the headlines from the men's attempts at glory, distracting the public from the reality that her male teammates had failed miserably. Reporters heralded Betty's grace, her defiance, and her athleticism. From coast to coast, and especially in Riverdale, she became an instant celebrity.

In a small, oil-soaked town in Texas, a wiry young girl devoured those reports from her father's newspapers. She had been doing so since learning her alphabet, her favorite section being the sports pages. During the summer of 1928, she closely followed the Olympians in Amsterdam. She did not know where Amsterdam was, or how anyone got there, but it sounded fun, exotic, and, according to the descriptions, as hot as it was in Beaumont. In late August, as the Olympics were nearing the end, she saw splattered across the pages photographs of and headlines about a young woman who'd recently made history.

The whole world had now seen a picture of Betty—not one of her in her running gear, crossing the finish line as she won the 100 meters (although that picture existed) but a fetching photograph showing her wearing a tidy stylish hat and little white gloves, her hands crossed demurely over her lap and a string of pearls falling from her neck. The image portrayed a well-behaved young woman who, according to some, had done a very unladylike thing in winning the first gold medal awarded to a woman in a very masculine endeavor.

It didn't take long for the young girl in Beaumont, and countless other young women across the country, to catch Olympic fever. She vowed to participate in the Games the very next year, to travel around the world, to win a medal, and to have her likeness splashed across every newspaper in the country. Only she didn't want a picture of herself with pearls dripping from her neck; she wanted one with a medal flashing gold.

When her father told her that those particular games would not come around again until 1932, the girl, whose nickname was Babe, threw one of her typical tantrums. But, as he often did, her father quickly appeased her. It was a good thing, he insisted; the interim years would give her time to practice, to hone her skills, to ensure victory over the rest of the competitors. Babe agreed, and set her sights on triumph.

MILDRED ELLA DIDRIKSON was born on June 26, 1911, in Port Arthur, Texas, the sixth of seven children of Norwegian immigrants. The family moved to Beaumont when she was three years old and lived in the shadows of the Magnolia Petroleum Company's refinery

in the oily grit of the city's south end—a small, harsh, somewhat big-
oted town whose attitudes would quickly become ingrained in Babe.

In the early 1900s, before the Didriksons' arrival, Beaumont was
a tiny dot on the map that consisted of little more than a few homes
lined up along a dry, lonely Main Street, most of whose stores had
been boarded up and left to deteriorate by owners seeking better fortune elsewhere. The more successful men in town eked out a living
making moonshine, illegal distilleries springing up across its bound-
ary lines, while the rest took odd jobs and handouts wherever they
could. Beaumont did have a small school and the requisite coffee
shop, called the Black Cat Café, which stood its ground against failure, a place where folks drank their coffee bitter and black, smoked
a cigarette or two pawned from a neighbor, read the local paper, and
complained about the temperature and the economy.

The town had had its origins in cattle and lumber, but eventually
those businesses, too, left. It was not known for its sports history, nor
any history, for that matter. In fact, it was better known for its racial
divide and bigotry, the lines that defined whites from everyone else,
and the various arguments that erupted on a daily basis. By the end
of the 1800s, Beaumont was a dismal community of less than ten
thousand people in wait of something bigger, the inhabitants guzzling
endless cups of coffee at the Black Cat and discussing the fortunate
event that would put them on the map and change their lives.

Such was their hope as they awoke each morning, and such was
their hope on a Sunday afternoon in January 1901 when a man in-
advertently struck a pickax into the arid earth of what many considered to be a worthless patch of land south of Beaumont officially
known as Spindle-Top. He did so halfheartedly, more out of frustra-
tion than anything else, but was rewarded with a large geyser of oil
that drenched him in a shiny coat. And it wasn't long before 100,000
barrels of oil were being churned out every day.

And so Beaumont grew. Refineries were built as far as the eye could see, the earth poked and prodded for miles around. The tiny town people had yearned to flee suddenly became a hot commodity. The price of land increased, spawning stretches of houses that went up as fast as lumber could be found and nailed together. Men and their families moved in, the booming economy bringing an influx of new blood from all over the country.

Ole Didriksen came as well. In 1905 the Norwegian man stepped off a tanker in Port Arthur, on the Texas-Louisiana border, a dusty town reeking of oil. For a man accustomed to Norwegian winters and summers cooled off by the breezes of the North Sea, Port Arthur was all but infernal. Yet he liked it—the bustle of the people moving about with purpose, the hardy stench of humidity, human sweat, and the oil distilleries going at full blast; it smelled like prosperity. Ole's wife, Hannah, and his three children, Ole Jr., Dora, and Esther, were still in Norway. Immigration laws didn't allow him to bring his family over for three years, and he reckoned that would give him enough time to find a job, make money, and build a house.

By trade, Ole was a cabinetmaker and furniture rebuilder, just as his father had been, though as a youth he had left his home early on and embarked on a career upon the high seas, spending years sailing around the world and even rounding Cape Horn several times, the vivid recollections of those travels eventually becoming family lore that his children never grew tired of hearing. But now his manual skills came in handy in this new and devilishly hot land.

As time passed, he framed his new home on 850 Doucette Street. The Magnolia refinery perpetually burped out smoke and fumes from the ugly smokestacks littering the skyline. It was not what Ole had wanted for his family. In his mind, they were going to live in a large, airy home, the children running around and playing in the wide expanse of their backyard, which would be dotted with tall trees and a patch of garden in a corner reserved for Hannah's laundry line, where her colorful linens would hang listlessly in the region's breezeless air. But the reality was much different.

The house Ole built was not large or luxurious, but it had a long wraparound porch he would enclose and turn into an additional bedroom, where his boys would eventually sleep, while the girls would share the only other bedroom in the house. The backyard was only a small, sad square, adjacent to other similar small, sad squares. Even though he routinely drifted through the house, fixing and hammering this or that, plucking nails poking out of the floorboards, or fastening squeaky kitchen cupboards, the fact would always remain: the house was too small and too crowded, and it could not grow any further.

Hannah Marie Olsen Didriksen and the children arrived from Oslo on a humid day in August 1908. A small, trim woman, she had during her childhood enjoyed sports, particularly figure skating and skiing, two winter activities her country was famed for. But she soon learned that there were no such pastimes in her new American home. As she disembarked in the United States, she tried to shield her eyes from the vicious sun. She stared at the refineries. There was a stickiness in the air and an odor that got to her right away. She felt it on her skin and in her throat, and the taste of oil never left her mouth.

Hannah was only five feet, four inches tall, very thin, and had a tendency to carry herself in the style many referred to as that of an athlete. (Several family members later suspected that Babe had inherited her athletic abilities from her.) Hannah did not speak or understand English and for the rest of her days would always have a problem with the language. But her small stature and poor English hid an inner complexity, toughness, and resolve few ever glimpsed.

In 1909, twin babies arrived, Lillie and Louis, the first Americans born to the family. And in June of 1911, Mildred Ella, to be known as Babe, made her appearance. No more babies came for a few years; thus Babe reveled in her nickname, which she held on to for the rest of her life.

Babe was raised no differently from her brothers, and it showed in her attitude, speech, and dress. Little girls were supposed to be quiet, delicate, prim, proper, and clean, but Babe was rude and loud and spewed obscenities and racial slurs she'd picked up from the adults around her, particularly toward the colored inhabitants of her neighborhood. She was seldom seen in anything but her brothers' short pants, which, like her bare feet, were always caked in mud. Neighbors didn't like her and thought of her as a gritty girl from the wrong side of town (not that Beaumont had a good side). They warned their children (who had already come to fear the saucy little girl) to stay away from her. And though her mother wished she'd behave and dress more like a lady and watch her tongue, Ole did not mind. Nor did he mind the fact that she stood up for herself against the boys and could usually do things better than they could.

Attuned to Babe's inner turmoil, Ole installed parallel bars, short obstacle courses, and a collection of weights in the small backyard behind their house. The tiny exercise field gave the children an opportunity to leave the confines of the tight house, to play, and to breathe the mucky air. Babe and her sister ran there, Lillie preferring smooth, flat terrain, while Babe made exuberant attempts to fly over the neighbors' hedges. Some hedges were taller than others, and the disparity caused her to develop a unique jumping style that forced her to crook her left knee; that style would remain with her, though it was later frowned upon.

Though the house lacked space, it did have plenty of windows, which every Saturday needed washing. It was on Babe and her sister Lillie that the weekly chores fell, so while the neighborhood children whose parents were better off spent their Saturdays at the cinema, for years Babe crawled on her hands and knees mopping floors and polishing windows. As she did so, she'd watch her mother beat the laundry—not only theirs but also other families', as she took in soiled washing to earn extra money. Her father's job as a furniture refinisher brought in about two hundred dollars a month. It wasn't terrible money back then, but with seven children, there never seemed to be enough.

Babe would recall the discipline she had learned, which she'd apply to other areas of her life, too. But she knew she wanted a different life from her mother's and assured herself that she would never be scrubbing someone else's dirty underwear for a living. In Norway, Hannah had been full of joy, Ole always said. But Texas wore her out; the lines on her face were evidence of that. Babe resolved that she would never allow her own face to tell the same story.

DANGLING FROM THE parallel bars in the backyard or sitting on the front steps of her house, Babe watched the neighborhood girls play their games, not with jealousy but with an expression of contempt that would accompany her throughout her life. Sissies, she thought; their girly games were just signs of weakness. She didn't have the time or the inclination for hopscotch or those stupid dolls of theirs, much less for the tiny plastic teacups in which they served imaginary beverages to one another. "I preferred baseball, football, foot walking, and jumping with the boys," she later explained. "I guess that habit of playing with the boys made me too rough for the girls' games. Anyhow, I found them too tame." She learned to shoot a rifle with the same expertise as any of the men in Beaumont. And as she grew, her intent became clear: sports were not only her preferred activity; they would also allow her both to stand out from the crowd and to eventually get away from Beaumont.

She attended the Magnolia Grade School, then the South End Junior High School, arriving at Beaumont High School with a reputation, especially her hankering for always wanting to pick a fight. She made no friends, feeling that she had nothing in common with her schoolmates, particularly the girls. She knew that some had dreams of a college education, followed by jobs that would make use of their studies. But for Babe, studying was useless. She had no intention of going to college, much less of finding a husband and birthing a pack of children. She joined the basketball team, the Miss Royal Purples, the only girls' team at Beaumont High, and, given that school never had a real place in her life, her grades reflected that fact: she merely kept them above the minimum required to allow her to play sports.

ON A BLEAK February night in 1930, a cold rain whipped down over the city of Houston. Colonel Melvirne Johnson McCombs, who managed a Dallas insurance company's athletic program and who was in Houston for business, was stranded in his hotel room by the weather when he picked up a local newspaper. He was cheered to read that a basketball game between two local girls' teams was taking place in a nearby auditorium. He recognized the name of one of the players, as he had been reading the latest newspaper articles and had started keeping tally on a girl who had been averaging more than thirty points per game, crushing the competition. Papers had been bragging about the local all-state athlete, and he had wanted to meet her for some time. Settling his Stetson onto his head, he headed out into the elements.

Looking every inch the "Colonel," as people referred to him, McCombs was a graduate of Texas A&M, where he had played baseball and basketball and had some success in track and field. He had followed his studies with a stint in the US Army Reserve but eventually became known to his acquaintances as much for his sense of duty as for his talent in scouting female athletes. His hair was now gray and short, cut in the military style he had favored during his army days (maintained by biweekly trimmings at a local barbershop); that, together with his tall, erect figure, gave an impression that he was devoid of any sense of humor. In truth, he was, though on occasion he would let out a barrage of sarcastic comments meant to be humorous but that came across only as biting. He now managed the Safety Department for the Employers Casualty Company and since

1925 had also been in charge of the company's athletic department, which included a semiprofessional female basketball team, the Dallas Golden Cyclones.

McCombs had initially utilized his talents as a coach in male teams all over Texas and Oklahoma. He had developed a keen eye for spotting real athletic talent; he knew ahead of his time that female athletes were also gifted with such capacity and often wondered why schools didn't take advantage of that pool of candidates. Most of his acquaintances were not even remotely interested in women's sports and declared them useless, but McCombs believed otherwise. He was the first coach in history to trade his team's uniform of long woolen bloomers, baggy blouses, and long stockings for lighter, shorter, cooler clothing. He recognized the former ensemble as too cumbersome for an athlete to play in, much less perform well.

HAVING MADE HIS way to the local auditorium to watch the girls' game, he stood in the bleachers and, as often happened on such occasions, felt a tingle run down his body. The discovery of new talent was visceral for the Colonel.

After the game, he followed the girl wearing a Beaumont High blouse with the number 7 stitched on her back to the rear of the auditorium. He found Babe chewing on two chocolate cream cakes and guzzling down a large container of chocolate milk. She was not very tall, standing no more than five feet, five inches, and probably weighed about a hundred pounds. A long scar ran down her right leg, a reminder of a childhood accident when, on a dare, she had jumped from a roof and a piece of scraggy wood had pierced the flesh. She looked ordinary, with sharp, angular features and a thin aquiline nose that the papers would later compare to a hawk's. A high forehead framed short, dark hair that fell over chestnut-colored eyes.

The Colonel introduced himself, gave her a vigorous handshake, and told her why he was there. Never stopping to clear the chocolate crumbs from her lips or to wipe away a chocolate mustache, she told him, in her heavy Texas twang, that he should meet her parents.

The following day McCombs arrived on dusty, smelly Doucette Street in a big yellow Cadillac, immediately impressing Ole and Hannah. He brought the smell of money and opportunity. Babe's parents greeted the Colonel as they always greeted visitors: by leading him toward the large kitchen table to partake in the Swedish meatballs Hannah had prepared. McCombs tilted his head toward Ole, while still keeping Hannah in the conversation, and promised them that if Babe was allowed to join his team—an all-female basketball team much in need of new talent—she would become a national champion and would never lack for money. For two immigrants who barely spoke English and whose conversations often revolved around finances, the idea of a child of theirs making good in America was beyond appealing.

Babe recognized this as a pivotal moment that could change the circumstances of her life. When McCombs left and the family was alone, she began to plead her case. She wouldn't even quit school, she told them; she would leave for just a few months to join the team until the end of the season and then return to Beaumont High to graduate. She directed her efforts toward Ole, who could never resist her begging and pouting. Although Hannah felt that Babe was too young to go out in the world alone, Ole gave in, even agreeing to travel to Dallas, some 275 miles from Beaumont, to help her settle in.

BABE'S FIRST APPEARANCE for the Golden Cyclones occurred on February 18, 1930. She had found a uniform in a pile of used ones with the number 7 stitched on the back—the same number she had worn in high school—and claimed it as her own. Her teammates weren't particularly friendly, but then, neither was she. Still, those "husky" girls seemed to resent her before their first game even started.

She entered the basketball court with typical dramatic flair, waving her arms and smiling from ear to ear. Outfitted in new uniforms, the team played against the Sun Oil Company team and beat it soundly. That was only the beginning. In the span of six games, Babe scored 195 points (a precursor to her being named all-American, twice).

As the team played more games, she became its standout, and people began talking about her, stunned not only by her gamesmanship but also by her brash personality. Newspapers and radio stations across Texas carried reports of her winning streak as a member of the Golden Cyclones. The games were heard on the radio throughout Texas, and in the region she became known as "Mighty Mildred." The articles splashed her picture front and center, relegating her teammates to the background. The taste of fame, if only regional, brought her closer to her goal of becoming rich and famous. She basked in the publicity, and it soon became apparent that her talents eclipsed those of all her teammates combined—a fact they somewhat appreciated, since she propelled them to win more games, but privately envied.

In fact, her teammates nurtured a fervent dislike for her; they thought this small girl from a backward town with a loud mouth and an oversized attitude was too strong-willed, too rough and insensitive, too uncouth. She had a penchant for cussing and a robust dislike for anything resembling authority. It was hard to reconcile that she was simultaneously an athletic asset and a burden to the team, especially when she felt no loyalty toward the others. She measured her success not by how many wins the *team* accumulated but by how many points *she* scored and how many times her name was mentioned in the newspapers, a preoccupation that grew with each game.

Babe didn't care about her teammates' feelings. She was not there to forge friendships; she was there to play while earning money and courting fame. From the start, it had been understood that she had been brought to Dallas for her basketball skills, even though she had officially been hired as a stenographer, a job for which she lacked the basic typewriting skills required. She earned seventy-five dollars a month, forty of which she immediately wired home to Ole and Hannah, spending thirty on rent and other necessities and keeping five for incidentals. Her diet continued to be inconsistent—or consistent in its own way—as her grades had been. She downed gallons of Coca-Cola throughout the day and subsisted mostly on cupcakes, either chocolate or toasted ones, her favorites being ones with the slightly charred marshmallow topping she bought at a local diner.

As the season neared its end, she thought about the plans she and her parents had made around the dinner table. She had promised that she would return to Beaumont and finish the required classes for graduation. But now, as her popularity grew after only a few months with the team, she wondered about her promise and the wisdom of returning to school at all. What was the point? She had never liked the place, had never fit in there. Now she was making money doing what she loved. And there was more to come, the Colonel and others promised her. So she drafted a letter to her parents and withdrew from Beaumont High School.

THE SEASON OFFICIALLY ended on a muggy late-spring day; even by Dallas standards, the heat was unbearable. That meant rest for most teams, but not for the Cyclones, who quickly transitioned to softball. The boredom the athletes, particularly Babe, displayed around a softball diamond stunned the Colonel. He needed a way to shake them out of their lassitude. On a lark, and as the temperatures climbed, he took Babe and several of her teammates to a track meet. He recalled his own days as a track star at Texas A&M, the pleasure he had felt as his feet bounced off the cinder tracks. There were several teams training at Lakeside Park, and he and his team sat on the bleachers and watched the strength and vigor on display.

McCombs explained that there were approximately nine events

in track and field, and though they were all under the same umbrella, they differed from one another, each requiring a particular set of skills and training. And aside from the relay competition, they were all individual events.

As Babe admired the athletes pushing their way down the tracks, she thought of her sister Lillie, who, about four years earlier, in the aftermath of the Amsterdam Olympics, had had aspirations of becoming a runner. Unlike Babe, Lillie had never practiced enough, thus never came near her goal. Now, watching the amateurs at Lakeside Park, Babe marveled at the possibilities: the athletics on display were a matter of personal control, she thought, as opposed to basketball, where she had none. These people played for their own sake, and were not reliant on others. In basketball, if one of her teammates had an off day, despite Babe's best efforts the team would lose, and she would blame that person or be blamed by the others. But track was different: there would be no one to blame but herself and, by default, no one else to congratulate. She felt drunk with the discovery of what this new world could offer. As she looked at her teammates and thought about the sniveling and gossiping she had endured since arriving in Dallas, she considered just how this sport could change all that.

BABE WATCHED THE hurdlers, mesmerized. She realized that she already knew the basics of the sport. Catapulting over the hedges in her neighborhood while trying to keep her speed between jumps came naturally to her, and hurdling was similar. She was not tall and knew that her stride would be shorter than that of the athletes she was observing. But she would make up for it by increasing her overall velocity.

Watching, she also realized that there were several tricks she could use to ensure a win: she could pummel her trunk across the ribbon, ensuring that it broke; or wave her hands wildly just prior to crossing the finish line, to confuse the officials and make it seem, from a distance, as though she had won. It was a decoy she employed once she started competing, and it would fool judges and audiences alike. Years later, she admitted it to a reporter. "All you have to do to win if it's close," she said with a smirk, "is to throw your arms just before the finish."

The Olympics would soon be held again; this time they would be in Los Angeles, relatively her own backyard. Perhaps Babe didn't know it, McCombs let slip during their conversation, although he suspected that she did. There was no female basketball Olympic try-out, but there was track.

Of course, Babe recalled the newsaper reports she had read in 1928 and the fuss that had been made over the new track-and-field starlet who'd won the 100 meters. As she admired the athletes push-ing their way down the tracks, she remembered sitting with her father on the front steps of their house on Doucette Street as he opened the newspaper, pausing at the sports section and marveling at the feats the athletes were accomplishing during the Amsterdam Olympics. She had never participated in track and field, nor had she ever worn spiked shoes, for that matter. But those were only small handicaps, in her mind. She began to concoct what seemed an implausible plan and told McCombs that she wanted to learn every technique involved in each track-and-field event. Her words provoked ridicule from her teammates. How could she take such an approach to a sport she had never participated in? She just smiled, confident that she would show them.

AS BABE BEGAN her new routine, there was a density to the air, coalescing with the expectation Babe had set up for herself. She prac-ticed her new track-and-field techniques until nightfall, arriving on the grounds of Dallas Lakeside Park after the team's practices and not leaving until the sun was low behind her, with training absorbing the better part of her days.

The time she spent running revealed a discipline and commitment that she had not shown before, not even in the team basketball games, and she became maniacal about her practices, intoxicated by the high she got from exercising. Following supper, she would don her running shoes again—or even go barefoot—and jog up and down a hill named Haines Street, stretching her legs and rotating her arms. She would run and run, faster and faster, alternating long sprints with short jumps, then moving on to a light jog. She would skip, then hop first on one foot and then on the other. Long walks and short ones, long runs and short ones. She would be tired by then, having practiced all day with the team and then run around Lakeside Park for hours on end. She always hoped for a bright moon, since its light allowed her to run even further into the night.

It was a punishing workout that left her little time for anything else. There were no shopping excursions, no diner meals, no breaks at the ice cream parlor, no fun at the swimming pool. It was tough and unrelenting; if anyone thought women could not take hard physical work, Babe proved them wrong.

Her resolve not only to improve but to perfect her introduction into track and field amazed McCombs, even as it worried him. He urged her to try to strike some kind of balance—the constant pounding on her body could be disastrous, he said, actually hindering her progress, both physically and mentally. Interact with teammates, he urged her, go out with some girlfriends, maybe even find a boyfriend. But she insisted she didn't have time to waste on such trivial pursuits, and she followed the simple philosophy her father had instilled in her: practice makes perfect. And so she trained until, as she later said, she "was seeing stars," her body aching but her mind soldiering on. Then, gasping and at the brink of inevitable collapse, she tumbled into bed, knowing that in a few hours everything would begin anew.

Babe was aware that there were dozens of little details to master to make it seem as if she had been born with wings on her feet. No one could see her struggle, the efforts she put into catapulting herself forward. She knew what the payoff for her labors would be: a trip to the Los Angeles Olympics in 1932.

CHAPTER TEN

WELCOME HOME

A great deal of fanfare greeted the 1928 Olympic athletes on their return to the United States, the port of New York full of pleasure boats and small vessels as the SS *President Roosevelt* made its way back into the pier. Spectators, assembled there since morning, were standing and yelling welcoming cheers while waving battered handkerchiefs and soggy newspapers. The athletes were awestruck as they passed the Statue of Liberty, skyscrapers looming large before them, the sound of bugles playing "The Star-Spangled Banner" reverberating in the air. Despite the inclement weather, shouts of delight resounded on the promenade, and although a parade had been planned for the athletes, they soon learned that the rain that was pelting the city had altered those festivities.

The enthusiastic gaiety displayed by the crowd seemed to contradict most of the written reports; not every American was thrilled by the athletes' performance in Amsterdam, particularly the men's. Many faulted General MacArthur, although he consistently hailed the mission as a success. "Our victorious team returned to New York with the plaudits of the country ringing in their ears. The team was feted out from coast to coast, both the press and my superiors being most gracious," MacArthur wrote in a telegram to T. V. O'Connor, chairman of the United States Shipping Board. "The American athletes not only have not failed, but have achieved a brilliant success comparable to those of past Olympics. Guests who were entertained on board the *Roosevelt* were served the same fare always served to passengers," he added, chiding the reporters who still blamed the lackluster results on the copious amounts of food.

In a letter to President Calvin Coolidge, MacArthur elaborated, "If I were required to indicate today that element of American life which is most characteristic of our nationality, my finger would unerringly point to our athletic escutcheon."

AFTER HAVING BEEN out of the country for forty-two days, Betty was ready to return home. Clutching her sweater, she looked anxiously over the crowd for her parents. Finally she spotted them and raced down the gangplank, virtually lunging at them, ignoring the rain and the chill, embracing her father and inhaling deeply the sharp smell of tobacco that always clung to him. Moments later, he whispered that there was something special waiting for her at home. At her urging, he revealed her birthday and Olympic-gold-winning present; he had purchased what every young person in the history of time has desired: a new car. The freedom that Betty craved, that she had come to enjoy during her early training in Chicago, would be hers.

Before she could test out her new car, the athletes were supposed to take part in a parade leading from the pier to City Hall. Nearly two thousand people had gathered to accompany them along the parade route, together with dozens of police officers who had been enlisted to escort them. But a sudden downpour changed all that. Instead, they were driven to City Hall, where, following numerous speeches, they were at last left to their own devices. Betty did not mind missing the fanfare of a formal ceremony; she was eager for a good night's sleep and a return home.

Shortly after her victory had been announced, thirty-five representatives from Riverdale and Dolton had met at the Bowen School to plan a celebration worthy of their winner. William A. Reich, a local businessman, had called the meeting to order and stated the purpose of it to be the organization of a parade and associated celebration to honor "our Elizabeth." It was decided that several other cities and villages should be involved in the plans, including Harvey, South Holland, and Calumet City. The gist of the parade and party was quickly decided on: all the homes and businesses along the route would have to adhere to strict regulations that included beautifying their facades with Olympic colors and banners, in addition to an abundance of streamers and balloons. Several bands would play, and thousands of noisemakers would be distributed. The state car Betty and her parents would ride in would lead the parade, beginning in Riverdale and winding its way through the surrounding towns before returning to Betty's proud hometown.

Getting hold of the plans on Friday, August 14, *The Pointer* declared, "Never before in the history of the community has there been such enthusiasm as is evident over the plans for next Tuesday evening when Elizabeth Robinson, local girl, is welcomed back to her 'hometown' in honor of her achievements."

"The parade," the paper informed, "will begin to assemble at 5:30 with its head at the Lincoln Avenue School. . . . Everyone is welcome and the more the merrier. Those who assemble in the formation on Lincoln Avenue will have the first opportunity to see Miss Robinson locally since her Olympic successes, and she will be right at the head at 7:15 and will begin a review of the assembly from an open car which will carry her to the rear of the procession. At 7:30 the procession will get underway. Both the arrival of Miss Robinson at the head of the parade and the start of the procession will be announced by bombs."

Betty arrived, flanked by her parents, well before the parade began. Nearly twenty thousand spectators elbowed one another for a better view of their golden girl as she was driven through a blizzard of confetti, banners, balloons, flowers, leaflets, and ribbons. She enjoyed the public adulation, craving it as she had craved it during her school plays.

The parade marched through Dolton, Riverdale, Highland, Ivanhoe, the West Pullman business district, Roseland, and the North Side. Inevitably, the parade passed the Thornton Township High School, the edifice Betty had left in a hurry only months earlier, eager to catch her train home. It was on that train that she had met Coach Price, a life-changing meeting, and now she was returning as an Olympian, a gold medal hanging from her neck.

Betty did not know if Coach Price was in the crowd, watching without being watched, as he always did, and barely nodding his head. She still had to complete her senior year; the beginning of the new semester was only a few weeks away. Naturally, the experience in Amsterdam had shifted her vision for her future.

The parade wound back to Riverdale Park, where it circled and made its way toward the gazebo built for the occasion. She felt the car slowing down as it reached the grounds, before stopping completely. She was ushered to a wooden stand by Paul Gull of the American Legion. Asher Parker of the Ivanhoe Civil Club presented her with a bouquet of flowers. Then, just before the mayor of Chicago introduced her to the waiting crowd, she was given "gifts and more gifts: diamond rings, wrist watches, pins, pendants . . . and a slick new roadster her parents purchased for her," *The Pointer* reported. Those were not small tokens from a grateful, proud community but expensive luxuries that a sixteen-year-old girl was not accustomed to receiving, and she was dazzled by them. (It was only a year later that Avery Brundage, then the president of the AAU, made a pronouncement regarding the types of gifts that should, and should not, be accepted by amateur athletes. He stated in no uncertain terms: "Expensive gifts and financial compensation for athletic skills beyond travel expenses must never be accepted by an American amateur-athlete." But the rule had not yet been set into motion when Betty received her gifts.)

As Betty raised her hand to the light, the diamond ring she'd been gifted shone as fiercely as her medal had in Amsterdam, as fiercely as her desire to recapture that winning moment.

LESS THAN TWO weeks after her return home, Betty went back to high school, now an Olympic gold medalist and a senior with what felt like too many responsibilities. Aside from her classes and physical training, she was in charge of mentoring the incoming freshmen students, in addition to serving as class secretary and Girls' Glee Club librarian. Much was the same; she still danced and performed in the theater club, participated in the Latin and French clubs, and maintained perfect grades. But she now had her future to think about. She had always imagined that her life would involve a career teaching the arts. But now, as she changed into her running outfit or glanced at her gold medal, she understood that new opportunities had opened up for her. She thought of going to college to study physical education; there was an emerging group of female physical education teachers and coaches, and she considered becoming one of them. Nothing was definite yet, but the possibilities enthralled her.

But more than anything, with the exuberance and optimism that had always ruled her life, she intended to secure another medal (preferably gold) at the 1932 Los Angeles Games before going on to coach the team herself in 1936. In a yearbook entry published later that year, under her name and photograph she wrote, as her aspiration, "to be a coach of the 1936 Olympic Team." It was a plan she herself had concocted, confident that she had no reason to assume that her goals would not come to fruition. Looking ahead, the whole world seemed conquerable.

UPON GRADUATING FROM Thornton Township High School, Betty did not enroll in a college away from home but remained on the grounds of Harvey, attending the recently opened Thornton Township Junior College. Her first semester progressed well; she enjoyed her English, chemistry, and French classes, followed by trigonometry and hygiene in the spring, receiving high marks (except for two C's in chemistry). Her commute was the same as it had been during high school. In fact, it seemed to her that nothing had changed in that regard; she left home early in the morning and took the train to the school, occasionally walking toward Harvey, trudging over grounds she had walked on since arriving there as a freshman years before.

She saw the same people she had always seen leave for work at the same hour they had always left, mostly on their way to the Acme Factory; the children who had stood waving to their parents behind the windows had now grown and were heading to their elementary school, while smaller toddlers assumed their places behind the same windows. The same women were pruning hedges and rosebushes or chatting with neighbors behind low white fences. And the trees changed colors at the same time every year, from vibrant green to russet and brown, then the decaying leaves fell on the ground before the snow buried them.

Though nothing around her had changed, she certainly had. It was not only the medal that had opened her eyes but the places she had seen, the people she had met. There was so much more to the world than the confines of Riverdale and Harvey, than the path she walked on every day. Luckily, running continued to afford her opportunities to experience new people and new surroundings.

. . .

IN SEPTEMBER 1930, Betty was listed as a participant in the Third World Championship, to be held in Prague. It was an exciting honor, as only the very best athletes had been selected to attend the competition. Helen Filkey would also be there, but more than anyone else, Betty was most eager to finally meet the athlete everyone was talking about: the Dallas dynamo Babe Didrikson.

One could not be a member of the track-and-field family without hearing the name of the brash Texan whose impact on the sport was being felt far and wide. Everyone looked forward to the challenge of meeting her face-to-face. It wasn't that long before that Betty herself had entered the competitions with a chip on her shoulder, perhaps not quite as oversized as Babe's but a chip nonetheless. And she still had one. But to Betty's disappointment, the young women were not fated to meet. No team was sent to Prague, disheartening the athletes—and Betty—even more.

In the spring of 1930, Betty transferred to Northwestern University and enrolled in a physical education program. Unlike Riverdale, Evanston was a vibrant and stimulating place, and she quickly felt a revived sense of freedom that the university had to offer.

Now, as she walked to class each morning, she was struck by the defining features of the South Quadrangle, which had been constructed by James Gamble Rogers, the architect who had also designed the vast vistas of Yale University. At Northwestern the sleeping quarters were arranged around smaller courtyards that branched away from a larger one.

As she acclimated to her new surroundings, Betty learned that it wasn't only running or her studies that interested her but also the typical pursuits of a college girl—including boys. While crossing one of the college's quadrangles, she noticed Bert "Ball Hawk" Riel, a young man well over six feet tall whose interests included football, tennis, and baseball. He was also the captain of the basketball team, which would become the most successful team in the school's history.

He had been playing since arriving at the school three years earlier, becoming the captain of the basketball team in 1931 and leading it to win the Big 10 Championship.

Betty spotted Bert the moment she stepped onto the lawn, watching as he threw a football high across the quad to one of his long-limbed friends. Bert was a lanky young man himself, a late bloomer whose body was still unsure of how to handle that height and the additional bulk that accompanied it. Betty had always appreciated a brawny physique and was not shy about admiring a man if he caught her eye. She had refined this taste on the SS *President Roosevelt*, where the male athletes, in nearly perfect shape, had strolled about wearing either tight training uniforms or almost nothing. She still remembered Johnny Weissmuller and his daily routine; in fact, her admiration for him would last a lifetime.

Bert had grown up in Watseka, Illinois, a small town at the mouth of the Iroquois River, a tributary of the Kankakee River. His father, Paul E. Riel, was a watchmaker, jewelry maker, and all-around tinkerer who had served Watseka as the sole eyeglass framer. The shop was attached to their house, leading to a continual stream of customers on the premises; the Riels came to know everyone in town—their stories, sorrows, tragedies, and loves becoming as familiar to the family as their own. Bert was a bit of a dabbler in the trade himself, learning to fit glasses and giving townspeople the impression that he would one day take over his father's trade and store. But he had other plans. He was aware that a whole world existed outside of Watseka, and upon graduating from high school he made a dash for Evanston, though he often returned home to help his father or wade through his hometown's rivers.

In the months between high school and college, Bert became a star athlete, a model student, and a handsome, muscular young man. When he did revisit Watseka, he did not lack for female attention or company.

By the time Betty reached Northwestern, she had become more noticeable than she had been in high school, her hair having grown longer and now tumbling in curls to her shoulders, her smile more pronounced, her body leaner, her stride emboldened by the confidence of an Olympian. She instantly reminded Bert of a Hollywood star, one of those women who made waves on the screen and took up the better part of the daily papers. The two bonded in local diners, chatting about their shared interests in sports, among other passions. He was a star at the university, and many believed he would have a long and glamorous future in sports. Meanwhile, as an Olympian, she brought to their relationship an alluring, elegant aura that other girls didn't possess.

AS THE 1932 Los Angeles Games approached, Betty reached out to a new coach named Frank Hill, who had seen her run at the 1928 Olympics. Though he normally coached only the Northwestern men's track team, Frank agreed to work with her. Betty did not know that Frank had already seen her win back in Amsterdam and taken notes on her, suspecting that they would cross paths one day.

Newspapers got wind of her new coach and quickly profiled the "girl sprinter" as she set her sights toward Los Angeles. She didn't smoke, drink, or stay out late, she told one reporter. None of that was true—she did all those things, and more. Frank Hill was not immediately impressed by her routine—or lack thereof. He saw her raw natural talent, but her erratic schedule needed structure, he told her, as her wide-ranging interests—the numerous clubs and extracurricular teams, including the rifle team, not to mention her boyfriend—were not going to help her earn another medal. She strung together training sessions whenever she could, which, at the end of the week, did not amount to much. Frank's training philosophy, on the other hand, was like "going into battle," he later explained. "Other forms of education should not be allowed to interfere too much with competitive athletes." When preparing to go to war, nothing stood in a soldier's way. Getting ready for a race was just like that, he felt.

Frank warned Betty that although her first medal had come easily, nearly seeking her out, the second time around would not be that simple. She needed daily training and conditioning, the likes of which she had never undergone. She now had a target on her back. There were other competitors out there who had been training far harder since the tryouts in Newark in 1928, eager to beat her. In anticipation of the Los Angeles Games, some athletes had made their intentions known in the papers, and Frank cautioned the cocky Betty that she should take those threats very seriously. (One of those athletes was Stella Walsh, whom Betty was scheduled to meet in Texas at the AAU National Championships.)

She considered his advice, and in quiet moments of reflection, when she allowed herself to ponder his words, she realized what the problem was, what it had always been: priorities. She lacked not the ambition but the discipline. Unlike Stella or Babe, for Betty running had remained the same, even after the Olympics—a pleasant activity she performed outside of classes, much like all the other enjoyable activities that took up the rest of her day. She could never conceive of leaving school to train full-time, nor could she imagine denying herself the joy of a date with Bert at the local diner in order to prepare for a race. She ran in small doses, breaking her training down to fit within the rest of her life.

What Frank was suggesting was radical. And every time they met he asked the same questions: How far did she want to go in her sport? What did she want to accomplish, and what was she willing to give up in order to get there? Something had to give in order for her to be able to fulfill her ambitions. It was not out of the realm of possibility for her to win longer races, too, to achieve greater glories and pile on more medals, he told her. But in order to do that, she would have to change her style of training. He would require total commitment from her; was she willing to give him that?

ALTHOUGH STELLA WALSH rarely dwelled much on past affairs, the loss she had suffered at Newark in 1928 still ate at her, years later. Undeterred, she had collected armfuls of ribbons in the intermittent years, intensifying her training to such a degree that the Cleveland papers began calling her "The Cleveland 20th Century Limited." As she trained in rain, heat, snow, and fog, her speed had increased, her stride lengthened, her body eventually fueled by such drive that on May 30, 1930, she became the first woman to run the 100-meter dash in less than 12 seconds. Just a month earlier she had defeated two Canadians, including Myrtle Cook, in the 50-yard dash at the Millrose Games in Madison Square Garden. Her supremacy continued at the Boston Garden, where she took the honors of the 220-yard dash at the AAU National Indoor Championships.

In 1929, Stella had competed in the Pan-Slovenia World Meet in Poland as part of the Polish Falcons of America team. There she had caused a stir by winning the 60 and the 100 meters, taking third place in the high jump and fourth place in the shot put, as well as anchoring the relay team.

Her native country had taken notice, the Polish government encouraging her to represent it at the international level, particularly in the upcoming games against Austria and Czechoslovakia. But she refused to run for Poland. Instead she upped her training even further, making 1930 one of her most productive years. All told, she competed in more than two dozen meets across the country and in Canada, bettering or equaling her own records.

The 1930 Outdoor Track and Field National Championships was held on July 4 in the Southern Methodist University Stadium in Dallas, Texas. More than two thousand spectators watched as six new world records were set, three of them by Stella. She also set a new world record in the 100-meter dash—11.2 seconds—outrunning Betty.

Betty had arrived in Texas feeling particularly exultant, as the training she was undergoing with Frank seemed to have placed her in a much better place, both physically and mentally. She had gained speed and several pounds of muscles, plus the confidence that she could win any race Frank put her in. The extra hours of training had also convinced her that a cinder track was where she belonged, causing her to streamline her schedule of activities, no longer wasting the little time she had on what she now considered frivolities.

ON THE EVENING of July 4, Betty and Stella met at the starting line and crouched for the "set" command. When the gun popped they dashed off at precisely the same instant, matching themselves stride for stride the entire length of the track. They traded the lead for several seconds, until at last Stella rapidly gained speed, crossing the finish line first. The move shocked Betty, who, unprepared for the surge, finished second.

Although the papers in Riverdale reported that only an inch or two had separated them, the reality was that it had actually been six. Reporters beyond Riverdale were only slightly fairer in their writing, claiming that "a slip at the starting line lost the 100 yard dash for Betty Robinson." The *Chicago Evening American* reported, "The only flaw in what otherwise would have been a most glorious Fourth was the defeat of Betty Robinson in the 100 yard dash by Stella Walsh, Cleveland's 'super woman,' who wound up the afternoon with two new records to her credit. Betty lost by a margin of six inches after getting away to a most horrible start, and even Stella's coach was frank to admit that the Chicago girl probably could take her measure the next time they met."

In an echo of years past, Betty slowly circled the track to regain her composure, looking over at the reporters as they gathered around Stella for photographs and interviews. To an outsider, the scene would have looked eerily familiar, similar to the tryouts in Newark in 1928 but with roles reversed. What Betty knew for certain this time was that she needed to train much harder to make it in Los Angeles, for she had experienced firsthand what she had read in the newspapers: Stella was becoming unbeatable.

Betty was still thinking about her loss weeks later—the more she dwelled on it, the more it stung. So when the Illinois Women's Athletic Club approached her with the idea of a rematch against Stella, Betty enthusiastically agreed. She increased her daily workouts with Frank, feeling secure that this time she could give Stella a good beating.

FEBRUARY 23, 1931, was a blustery evening. Spectators gathered at the 124th Field Artillery Armory on the South Side of Chicago, taking and making bets. Their money was on Betty, the hometown favorite, although for the first ninety-five yards it was a dead heat, the two athletes battling it down the track on equal stride, as though they were attached to each other by an invisible string. The crowd grew agitated when no clear winner seemed to move ahead, until, as the final ribbon loomed into view, Betty seemed to gain a final burst of energy, hitting and breaking the ribbon nearly a foot ahead of Stella, enough of a distance to dismiss any controversy. Her time was clocked at 11.1 seconds. But expecting that they would meet again in Los Angeles, each vowed to take the other one out, even if it killed her.

WHEN TIDYE PICKETT heard that Los Angeles had been named the next host city for the Olympics, she knew that she had to be a part of them. Deep down in her gut she felt that *these* were the games where she would make her mark. Of course, she was aware of the obstacles, not the least of which was the color of her skin, but she was determined nonetheless to heed the call of the West.

Like Betty, Tidye had been born in Illinois, on November 3, 1914, in Chicago. As she so often ran over the city parks' cinder tracks, she'd recall the athletic programs she had participated in as a child, held by the Park District. Not everything had been open to African American children, but the park programs were. One had been held at the Carter School Playground, where Tidye had befriended Pearl Green, the girls' athletic director. Impressed by Tidye's abilities, Green had entered her in all the meets she could find, including those at the YMCA, the church organizations, and the Chicago Park District's South Track Team. Tidye excelled in all of them.

Slight, standing only five feet, three inches, she had never weighed more than a hundred pounds. She knew that her size should have hindered her, yet she learned early on that being small meant that she could run even faster than her competitors. During an early 1932 meet at the Armory Cottage on Grove Avenue, she met John Brooks, a young track-and-field hopeful who would eventually go on to qualify for the Olympic long jump competition. Watching Tidye, Brooks saw not only fresh potential but also the determination to break boundaries, a mentality he shared. He would work with her and push her to become one of the first African American women to grace the Olympic stage.

IN MALDEN, MASSACHUSETTS, a suburb not five miles north of Boston and on the banks of the nearby Mystic River, another young African American athlete, Louise Stokes, also had her sights set on Los Angeles. Born in Malden in 1913 to William Stokes, a gardener, and Mary Wesley Stokes, a domestic, Louise was the oldest of six children and began her athletic career while still a student at Beebe

Junior High School. While she was a star of the high school basketball team, her coach, noticing how fast she was, suggested that she join the prestigious Onteora Track Club, sponsored by William H. Quaine. Although Quaine was a postal worker, he had once been an athlete, and he now coached those in whom he saw burgeoning talent.

Louise joined the athletes who looked to Los Angeles as an opportunity, a place where all of her hopes would coalesce; but before reaching the City of Angels, she would have to make it to Evanston, where the tryouts would take place in the summer of 1932.

IT SEEMED ONLY one thing could have kept these athletes from their goal: the possibility that women's track and field would not be on the Olympic roster, as its omission was still very much on the table. Old-fashioned beliefs about women's ability to compete alongside men persisted, that belief dictating that women participating in what were considered masculine sports jeopardized their femininity and rendered them unappealing to men. Mrs. H. E. Schoenhut, a physical education teacher, was quoted in a newspaper as saying, "Running in particular, either sprinting or distance, quickly destroys the feminine musculature and develops a condition of the muscles similar to that of a male runner of like experience. Again, if one thinks of the future, the strain of such physical exertion writes its story on the face of an athlete, and that is the only face one has, you know, to carry her through the rest of her life."

One infamous journalist, Paul Gallico, reflected the feelings of many men who had witnessed track and field in 1928. "There is no girl living who can manage to look anything but awful during the process of some strenuous game played on a hot day," he wrote, zeroing in not on the physical harm sports were said to cause but on the supposed compromising of women's looks. "If there is anything more dreadful aesthetically or more depressing than the fatigue-distorted face of a girl runner at the finish line, I have never seen it." (Not surprisingly, Gallico was dating a dainty swimmer, the petite Josephine McKim.)

Although Pierre de Coubertin had retired in 1925, he continued to argue that women should have been excluded not only from track-and-field events but from the Olympics altogether. He also suggested that women were not physically built to withstand the demands of strenuous exercise: "No matter how toughened a sportswoman may be, her organism is not cut out to sustain certain shocks," he insisted. "Her nerves rule her muscles, nature wanted it that way."

And he had his supporters. About a year after the Amsterdam Olympics, on August 10, 1929, an article with the incredulous title "Olympics for Girls?" (by Frederick Rand Rogers) was published; it offered up dubious science that "perhaps the most obvious physical difference of all is that men are more animal-like, mobile, energetic, aware, while women are more plant-like, more closely attached to the soil, to home, and quieter by nature." It went on: "Man combats, but woman tends to conform. Man destroys, but woman more truly loves. Man makes history, but woman is history. Competition, even though undesirable socially, is at least natural to men. In women it is profoundly unnatural. Man wins through struggle, but woman stoops to conquer."

Aside from the idea that sports such as track and field seemed to cause women to develop muscles deemed "too masculine," which in turn supposedly prevented them from attracting a male suitor and producing babies with him, there was also the absurd belief that some of those women were not only taking on the appearance of men but *becoming* men themselves, their gender and sexuality interwoven.

Rogers continued in his article: "It is almost futile to argue this point with either feminists, many of them violate nature themselves, or psychologists, whose measuring instruments are unfortunately still too crude to discover emotional and mental sex offences. Nothing is so tragic as the so-called 'divided self,' when the self is divided between male and female impulses and interests. 'Manly' women, no less than 'effeminate' men may constitute nature's greatest failures, which should, perhaps, be corrected by drastic means as those by which the most hideous deformities are treated."

As opportunities for women grew despite staunch opposition, female athletes also learned that they had an unlikely antagonist: Mrs. Herbert Hoover, Lou Henry Hoover herself. The president's wife headed the Women's Division of the National Amateur Athletic Federation (NAAF), and, like those who had held the post before her, she felt that women should be involved in sports simply as "play for play's sake."

In 1929, Mrs. Hoover called the Conference on Athletics and Physical Education for Women and Girls. On April 6 and 7, seven representatives met to discuss "Limitations for Women and Girls in Athletics," along with other related topics. Mrs. Hoover and other like-minded individuals hypothesized that women benefited from physical education and sports not in a competitive environment, but only when they stressed pleasure and the opportunity to socialize. A woman's involvement in such activities for any other reason, Mrs. Hoover suspected, would derail her from her true path: marriage and motherhood. The conference representatives further asked that they be allowed to address the IOC members in the hope of convincing them to take women's track and field out of the schedule of the Olympic events permanently. It was a particularly odd request coming from Mrs. Hoover, as she had grown up a sort of tomboy herself, in her youth participating in many activities that had not been classified as typically feminine.

BY THE TIME "Olympics for Girls?" was published, women had already received the right to vote. By 1930, more than a quarter over the age of sixteen were working, and the divorce rate was rising, thanks in part to women's newfound ability to work and take care of themselves. Physically, some women were also doing away with tradition altogether, chopping their hair off and grooving to the sound of the Charleston, at the same time engaging in sexual promiscuity. Yet it seemed that, despite such advances, the world of sports still refused to allow them full admittance, feeling perhaps that equality would hurt sports' reputation. But whose reputation their exclusion was protecting, no one knew.

Still, women athletes soldiered on. And with the Los Angeles Games ahead, a greater number of them found themselves on the cusp of becoming household names.

PART TWO

LOS ANGELES, 1932

CHAPTER ELEVEN

FLYING HIGH

B y June 1931, a dangerous heat wave was spreading across the country, working its way steadily from the East Coast to the West. The papers reported that throughout the Midwest, and particularly in the Chicago area, the temperature would continue to rise alarmingly, producing several more days of record-breaking heat before relief came in the shape of storms. Meanwhile, the Depression was continuing to take its toll, and by late 1931, nearly two million Americans were without any form of income.

As jobs disappeared, there was little that people could do to better their situation. Unemployment lines lengthened, food became scarce, thousands joined the long lines at the soup kitchens, and thousands more fell behind on their mortgage payments, the prospect of homelessness soon going hand in hand with that of hunger. Even the shelters were overcrowded, and looting became commonplace. Matters were dark and turning darker, so much so that even the gangster Al Capone opened a soup kitchen in Chicago to help his fellow Chicagoans.

President Hoover, on the other hand, did not agree that matters were as dire as everyone made them out to be. The country was on its way up, he said, if people would only find humor in the situation. "What the country needs is a good laugh," he told Senator James R. Clapper in February 1931. "If someone could get off a good laugh every ten days, I think our trouble would be over." But no one felt like laughing.

Despite the bleakness across the country, on the grounds of Northwestern University Betty's training had redoubled; she wanted to participate in more meets, and the forthcoming Ninth National Track and Field Championships in nearby Chicago—where eleven of the athletes participating were defending champions—especially excited her. Everyone was expecting a terrific competition—Babe Didrikson had been making waves and was being touted by her hometown newspapers as the runner to watch. But for Betty, Stella was still the one to beat, the potential troublesome splinter on her road to another medal.

ALTHOUGH AS A young girl Betty had tolerated and even enjoyed the heat, with age she was becoming sensitive to summers, bothered by the hot spells, especially the recent oppressive heaviness. She yearned for a cool dip in the Illinois Women's Athletic Club pool or a swim in Stone Lake. But her coaches, including Frank, cautioned against swimming. Water sports used entirely different muscle groups from running, and despite studies proving otherwise, it was still thought that overtraining those muscles would permanently damage the heart and other internal organs. Betty understood their worries, and though she did not like being reprimanded, nothing could jeopardize her training for the Olympics, so she mostly obliged.

The morning of June 28, she practiced for hours with the rest of the group at the IWAC, breaking at midday. Her mother and nephew had been watching. The heat was unbearable, and by the end of the session she needed a respite.

It was then that an idea struck her. She proposed to her mother and nephew that they all return to Riverdale, perhaps for a very short dip in the Calumet, though she had other intentions in mind. Her real plan was to call on her cousin Wilson Palmer, who was a year younger and part owner of an airplane. She piled her family into her car and rumbled away from Chicago, driving toward Riverdale, as she always did, at a dizzying, almost terrifying speed, the freedom she felt on the road akin to that of running a race.

SMALL-FRAMED, FRECKLED, AND with a shock of red hair that revealed his Irish ancestry, Wilson, or Wil, as he liked to be called, loved his plane. A year ago, he and two of his friends had purchased the red Waco biplane fresh off the assembly line. He was a calm, warm young man with a slight streak of mischief, and the plane allowed him to spend time on his own, which he sometimes yearned to do, given the size of his large family. But he never minded joyriding with Betty, one of his many cousins and—truth be told—his favorite.

The plane, a new version of a three-seater open-cockpit biplane that had been introduced in 1927 by the Advance Aircraft Company, was widely used by amateurs for pleasure. It appealed to Wil, and to Betty, the freedom the flight offered from the constraints she sometimes felt; the abandonment of worries she experienced as she breathed a different air up above. She liked to look at the town, spread out before and below her. For such occasions, she had even purchased a helmet that reminded her of Amelia Earhart's. Within the compact plane, Betty felt the same exhilaration that she imagined Earhart experienced.

Betty and Wil had gone up together ever since he'd become part owner of the "flying machine," as some people in town called it. Like dozens of Americans, Betty was fascinated by aviation, and when Wil could not take her up, she often found someone else who could.

Earlier that morning, Wil and his father had gone to the field to check on the plane and decided to take it for a short flight. The two flew together often, so the short trip over Riverdale and Harvey was a familiar excursion. On returning to the field, they drank from flasks of lemonade, and Wil mentioned that he was going to take a longer solo flight a little farther out. But this time, the engine would not start. Wil tried several more times, as did his father, but there was no response. Unable to figure out the problem, Wil ran toward Harold Brown's home in the hope that he might be able to help them.

Harold, who owned a third of the plane, was awakened by knocks on the door of his 155th Street home. All of the partners had flown before, although Wil was the most unseasoned of the three, having been a pilot for less than a year. Harold and the other partner owned another plane together, which they kept in a bunker located at the edge of a field in Harvey, one they often took out for jaunts with their lady friends. Harold opened the front door to the breathless Wil, who asked him to go over to the field and help him restart the engine. Given the heat, he invited Wil inside for a glass of cold water while he went to dress.

MEANWHILE, BETTY SAT behind the wheel of her Model T and cruised down the road toward the Riverdale airstrip, her mother and nephew in tow. As soon as she arrived, her automobile got stuck in one of the ditches skirting the airstrip; consequently, Wil and Harold had to push it out of the muck before returning to the plane, while Betty and her family looked on from the side of the road.

No one was worried, least of all Betty, that the plane was having difficulties starting, nor did they believe that their excursion should be postponed until a mechanic gave its engine a thorough look. Dusty and sweaty from the car ride, Betty was eager to leave the ground behind, and, streaking her shoes with mud as she climbed out of her car, she kissed her mother and nephew and impatiently hurried toward the plane.

Clambering inside, she settled into the front while Wil hopped in behind her, taking the pilot's seat. He flipped a switch, the engine finally groaning to life, and Betty felt a jolt as the plane roared down the short runway. She waved enthusiastically at her mother and her nephew, who watched as the plane careened unsteadily before slowly lifting off.

Although the air was stale, Betty reckoned that it had to be cooler up above, and soon the world shrank beneath her and Wil as he began a series of maneuvers that delighted her, soaring faster and higher, then dropping at a 45-degree angle toward the earth. The horizon opened up as they flew over places they knew so well. Betty watched the streets spread out like veins, noted the urban squalor of the abandoned Main Street, its foreclosed storefronts now occupied by dogs and transients. Factories were strewn across the dry, arid landscape, the blue-gray waters of the Calumet calmly rushing through the city beneath them, as the exhaust from the Acme Steel factory rose through its smokestacks and billowed along the adjacent lots now overgrown with weeds, the thick layer of humidity blanketing the area with a further sheen of dreariness.

Wil made a quarter turn to the left and continued his stunts, ascending and descending, higher and lower, rising four, five, six hundred feet, until they both felt a jolt. Time stopped for a moment before their sudden, steep decline; a harrowing descent, the earth rapidly becoming closer.

THE POLICE DEPARTMENT received an anonymous call stating that an aerial accident had just occurred. Quickly, the desk sergeant on duty placed a call to the Kerr Ambulance Service and the county police, who were immediately dispatched to the scene. But when the ambulance arrived, the personnel found only the remains of an empty plane, no trace of the pilot or his passenger. They soon learned that a boy and girl, both in extremely critical condition, had been taken to two area hospitals.

Once word spread that the girl was alive and who she was, *The Harvey Tribune* began a vigil outside the hospital, keeping tabs on her condition. Reporters had initially been told that she had been mistaken for dead and taken to the local funeral parlor. The dreary story began to circulate around Riverdale, taking hold of people's imagination.

Betty's doctor, Jacob Minke, freely spoke to the press, acknowledging that her situation was desperate. If she lived, he said, her chances of running again were highly improbable, given that the injured leg would likely remain shorter than the other one. Even walking seemed doubtful. Her thighbone had fractured in numerous places, and a number of silver pins had been inserted. They would cause her pain but also act as a barometer, aches commencing as the weather changed. Her left arm had been mangled—shattered in at least three places—and her right was also injured, though not as badly as her left. She had suffered a laceration over the right eye and had internal injuries too many to list, though the damage to her vital organs was still being assessed.

Giving an interview to the *Chicago Tribune*, Betty's sister Jean acknowledged that Betty's love of flying had developed nearly two years earlier. "She has been up before with Palmer," she told a *Chicago Tribune* reporter. Despite being frightened by her flying curiosity, none of the family had imagined an accident like this occurring.

Wil had also been injured and was later taken to Ingalls Memorial Hospital, where members of his family gathered nearby to offer support. Not only had he suffered a severe injury to his lower leg, which doctors insisted on amputating in the hope of saving part of it, but the impact had also smashed his body against the plane's instrument panel, causing grave damage to his face and skull. His jaw and nose were broken, he had a skull fracture, and he had yet to wake up from a coma.

As Betty and Wil lay in their hospital beds, people who had heard of the accident hurried to the scene to view what remained of the plane, but to their disappointment the machine had already been removed. As was standard for all plane crashes in the United States, the wreckage had been taken away just moments after the accident by officials from the Aeronautics Division of the US Department of Commerce for inspection. The inquest revealed that nothing had been amiss with the plane; all parts had been functioning properly. Harold Brown, who had helped Wil start the plane and watched it take off from the small airstrip, agreed that the plane was not to blame. Though he did not directly fault Wil for the accident, he believed Wil might have had difficulty gaining altitude due to the weather or that he might have fainted because of dehydration. A stalled motor didn't explain the crash, he said.

All that remained of the crash was a hollow depression imprinted in the earth, upon which reporters flashed camera bulbs from various angles. They planned on using their stark photographs next to the articles appearing on the following day, alongside the one of Betty wearing the string of pearls gifted to her after the Olympics.

VISITORS ARRIVED DAILY at Betty's room, her mother a constant companion. On hearing of the accident, Helen Filkey made her way to the hospital, eager to see for herself how Betty was faring. Helen knew that newspapers had a tendency toward the dramatic and hoped they were also exaggerating Betty's accident. But as she watched her unconscious competitor, her head bandaged as well as her arm, her leg in a brace, stretched out in front of her, Helen felt certain Betty would never run again. Helen had seen athletes sidelined by injuries that were far less severe than the ones Betty was now suffering from and knew that they were impossible to overcome.

On her way into and out of the hospital, Helen often encountered Bert Riel, whom Betty's family had not known she had been dating but who had been by Betty's side since hearing of the accident. Bert spoke tenderly to Betty, hoping she could hear him. Her gaiety and enthusiasm had always overwhelmed him; now she was unrecognizable. He often looked pained when he left the hospital, but others surmised that Betty would be even more pained when she woke up— if she woke up—when she learned that she would never run again, possibly not even walk.

CHAPTER TWELVE

SUMMER WOES

While in Riverdale, immediately after the accident, doctors were focused on trying to get Betty to recover, roughly 350 miles east of Riverdale, in Cleveland, Stella Walsh prepared for her upcoming meets. Aside from the games, she had other considerations on her mind, which had nothing to do with sports. She had decided to heed the advice of her family, friends, and foes alike and try to become—in their words—more feminine, more attractive to her male counterparts. In that pursuit she set out to win the title of "Miss Stadium," or "Queen of Cleveland," which was bestowed as part of Cleveland's 135th anniversary celebrations, in conjunction with the opening of the new stadium on Lake Erie.

She hoped that winning the competition would put a stop to the controversy that had arisen a few weeks earlier, following an incident at Pershing Stadium in New Jersey, on July 25. It had been an accident, but enough of an event to ruin her stay there. She had arrived at the competition as the nation's best-known track star, but by the end of the meet her athletic power was not what the spectators would leave the stadium talking about.

A few moments before the games were to begin, as Stella warmed up for her discus routine, she misjudged the distance between herself and center field, throwing too far and striking a twenty-eight-year-old spectator. He keeled over, unconscious, blood oozing from a fractured skull. Many feared that he had died on the spot; when the paramedics arrived, though, he was still alive, albeit in serious condition, and he was rushed to a nearby hospital.

Back at the stadium, police officers planned on arresting Stella immediately but were persuaded to let her finish the events; she did so, even winning the 220-yard dash, despite her distressed condition. It was her only medal that day. Immediately afterward, she was handcuffed, led away from the arena, and taken to the police department, from which she was released several hours later, though the story was already circulating. Press reported on the accident, citing the unusual strength Stella had displayed in throwing the discus, something spectators had never before seen in a woman.

She was hopeful that winning the "Queen of Cleveland" title and crown would help her move past the accident, "prove" her womanhood, and halt the ugly rumors swirling around her. In addition, she knew that the prize included a new car and a trip. She coveted both those things, as she couldn't afford either of them. But in getting wind of Stella's entry, reporters insinuated that she was out of her league, suggesting that although no one could deny the fact that she dominated on the track, the Miss Stadium competition was clearly a contest devoted in equal parts to beauty and popularity, neither of which she possessed.

"Girls with lots of dimples and personality usually become queens in this sort of thing," a Cleveland *Plain Dealer* reporter wrote, reminding readers that Stella had never possessed any dimples and was as cuddly as a prickly pear. But, accustomed to insults, she approached the challenge as she did everything else—with pure logic, devising a step-by-step plan, sizing up the competition, and looking for vulnerabilities in them, while scouting out any advantages that might be available to her.

When the day arrived and her name was called along with those of the other four finalists, Stella walked up to the stage wearing a new dress and heels she wobbled in, as surprised as everybody else was when she was bedecked in a crown and a glittering robe. She seemed awkward standing next to pretty, blushing Anna Griffith, the girl who had already been pegged as the winner. But Anna had earned a total of 200,900 votes, while Stella—muscular, rugged, boyish-looking Stella—had earned 327,400, thanks in part to her lobbying her Polish neighbors.

FOR DAYS AFTERWARD, Stella reveled in her new token of femininity with equal parts triumph and sadness. For as far back as she could remember, her lack of delicate features had been a topic of discussion, particularly during track meets, the sarcastic remarks in the locker rooms becoming increasingly common banter. As she had grown with age, she had expected the lines on her face to soften. Instead, they had become more pronounced, sharp and angular, setting her apart from the rest, though her physical attributes weren't the only thing that was different. She had a penchant for playing basketball with the boys rather than accompanying the girls in their excursions to the cinema or beauty parlors. When she had joined yet another boys' sports team, she only reinforced the notion that she belonged with men. Because of those ambiguities, she had been given the painful nickname of "Bull Montana," after the wrestler who'd eventually become an actor playing assassins and pimps.

And it wasn't just her schoolmates; later, even her competitors began to harbor their own doubts about her. She had a face without expression, some said. They couldn't read her, and they distrusted her because of it. But when she heard their disparaging remarks, she pretended not to care, or not to show it when they bothered her. Truthfully, her teammates would have preferred an angry rebuttal, shouting, an argument; even cussing would have been better than her staring at them with the coldest, hardest pair of eyes they had ever seen.

Stella had never been inclined to socializing, and the silly discussions some of her competitors indulged in didn't really appeal to her; she thought them petty and useless in an athletic environment where strength of body and mind reigned supreme. Not that she would have been able to carry on a conversation with them; even in that she was lacking. She arrived at her meets already dressed for competition, which spurred rumors. But it was the fact that she always left the locker room without showering with the rest, a wave of perfume in her wake, that got them talking. Her teammates knew she doused herself in large quantities of perfume instead of stripping naked in front of others, some of them mocking her modesty, others suggesting that it was not shyness but something more profound, the result being that they stared at her with not only unabashed contempt but even a touch of revulsion. Throughout her youth and early running days, Stella had achieved legendary status in her neighborhood and around the city of Cleveland, winning races against local opponents who quickly had offered her no competition at all. Very odd, many of her teammates surmised. And though she had no desire to reveal personal matters, she still craved the spotlight she would gain as an Olympian.

ONLY ONCE HAD Stella been forced to show vulnerability, and even that had been out of her hands. Even as she sported her crown and high heels, that episode pained her three years later. In the locker room of the old Woodland Bathhouse in Cleveland, where she often discreetly bathed herself, after she thought everybody else had gone home, an older girl named Beverly Perret had crept in and startled her. Only when Stella heard the whisper of the door opening had she turned around. The terry-cloth towel had slipped from around her chest, revealing a body seemingly at odds with itself. Stella remembered the expression on Beverly's face as she took in the nonexistent breasts and the limp little stump between her legs. Beverly, who had indeed been startled at first, was unable to speak as Stella hurried to gather up the towel at her feet and hastily tried to cover herself.

Beverly had sensed her discomfort and drawn closer, wanting to touch her, but much as others before her had learned, Stella had an aversion to physical contact. It was the only time anyone had seen her body for what it was—what she thought was a freakish abnormality, one with which she was growing increasingly uncomfortable. She had worked so hard to bury her secret, somewhere where people could not see it; she had learned to pretend that it could not hurt her, but it haunted her every time she changed or showered and stole a glance at her naked self. She no longer did that—she avoided reflecting surfaces as much as possible, and, most of all, she avoided the possibility of anyone else catching a look at her body.

She did not know it, but though her condition was rare, it was not unique to her. She was not "a freak of nature," as she often described herself in private or to Beverly. (Children with mixed anatomical structures had been born before and would be born again, labeled either intersex or hermaphrodite. But Stella was not aware of any of that back then, nor did she bother to find out much about her condition.) Only one thing occupied her mind: hiding her naked body from anyone in sight, while making certain everybody knew she was a female.

AS STELLA WAS relishing her new title, Betty was awakening to her painful new reality. Her head was tightly bandaged, her leg tied straight up in the air. She could barely move, and when she did, pain shot through her like an arrow, wrenching and unforgiving. She could not recall what had happened, and when she tried, she only remembered wanting to go up in her cousin's plane, the freedom of flying above Riverdale, the clouds surrounding them, then—nothing. Her family carefully explained that there had been an accident. She couldn't grasp that weeks had passed while she had been asleep. She was now at the Oak Forest Infirmary, an institution she knew from her time in high school, when she had volunteered there.

She was not comforted by the idea of being in the place, nor had she ever liked it. Located in Dumming, a few miles from Riverdale, the facility had started off as a sort of poorhouse or almshouse, even though eventually people who were mentally incapacitated had also been placed there. Those in the area had heard of its horror stories, a turn-of-the-century article in the *Chicago Tribune* condemning it as a "crumbling, helter-skelter series of wooden buildings," whose "inmates" were "crowded and herded together like sheep in shambles, or hogs in the slaughter pens."

Betty asked about Wil. Both of his legs had been crushed, and though his doctors still suggested amputating his right limb to relieve some of the soreness, Wil's mother continued to refuse to grant permission. She thought it better for her son to deal with the pain than to lose the extremity.

ONCE SHE COULD sit and speak for herself, Betty put up a good front. "Of course, I'm going to try to run again," she told the *Tribune*. "After spending the last eight years in preparation for an athletic career, it would be useless for me to give up without at least an attempt to run. But just when I will be able to begin strenuous training is up to the doctors. In the meantime, I'm going to continue my course in physical education at Northwestern," she said, flashing one of her trademark smiles. But beneath her brave facade, matters were different.

She knew, for starters, that she would not be repeating her medal run in Los Angeles. Her right leg was now half an inch shorter than the left—her ability to crouch down for the set position had gone.

Without that, there was no hope that she would ever run the 100-meter dash. Besides, she should not aim too high, doctors warned her; even walking seemed like a long shot. She should concentrate on merely getting up from the wheelchair, they insisted, discouraging movements they felt would cause her undue pain.

Wil had not fared any better. The wound on his leg was slow to heal, and infection had set in. That November, he would return to the Ingalls Memorial Hospital to have additional surgery, doctors still insisting on the amputation, if only for pain relief. But his mother still refused, and he listened to her arguments.

Betty returned to Riverdale to heal and recuperate but found that her recovery was slow. Most mornings, it was difficult to get up and force her tennis shoes onto her feet. Even if her mind willed it, her body would not cooperate. And there were times when her mind didn't want it, either. On those dark days, she told herself that she could walk in the afternoon or go out in the evening, when the children were playing ball and the sun was waning. Besides, tomorrow morning was just around the corner; she could wait until then. She was recuperating, after all, not training. She had time.

BERT MADE THE trip from Evanston to Riverdale, what seemed daily at first, though in time his visits dwindled. He sat in a chair in her parents' living room, across from her, and spoke of the athletes who had remained on campus throughout the summer, their long days of jumping, running, playing—seemingly unaware that those stories were the worst kind to share. Betty sat quietly, her leg tightly bandaged, and made no effort to be pleasant. She wasn't surprised when he curtailed his visits, nor was she surprised or hurt when he no longer came at all. Oddly, it brought her some relief to have all reminders of a previous life finally behind her.

She dreaded most days, finding no comfort in being home, surrounded by her family. Instead, a heaviness had settled on her, pressing on her head and squeezing her chest. More than anything, though, she cringed on hearing the footsteps of her brother-in-law Jim Rochfort coming down the stairs, the knocks that followed, his persistent urging that they go outside for a walk, which in time, he promised, would become a short run. She complied, but only out of exhaustion or to avoid arguing, her unhappiness oozing out of her with each step. Much like the ability to run, her willingness to argue had dissipated.

There were days when her legs pained her more than usual, and it was then that Jim would pick her up in his arms and carry her down the steps himself, all the way across the street to the park, where the cold morning air filled her lungs and the darkness of night still lingered. They would sit on a bench for a few minutes, listening to the birds, the wind so blustery that it stung her eyes, and she would attribute any tears to that. Eventually they would begin to walk, her knees popping as she took her first steps. She suspected that Jim could hear her bones cracking as he marched a few paces ahead. He made light of it, telling her that he just imagined having a popcorn machine trailing him. Around a gravel path they strode, her flat-soled tennis shoes wearing thin, Jim measuring her stride and in time clocking her speed, eventually bringing more intensity to her training. She trusted him; he instilled hope, whereas her doctors had given her none, Jim allowing her to progress at her own pace, which was as slow as that of a toddler trying to find her balance for the first time.

There were times she couldn't help feeling sorry for him, up so early every morning to help her, hoping that one day she would improve enough to get back onto a track field. Didn't he mind, she asked one cold morning as they stretched her stiff limbs—which seemed unyielding—didn't he mind training with her? Why should they try so hard when the likelihood of her returning to the track, let alone to the Olympic Games, was virtually nil? But Jim, ever the idealist, did not consider the hours with her a sacrifice; he had endured much, much worse during the war.

It was during those early mornings, as she ground forward and struggled to keep up with Jim, that she realized that nothing about her previous life had ever involved sacrifice, including her track-and-field runs—even her wins. Those had come so easily to her, so effortlessly, through luck as much as talent. Had she truly *earned* any of them? Having trained for less than four months before going to Amsterdam, she had fit practices in between her other commitments—even bake sales had on occasion taken precedence. She had also never truly taken the time to get to know the other athletes in Newark, the ones who had been training and running for years. Instead, she had strutted onto the field, expecting to win it all with confidence.

Now, she mused, trudging around the park in the cool morning air, history seemed in danger of repeating itself. She wasn't working as hard as she should be in order to get better. She pouted when Jim arrived early to call on her, as if the act of walking again were a matter of course, and not an opportunity she had to earn again.

The recognition of that must have been a shock so severe that it was viscerally painful. Weeks after she returned home, she made a pact with herself that she would not let time slip away but would become a participant again; she would defy those doctors who had not believed in her. She began to wake up even before Jim and quietly make her way outside, heading toward the park when only a few of the neighbors' windows were illuminated in the predawn darkness. Alone, the echo of her shoes crunching on the gravel, she looked straight ahead as she counted her breaths, attuning her mind to her body, walking slowly at first, a bit faster in the days that followed, trying to push herself that much further with each passing morning. There were no records to break, no stopwatch to count the seconds against her—just the simple pleasure of trying to run as she had years earlier, when running behind Riverdale's homes with her face slamming into flapping laundry was all there was.

She came to like that early-morning darkness, its familiar sounds: the birds flitting among the tall branches, the motorcars in the distance, and the bustle of Riverdale's inhabitants as they shook off the night's sleep and readied for the day ahead. But mostly she reveled in the sounds of her own two feet pounding over the road, the crunching of twigs and leaves underneath, her heart beating with exertion, for that was when she knew that she was working hard, that she was resuming some version of the life she had led before. Jim often found her there, alone in the park or on the short graveled path, sometimes jogging in place, other times doubling over in pain and exhaustion, nausea overtaking her. But all the while she was learning that her broken body could withstand hardships and discomfort that she had never had to endure before, the pain teaching her the meaning of resilience.

WHEN BETTY RETURNED to Northwestern in 1932, she found Frank Hill awaiting her. He was kinder this time and, beginning her training slowly, patiently determined to get her into fighting shape. Right away he could see that the old Betty was no longer there. Her form was entirely different, as was her overall technique. Her forward lean, having lost its natural bent, seemed forced and rigid. Her sore legs, different in length, possessed a stiffness that only time would ameliorate. She complained that her back was on fire, a burning spreading from deep within it, gradually overtaking the rest of her body. And she could no longer crouch for her sprints; the muscles in her legs no longer supported doing so.

It would take years of consistent hard work, Frank cautioned her, to regain a fraction of the conditioning and strength that had been hers prior to her accident. By the time she did, many younger, faster athletes would have come onto the scene. He doubted that a full return to the Olympic Games was possible, given that the only thing that appeared the same was her smile, he sadly told reporters; her smile and her unwavering spirit.

Betty had always appreciated Frank's advice, as much as she had appreciated anyone else's. But she had never taken other people's words as gospel, and she did not let herself believe him now. She possessed a resilience that had taken her this far, a willful streak that she referred to as determination and that she relied on. She was slouchy at first, as she could see in her reflection in the store windows she passed as she ran down Main Street, but she also saw improvement.

Physically, she could never be her old self, but she did not mind that, for mentally she did not feel like the old self, either. She could run, and that was enough for the moment. "I couldn't bend down," she recalled some forty years later. "But I could still run." She had won the Olympics once before, she reflected while jogging along Riverdale's sidewalks or Northwestern's track. Could there be any way to participate in the Games again? It was too late for Los Angeles, but what about Berlin in 1936? Could she dare to hope for a place on the team, regardless of what form that would entail?

The papers urged her on. A *Chicago Tribune* article read, "Betty Robinson, Olympic track star, ready to run again. . . . Every day now finds this Northwestern University junior exercising with dumbbells, on bars and on a bicycle to limber up stiff muscles resulting from torn ligaments, a broken left arm, and a fractured leg." Yes, she determined as she made her way around Riverdale, she could at the very least allow herself to imagine returning to the track where she had first become a champion.

CHAPTER THIRTEEN

CALIFORNIA DREAMING

While Betty continued to rehabilitate, Northwestern's Dyche Stadium became the site of two major events (technically, it was only one, with a dual purpose): the AAU Women's Track and Field Championships, which simultaneously served as the trials for the Los Angeles Olympic Games during the summer of 1932.

Three of Betty's former teammates were going to participate: Jean Shiley, Lillian Copeland, and Margaret Jenkins. She religiously followed their arrival in Chicago, as well as their doings. The Chicago papers were devoting enormous time and column space to them, and it seemed to Betty that she had grown to living vicariously through the abundant coverage, devouring the articles with a hunger she hadn't known until then.

Chicago was the place to be during that summer of 1932. Franklin Delano Roosevelt had been in town on July 2 for the Democratic National Convention at the Chicago Stadium, to accept his party's nomination for president. This event vied for attention with the Olympic tryouts, held only days later. But neither the political story nor the sporting event received as much attention as Equipoise, the horse that had become more famous than the presidential hopeful or any future Olympian could ever wish to be. Betty also certainly took note that the newspapers concentrated on two women who stood out from the pack: Stella and Babe.

Life for Stella had always been tough, and it continued to be so. She had recently lost her job at the Cleveland Railroad System, and, much like her track defeats, it hurt her. Although reports claimed that participating in the Olympics was still her primary goal, she realized, as most people did, that in these turbulent times gainful employment was of the utmost necessity. Factories in Ohio had closed, and the one where Stella's father had been employed since arriving from Poland had cut back his hours to less than half-time. He had found it impossible to keep up the monthly mortgage on their home while supporting his wife and daughters.

But there was a bright spot on the horizon. Throughout her life, Stella had looked forward to becoming a naturalized American citizen. She had submitted her paperwork in 1930, nearly two years earlier—her desire for citizenship fueled not as much by a great attachment to her new country as by her eagerness to run the Olympics as an American rather than Pole. Her citizenship exam was scheduled for June, just days prior to the Olympic trials.

On the day of the exam, she was awakened by a knock on the door. A messenger held an envelope from the Polish Consulate in New York, with a letter offering her employment inside. She was not the most qualified person to perform the job it was offering, but the letter hinted that if she kept her Polish citizenship, she would be given not only a good job but also benefits that extended to her family. No one would decline a secure, well-paid position, even if—in this case—it meant sacrificing one's dreams and running for Poland instead of the United States. She quickly packed a bag and caught a train to New York.

As she climbed into her private train compartment at the Union Terminal train station, Stella concluded that the Polish Consulate had offered her something that American citizenship could not: not only employment and benefits but also the promise of money to finish her education. She decided that after the Olympics she would move back to her native country to study, find a job, and continue running under the Polish flag. Only hours earlier she had been looking forward to becoming an American and finally gaining full acceptance as one, but as she settled into the train's compartment at Union Terminal, she found the prospect of leaving the country and all that noise behind refreshing, even uplifting.

"I'm not trying to duck the United States," she told a reporter who cornered her at the station. "But I've got myself to look out for." Days later, following her announcement that she would be permanently leaving Ohio to take the job in New York, she publicly declared that she would be running for Poland in the upcoming Olympics. The papers had anticipated as much, yet to hear her say so came as a jolt. "I will always have a warm spot in my heart for Cleveland," she said.

Her decision would have long-term implications, but at that moment she did not worry about them. She was severely criticized for it, especially when it came to light that the Polish Consulate was not the only business that had offered her a job. Cleveland's Recreation Department had also come forward with a proposal, one that she had turned down. Her fans were stymied, but the choice had been a simple one: working for the Recreation Department meant being associated with physical education, which would go against the IOC's regulations on amateurism. The rule stated that athletes could not involve themselves in sports-related work. Had she taken the position, she would have forfeited her status as an amateur and automatically become a professional, denying herself participation in the Olympics. She was not willing to make that sacrifice just yet.

AS STELLA BOARDED the train to New York, relieved to have found a job but a pariah in the eyes of many, Babe Didrikson arrived at the trials, intending to win all eight of the events. She had already made a big splash in the papers. Unfolding *The New York Times* in her compartment as her train sped north, she read, "Miss Mildred Didrikson, the sensational young lady from Dallas, Texas, is expected to be the standout of the meet."

It was an odd position to be in. Earlier in the year, Colonel McCombs had strategized a radical plan to improve her chances at a championship and had come up with a scheme that was unlike any he had ever seen or executed before, and that he soon proposed to Babe. Most of the other teams from across the country were composed of a dozen or more athletes. Each took part in one or two events, based less on their preferences and more on their skill set. Thus team members not only earned points toward a total number required for the team to win but also won based on their individual scores.

But what if they did not follow the usual rule regarding their team? McCombs proposed. What if Babe, alone, represented the whole team and participated in all the events by herself, permitting a full display of her talents? It seemed simple to him, if not for the opposition of Fred Steers—the AAU Rules Committee chairman and manager of the US Women's Track and Field Team—who would doubtless bring up arguments against the plan. Steers had good reasons to do so, for the AAU governed the competition and its rule book specified that no athlete, under any circumstances, could compete in more than three events.

And Steers had a reputation for being obstinate. He would refuse Babe's participation in all the events, McCombs knew, and the only way of circumventing this was to beat him to the punch. So McCombs self-assuredly told the press that Babe would be the only representative of the team attending the tryouts and that she would be participating in all of the events herself. Steers had no time to react, much less refuse.

From the very beginning, Babe had liked the Colonel's demeanor, that of a self-assured, confident, presumptuous man who commanded respect, a respect he acquired without yelling or screaming but simply by the strength of his words. But by nature, he was neither calm nor confident. He had been advised to cultivate patience and composure, even in the midst of the most strenuous circumstances and while enduring the most pressure-ridden situations. While in the army, a physician had discovered a heart defect, which had immediately prompted McCombs's dismissal. The condition could kill him, the doctor had told him, and he'd better learn to handle himself with a little more tact.

In sending Babe alone, McCombs was creating an awkward situation for her. Her teammates, who already disliked her, felt ripped off. Why shouldn't they be given the same chance to try out for the Olympics? Oddly enough, they did not blame McCombs for the turn of events but insisted that Babe had instigated it. And other competitors did not appreciate her blatant disregard for rules, either. If they could compete in only a handful of events, why shouldn't the same be true for Babe? Why was she deemed so important and given so much freedom? So in essence, and by no fault of her own, she was leaving an awkward situation behind, only to find a similar one in Evanston.

THE GIRL WHO left the Dallas train station that hot, humid July day was markedly different from the one about whom reporters had been writing recently. As the five o'clock train awaited departure, there stood Babe, dressed uncomfortably in a pink midcalf dress (an anomaly considering her usual attire), holding a small white leather purse in the crook of her arm. On her head sat a large pink hat, and the grin on her face seemed to radiate both excitement and a shade of uneasiness, most likely because she was standing on high heels for the first time in her life.

She arrived in Chicago when the temperature had climbed to over 100 degrees Fahrenheit and felt even stickier. Waiting for her were dozens of reporters and AOC president Avery Brundage, who fawned over her. Following cordial greetings, Babe self-consciously ran her fingers through her hair and over her dress, both now limp from the heat of the train compartment, and tried to put them in order. It had been an unusual welcome: Brundage prided himself on remaining detached from the athletes, on not showing any preference toward them in public, regardless of his private feelings. Yet the image of him shaking hands with Babe was published in papers nationwide, signaling his obvious favorite to readers and athletes alike.

Brundage was born in Detroit in 1887 and graduated from the University of Illinois in 1909 with an honors degree in civil engineering. He had excelled both academically and athletically, afterward qualifying for the 1912 Stockholm Games in the pentathlon, where he finished sixth, and in the decathlon, where he came in sixteenth.

Following his training as an engineer, Brundage went on to build a construction business and quickly became a millionaire, though despite his financial success, or perhaps because of it, his first love always remained amateur sports, which he could now pursue with abandon. He was adamant that sports should be followed as recreation, not for profit, that amateurs should live up to the "highest moral laws," their lives imbued not only with self-discipline but also with a principled outlook. Professional athletes, in his opinion, were nothing more than "a troop of trained seals." Not surprisingly, the Olympics became a particular obsession of his, especially the participation of female athletes, and he took particular issue with the track-and-field stars. In 1936, during some private correspondence, he would write, "I am fed up to the ears with women as track and field competitors. Their charms sink to something less than zero. As swimmers and divers girls are beautiful . . . as they are ineffective and unpleasing on the track." Yet he made an exception for Babe—for even he thought that she was exceptional.

Babe's luggage was whisked away as she followed the crowd out of the station. Everywhere she went, she heard people complaining about the heat, fearing that it would hinder the athletes' performances. But she was used to training in temperatures that rocketed even higher than the ones in Chicago. Neither heat nor humidity would be an issue for her, and she knew it. While the others took light workouts at Dyche Stadium in the hope of acclimating themselves, she preferred to walk alone, calming herself by visualizing the meets ahead.

But there was one thing that nagged at her. Earlier, while speaking to the Colonel, she had decided to enter every available event at the trials except the 200 meters and the 50-yard dash (her weakest events). Still, there were eight others that she could win.

Although she felt that she would come out victorious, the night before the trials she slept fitfully, plagued by nervous energy. Her stomach cramped so severely that her chaperone, Mrs. Wood, fearing appendicitis, summoned a physician. He examined her while she writhed on her bed in agony. He promptly diagnosed her illness: anxiety. She was too edgy, he told Mrs. Wood; her nerves were even causing a sickly pallor to spread across her face. She was letting her fears and emotions get the best of her, making herself sick. She'd better calm down, or she would not be good to race tomorrow.

The doctor's ministrations did little to wash away the tension Babe felt. If anything, she felt worse than ever. She rested her back against the headboard and remained awake most of the night, mentally running her races, half of which she imagined she lost, her brain churning and finally quieting near dawn, when she slept fitfully.

Not surprisingly, she woke up later than intended, the horror of arriving late to the meets increasing her uneasiness. She hurried to catch a taxi to the stadium, quickly stripping most of her clothes off and climbing into her uniform as the cab drew near the stadium.

FIVE THOUSAND SPECTATORS had braved the hot spell and bought tickets to the events. They sat fanning themselves as the athletes marched around the stadium, a somewhat scaled-down version of the Olympic parade. The teams consisted of groups of fifteen to twenty-two athletes, clogging the center field. Representing the Dallas contingent was only one small woman, a girl really. Waving her arms frantically, Babe entered the stadium to thunderous applause. It was noisy, rowdy, and completely unlike anything she had experienced back in Texas.

Since she'd embarked on track and field, her body had changed dramatically. Always small, she was now leaner than ever, though her leg muscles were more clearly defined. She did not possess the curves that women craved and men favored; instead, she had a strong athlete's body of which she was proud. She held herself with confidence, which was even more evident when she donned the neon orange uniform emblazoned with the Employers Casualty logo. No one would miss her amid that mob of athletes hovering around her. As the athletes took their places in the stadium, she ran circles, stretched her legs, laced and unlaced her shoes. Her cocky attitude amused the crowd yet unnerved her competitors.

THE MEETS BEGAN at two o'clock, the animated onlookers taking particular notice as Babe hastily ran from one event to the next. Some of the meets had to be delayed in order for her to finish competing in one before making her way to the next, which resulted in many of the athletes having to wait to compete. So many allowances were being made for her, they felt. It was all about Babe. Employers Casualty, her team's sponsor, had also given her an extremely expensive pair of track shoes, banking on her winning and bringing more prestige for the firm—along with the title—back to Dallas. They were shiny and supple, with the longest, sharpest spikes on the field. The other athletes took stock of her shoes with envy, knowing that they gave her a clear advantage and despising their own, as most of them had been run to the ground months earlier. They also did not appreciate the hiatus between heats, much less the fact that the crowds were so busy following Babe that they did not care to follow any other athlete.

Spectators drew their breath as they watched Babe's hurdling skills elevate her to a world record that was two-fifths of a second faster than the existing one. (She was timed at 12 seconds sharp by five of the six timekeepers; the sixth timed her at 11.8 seconds.) Prancing to victory in the broad jump, she managed to win that event as well. Her talents were unquestionable and made headlines, but so did her cocky personality and appearance; unlike her competitors, she refused to fit into any feminine ideals advocated at the time. One fervent home-town supporter, Grantland Rice, wrote, "She is an incredible human being. She is beyond all belief until you see her perform. Then you fully understand that you are looking at the most flawless section of muscle harmony, of complete mental and physical coordination the world of sport has ever known."

BY THE END of the tryouts, Babe had won the AAU National Championships on her own; of the events she had participated in, she had cinched five wins, tied for a sixth, and placed in a seventh. No one had ever witnessed anything like it.

"A new feminine athletic marvel catapulted herself to the fore-front as an American Olympic possibility," a July 26 *New York Times* article reported, "when 19 year old [*sic*] Miss Mildred (Babe) Didrick-son of Dallas broke the world's record for the 80 meter high hurdles, shattered the American mark for the baseball throw and topped off her activities with a victory in the running jump."

The Olympic trials assured Babe's place in history. Newspapers across the country, particularly back in Dallas, lauded her at length without ever mentioning any of her teammates. As far as Babe was concerned, that was fine, as there was no reason to reference them. The Colonel had denied them an opportunity to try out in order to highlight Babe's name in connection to his. From Dallas, her team-mates followed Babe's rise in anger, stung by both her and the Colo-nel. Now that she had achieved glory without them, their animosity

only grew. "She was built up by this man, McCombs," an anonymous Golden Cyclone teammate moaned. "She was out for Babe,
just Babe. . . . She was not a team player. . . . Babe was out for fame."

But their words did not faze her. Having collected her victories in
Evanston, she discarded reports of her teammates' nastiness, concen-
trating on one thing: Los Angeles.

CHAPTER FOURTEEN

GO WEST, YOUNG WOMEN, GO WEST

E ven before winning the Olympic bid, Los Angeles had been enjoying a worldwide reputation as the center of American glamour, citizens seduced by the allure of Hollywood. City officials were aware that only a select few were able to capitalize on opportunities associated with the movies but knew that sports, too, had a way of bringing people together, if promoted correctly; why shouldn't the city, with its verdant hills and abundant sunshine, become a leader in athletics as well? That, at least, was what Harry Chandler—the *Los Angeles Times*' publisher and perpetual bolsterer of southern California—had in mind.

Born in Landaff, New Hampshire, on May 17, 1864, and educated at Dartmouth College, Chandler began a stint at the *Times* in 1884. Serendipity had played a part in enabling him to get the job there; having built a small dispatching service outside Los Angeles that eventually took over the delivery of Los Angeles' morning papers, including the *Times*, he had come to the attention of Harrison Gray Otis, then its publisher. The two struck up a friendship, and it wasn't long before Otis offered Chandler a job.

Chandler was married at the time, but when his wife, Magdalena, died in 1892, he hurried to marry his boss's daughter, Marian Otis, in 1894; in time she bore him six children and helped him raise the two he had fathered during his first marriage.

In 1917, his father-in-law died, leaving Chandler in charge of the *Times*, and along with more modern views, his visionary ideas allowed the paper to become one of the most successful ones in the West. One of Chandler's goals was to promote not only Los Angeles but also the entire southern California region. When the prospect of an Olympic bid had come along, in fact, he had been among the first to argue that holding the Games in Los Angeles could boost the entire region's economic prospects.

The proposal to host the Olympics in Los Angeles was first presented at a meeting of the Community Development Association (CDA). Max Ihmden detailed the free publicity the city would receive and outlined the financial boom that would follow. While the members of the CDA entertained the idea, the reality was that most of them had no clue how to proceed. How could a city secure an invitation? That's when William May Garland entered the picture.

ITS DISTINCTIVE URBAN sprawl made Los Angeles unlike most cities that had hosted the Olympics. Its great distance—nearly six thousand miles—from the nearest European city made it less attractive not only to the IOC officials but also to the athletes who would eventually participate in the Games. In 1904, St. Louis had played host to the Games, the first time the Olympics had been held outside Europe, and those Games, as many Europeans and reporters had predicted, had turned out to be a dismal failure.

Initially Chicago had won the bid for 1904, but at the time St. Louis was in the process of organizing the Louisiana Purchase Exposition, to be held around the same time that Chicago intended to host the Olympics; it seemed inconvenient, as alongside the

Exposition St. Louis planned to host sporting activities that would likely mimic the Olympics. Arguments ensued among St. Louis and Chicago's officials, each city unwilling to back down, until Pierre de Coubertin became involved in the scuffle and decided to strip Chicago of its privileges, awarding the Games to St. Louis, with disastrous results.

The failure of those Games was attributed to several things: because the Olympics were held in conjunction with the Exposition, the sports events were demoted to being some sort of minor attraction, the attendees preferring to spend their time in other venues. The weather also played a vital role, the oppressive heat creating dust clouds as tall as tornadoes, preventing runners and other athletes from performing at their best. Coubertin, as well as other IOC officials, were enraged by all this, vowing that the Olympics would thenceforth remain on European soil.

STILL, CALIFORNIA WAS now a more attractive location than St. Louis. In the 1920s, it had been enjoying unprecedented prosperity, its abundance of sunshine and moderate temperatures adding to its good fortune. Economically, the state was booming, and real estate was at its peak. And with Hollywood churning out talkies with a speed that was matched only by its imagination, the city seemed to have no limit as to what it could accomplish. But Los Angeles officials were also aware of the strikes against it as a host city, including the fact that it did not have a large stadium to host major sporting events (although plans for building one were in the works). Regardless of those apparent inadequacies, as the 1920 Games in Antwerp neared, Garland boarded a ship and made his way to Europe to bid on behalf of Los Angeles. In his briefcase he held proposals for bids on the 1924 and 1928 Games, unaware that they had already been committed to Paris and Amsterdam, respectively. Arriving in Antwerp, he was unable to hide his disappointment from Coubertin when he learned this. But despite the failure in St. Louis, Coubertin assured Garland he believed that Los Angeles's plans had merit.

Coubertin was the only one to feel that way. Other members of the IOC, mostly European men, were not keen on Los Angeles. City officials would have to relieve the issues they'd already identified quickly; but Garland, backed by Coubertin, took pains to assure them that that would be done. He promised the Olympics would not be held in conjunction with anything else—no other fair or exhibition was scheduled to take place. The Games would be an individual entity, as they had always been. Garland informed the IOC members that the CDA had agreed on the need to bolster the city's international sporting reputation, and settled on a plan to build a stadium that would hold at least seventy-five thousand people. The athletic arena, called the Los Angeles Memorial Coliseum, was located in Exposition Park, just a few blocks from the campus of the University of Southern California. In May 1923, Los Angeles finally secured the invitation to host the Tenth Olympic Games.

AS PREPARATIONS FOR the Olympics churned ahead, a large black cloud loomed: the stock market crashed and unemployment soared; soup kitchens sprang up everywhere. Resentment of sporting pageantry grew, and anger toward officials who were spending so much money on the Games' preparations instead of helping the needy and the hungry reached its peak. Posters appeared around Los Angeles crying out, "Groceries Not Games!"; others were already plastered near the Coliseum proclaiming, "Olympics Are Outrageous!" as army officers were called in to keep the crowds at bay. It was not the most conducive backdrop for an Olympic spectacle.

Despite the hardship of the Depression, the preparations continued, and by 1931, as the Games neared their starting date, a degree of caution and pessimism about the new American dream trickled in. In view of the hard times, protesters urged the governor of California,

James Rolph, to put an end to the Games. The climate was one of cynicism, not one of big dreams, they agreed; it was time to figure out how to make ends meet, where to find work, how to fill a belly with food, not to jump around a track or swim in a pool.

Thus, it was not surprising that by April 1932, just three months shy of the scheduled July 30 opening ceremonies, the total number of tickets sold for the events was nearly zero. If that were to continue, IOC organizers would surely be unwilling to return to the United States anytime soon.

Planners strategized, trying to find ways to cut costs not only for American athletes traveling to Los Angeles but also for those coming from Asia, Europe, and South America. They arranged for rail and ship discounts to offset travel costs and found the best inexpensive accommodations in order to save on budgets.

The press finally began its coverage of the forthcoming Games, dedicating columns of space to them not only in the sports sections but also in the travel and society pages. Intimate profiles and in-depth interviews detailing the lives of the more prominent athletes were published. Bookies took bets on who would win, whose stride would be longer, if romance would blossom between any of the athletes, whether any of the women would earn a contract from Hollywood.

Despite the early strikes against it, by the middle of July, the community seemed to line up behind the Olympics. In a three-day period, nearly forty thousand tickets were snatched up, followed by more than thirty thousand the following two days. Olympic fever was in full swing, and by July 20, ten days prior to the opening ceremonies, ticket sales had reached 1.3 million.

Aside from all that, the Southern California Committee for the Olympic Games had another matter to deal with that was really out of its hands: the weather. The temperature had risen to 100 degrees Fahrenheit and was expected to climb higher, once again affecting athletes unaccustomed to extreme heat. Dehydration, muscle cramps, nausea, fatigue, dizziness, and nosebleeds were all health issues medics feared they'd have to contend with—and those were the less serious ailments.

BACK IN EVANSTON, the female athletes began to make their way to Los Angeles on the evening of July 16. Fred Steers, their manager, believed it was the best women's team ever (albeit only the second ever assembled): "The United States Women's Track and Field of 1932 is the strongest of its kind in the history of athletics . . . easily outclassing the combined Women's Track and Field teams of the world," he wrote in a report.

Coach George Vreeland agreed. As he stepped onto the train, he had to admit (at the very least to himself) that he was anticipating the next phase of an exhilarating journey, however bittersweet. He had hoped that a few of his Newark team's athletes would qualify, but none had. Thus, all the athletes he was to coach for the international Games were new to him.

He had heard rumors about a handful of them—one in particular, who was now heading into the Games with a lot of hype associated with her name and who apparently felt the need to journey across the country running up and down the train performing all sorts of exercises, be they jumping jacks or splits. When she tired of that, Babe either blew away at her harmonica or whistled tunes from her home state of Texas: long, bitter, mournful cowboy ballads that irritated those who were trying to rest. Although he hadn't coached Babe before, Vreeland reasoned, and perhaps did not entirely agree with how she had behaved in Chicago, at least he felt secure in the knowledge that she would be bringing home a gold medal or two. Those wins would make up for the loss his Newark girls had suffered in Chicago.

As the train sped west, each athlete and coach cocooned in his or her thoughts, they were met along the tracks by waving fans who had noticed the large visible sign trumpeting "The US Olympic Team" on the side of the car, proudly announcing itself in every town it passed through. For most of them, it was a new and overwhelming experience.

On reaching Denver, Babe was whisked away to radio and print interviews, while the rest of the team was taken to the Brown Palace Hotel, where they would spend the night and take part in a banquet. The athletes were looking forward to a luxurious meal and festivities planned in their honor, but it was there that they encountered racism—some of them for the first time. The hotel had a policy of not allowing African Americans through is front entrance, whether they were Olympic hopefuls or not. Most of the athletes were ushered toward the main door, but Tidye Pickett and Louise Stokes were directed toward the rear entrance. In a show of solidarity, all of the athletes accompanied Tidye and Louise through the back.

Their alliance to the two women lasted only so long. Though most of them were given single rooms on the main floors of the hotel, Tidye and Louise were escorted to an attic room to share, and they were not allowed to participate or mingle with the rest, though none of their teammates spoke out about that. "All the other girls had private rooms, went to the banquet, were interviewed by the reporters," Tidye recalled later. "Louise and I shared a room in the attic and ate our dinner upstairs on trays."

Leaving Denver for Los Angeles, the team was in high spirits as they prepared for the last leg of their journey. With the athletes cooped up in the heat of the train compartments, tensions rose, hostilities were renewed, and jokes fell flat. Just as the train pulled away from the station, an incident occurred that compounded Louise and Tidye's unhappiness. The two athletes were sharing a compartment, Louise resting on the top berth while Tidye had the bottom. Although most who witnessed the event believed it nothing more than a prank, several felt that Babe went too far by walking up to them and emptying a pitcher of cold water all over Tidye. The two argued, accusing each other of incivility, Babe blaming Tidye for being unable to take a joke and Tidye accusing Babe of being a racist. No apologies were offered.

THE TEAM ARRIVED at the Union Pacific's Los Angeles station at 8:30 on the morning of July 23 and disembarked the train to loud hoots and cheers. Immediately they were enthralled by the glitz of Hollywood, its movie stars, the full, luscious citrus trees, the perfectly manicured lawns and palm trees, even the heat that greeted them. The open spaces were punctuated by cheerful bungalow-style homes in pastel colors, the sky as blue as they had imagined. It was a large city. By the early 1930s, Los Angeles and its suburbs held nearly a million and a half inhabitants, many of them owning Model Ts, which they used for work and leisure, congesting the streets with the cars and their loud honking sounds.

Right away, the teams were segregated according to gender; the women were sent to the Chapman Park Hotel, while the men settled into the so-called Olympic Village, built around a circular road and separated in equal numbers along quadrangles on nearly 250 acres of land donated by Elias Jackson "Lucky" Baldwin in the Baldwin area of Los Angeles. To accommodate the nearly nineteen hundred male athletes, builders had constructed more than 550 bungalows, each one able to house between ten and twelve athletes from various countries.

This was a new concept in Olympic accommodations. Up until that point, most nations had preferred keeping their athletes in discrete quarters, where they could train in private and befriend only other athletes from their own countries. But this new Olympic Village would allow competitors to get to know one another, to break bread together, maybe to become friends and share experiences. Though IOC bureaucrats had originally shunned the idea, when Zack J. Farmer, who sat on the Organizing Committee, proposed it again, they reconsidered it. Going back to Coubertin's notion of the Games, the Olympics, they thought, were meant as an opportunity for youths of many nations to come together and foster intimacies. What better way to achieve that than to live under the same roof? Farmer's proposal not only gained ground but this time was accepted, reenergizing interest in the Games. The village also served a dual purpose. By allowing only men and by fostering an air of mystery, it would, ideally, attract tourists to the area, particularly young women, thus becoming one of the many attractions of Los Angeles. The scheme worked. That the village was designed to be bulldozed soon afterward was also ideal, as no trace of it would be left.

THE WOMEN, ON the other hand, would not benefit from the Olympic Village. They were relegated to the luxurious Chapman Park Hotel on Wilshire Boulevard, located within a safe area of the district but also along a stretch of road with plenty of shopping opportunities. The women would appreciate that, the organizers felt. Newspapers would be allowed to cover their buying expeditions throughout the many stores in the area, photographing many of the athletes as they looked over silk hose and discounted hats and purses. Reporters were also granted permission to visit the athletes at the hotel, where they could chat or have a drink. Male photographers planned to take pictures of the athletes while lounging on chaise longues, fretting with clothes and panty hose, drinking cups of tea and eating sandwiches, or sipping cocktails in their brightly patterned kimonos, those little activities that made such a difference to women, they said; or perhaps as they knitted, as a few of them were inclined to such hobbies. The photos, the reporters believed, would send a clear message that although the athletes were taking a break from their lives in order to participate in the Games, they had not forgotten about their feminine duties, to which they would return promptly after the Olympics.

.   .   .

BABE WAS SO unpopular with her teammates that no one would even share a room with her. She had no modesty, false or otherwise, and the athletes had grown to detest that, seeing her only as a stuck-up, bragging prima donna. Never shy about revealing a good measure of self-confidence, she smirked as they stood back, fidgeting nervously while names were called as possible roommates for her. They couldn't have known that her brash exterior and attitude concealed a young woman plagued by self-doubt or that all of her seeming bravery was nothing more than a fabrication. She feared disappointing her team, but mostly she feared disappointing her parents. She rehearsed her meets over and over in her head, her opponents never knowing that she was hypervigilant in monitoring her opponents' progress, memorizing every record they had set, broken down to the inch and the second; the improvements they were trying to make as the season wore on; and their tactics, both those that had worked and those that hadn't. They had no idea that if she even sniffed the possibility of anyone outperforming her, she increased her already strenuous workout schedule to inhumane levels.

Eventually, when no one volunteered or agreed to room with Babe, Mary Carew was picked as the sacrificial lamb. Eighteen years old, Mary hailed from Medford, Massachusetts, and had competed at the Olympic trials in 1928, alongside Betty and the others, though an illness had prevented her from earning a place on the team.

When Mary was six, her parents had died within months of each other, and she and her three younger siblings had been farmed out to various relatives across New England. Her siblings had remained in Medford, while she was sent to an aunt's farm in Connecticut. Right away, she understood that life would be a shade more horrific for her than it had already been. Her aunt made up a room for her in a pigsty, often tying her to a wooden post, and left her to sleep with the animals. Although Mary was allowed to attend school, she quickly fell behind the rest, teachers assuming that she had either not developed properly or was suffering from psychological wounds due to the death of her parents. They also could not grasp why she always had welts on her body, though the aunt assured them that she was only suffering from poison ivy.

Mary developed running as an escape mechanism, and also a method of quickly getting out of her aunt's way. When she was ten, an uncle from Medford arrived at the farm to check on her and, on seeing the situation, removed her from the place and took her to his house. She was enrolled in the Medford Public Schools District, where she thrived in sports, becoming the star of her new school's first girls' track team, setting records in the 40-, 50-, and 100-yard dashes.

At five foot two and barely one hundred pounds, she was an unimposing figure. Though she gained a spot on the Olympic track team, she was timid and quiet, and no one expected her to make much of a splash. She was seen as insignificant by the other athletes, always so taciturn as to make them forget when she was around.

As she and Babe headed up to their room, Mary could hear the rest of her teammates laughing behind them. She was soon overwhelmed by Babe's grandstanding. Babe would not shut up. But "everything she bragged about, she could do," Mary said. "And she bragged all the time. She wasn't liked by the other girls because nobody likes a bragger, but she didn't care."

Yet after that inauspicious start, the two developed a close friendship—Mary learning that Babe's act was just that, a front she put up when people were around. Mary confided in Babe about her anxiety over the upcoming competition; she was set to run against Stella Walsh. And Mary knew she would never beat Stella.

AS JULY 30 approached, even those who had not expressed an interest in the Olympics suddenly found themselves looking forward to them. There was a last rush for tickets, but not enough to be found.

Hotels, boardinghouses, and bed-and-breakfasts were full; those who had arrived late struggled to find a place to stay. Though signs of the Depression still lurked, the Olympic Committee tried to add sparks of goodwill to an otherwise gloomy era. There was a festive feeling in the air, and for a short while, at least, everybody's worries seemed lightened.

THOUSANDS OF PEOPLE descended on Los Angeles, traffic and crowds beginning at dawn on July 30. Everyone who owned a car also seemed to own tickets to the opening ceremony, and by early morning heavy traffic choked the roads leading to the Coliseum. Giggling children sat atop their fathers' shoulders, pointing at the flags and blow horns and trinkets galore being sold by entrepreneurial vendors. Stylish ladies had carefully donned their Sunday best, while men sported their finest ties. Movie stars added a further touch of glamour. The crowds munched on roasted peanuts and guzzled down gallons of lemonade.

By noon on the big day, nearly twenty thousand people were seated, while outside thousands of visitors who had been unable to secure tickets milled about, hoping to catch a glimpse of the hoopla inside the stadium.

President Hoover had declined the invitation to attend the ceremonies, remaining in Washington to deal with what many considered to be more pressing matters. No one missed him. Those were grim days for most Americans, and many felt the president, who seemed oblivious to the suffering that the country was undergoing, bore much of the blame for the Depression. Few were surprised that he sent in his place Vice President Charles Curtis, who arrived from Washington to cheering crowds and carried an official welcoming letter from Hoover.

A loud cheer arose in the stadium as the clock struck two thirty. Vice President Curtis read Hoover's letter, declaring the Games open.

The national anthem was sung, led by nearly twelve hundred choir members and accompanied by a 2,050-piece orchestra. The crowd rose as the athletes marched out of the narrow concrete tunnel into the open stadium and the parade of nations began: Greece led the way, with the United States—the host nation—closing it out. Thirty-seven women in total were competing in Los Angeles: seventeen track-and-field athletes, seventeen swimmers, and three fencers. Anyone who was interested in women's sports, however, was there to see only one: the famed Babe.

The American female athletes came from far and wide, from Massachusetts and Colorado, from Texas and Ohio, and from everywhere else in between. Those who had not previously attended the ceremonies entered the stadium grinning widely in their uniforms of white skirts and blouses and red vests. Like the rest of the women's team, Babe had been forced to wear panty hose, an aberration for her, and her legs itched as if she were being bitten by fire ants. She stood scratching the back of one leg with the opposite foot, then repeating the action on the other leg. Yet, like everyone else, she was in awe as the flag was raised to the sound of the Olympic hymn and doves were released in the arena. The circular stadium gave her a sense of the scale of the event, and as her eyes swept over the crowds, she was overwhelmed. She marveled at how different all of it looked from Beaumont, even from Dallas. But she was aware that a darkness was still festering underneath.

Though there were many spectators who were thrilled to see women take part in the Games, discussions were still under way about whether or not they truly belonged alongside the men. Babe was not clueless; she read the papers and knew of the debates taking place around her. She also knew that track-and-field athletes, in particular women like her, were even more brutally judged than the other female competitors, and that, as the discipline's most visible star, she often took the brunt of the insults. The short hairstyles most of the runners sported provoked unsavory taunts from reporters, who did not seem as skeptical about the women on the swim team as they did about them.

Babe did not need an explanation as to why reporters had taken a shine to the swimmers. Dubbed by the press the "American Mermaids," they were admired, for they were slender, tall, and perfectly coiffed, manicured and perfumed, slick in the clingy bathing suits and pointy sandals they enjoyed wearing for no reason at all. One could not help but notice them, praised as examples of femininity, glamour, and style, and reporters appreciated them for their beauty more than they did for their athletic abilities. "They strut—and strut," a reporter from the Associated Press wrote. "The sprinters, jumpers, and weight heavers never appeared until the time to do their stuff, and disappeared immediately afterward, [but] the femmes who gain fame . . . in aqua, are never out of sight. . . . Many of them make a habit of parading—and then parading some more."

The swimmers took great pride in their appearance, sometimes more than they did in their sport, they admitted. Eleanor Holm, in fact, told a reporter, "My appearance is more important to my life as a woman than my swimming championship." Showing no reservation or shame, she continued, "If I had to choose between swimming cups and honors, and the loss of looks . . . I'd give up the championship."

Babe was aware of what newspapers wrote of her, often not in flattering terms. They described her nose as too pointy and birdlike, her lips as too skimpy, and her eyes as too watery to be alluring. None of the reporters thought her pretty or attractive, and none had anything pleasant to relay to their readers. That she had no time for boyfriends or the intimacies that girlfriends shared seemed unusual to them, leading some to publicly speculate that she was a lesbian or maybe even a man masquerading as a woman. The prominent sports reporter Paul Gallico fueled the rumors the most. At one point he referred to her as a "Muscle Moll" and, puzzled, asked his readers whether they, too, thought she belonged to a third sex, neither male nor female but something in between. He was curious, he said, as curious as he was about "the bearded lady and the albino girl at the circus sideshow." He further went on to describe her as "a hard-bitten, hawk-nosed, thin-mouthed little hodgen from Texas." What struck him, and perhaps infuriated him more than anything else, was the fact that she refused to acknowledge the questions he asked, apparently lacking the emotions he was trying to elicit from her.

But it did bother her. She was a woman. But she suspected that her words would not have mattered; nor did she feel the need to explain herself. After all, it was her athletic skills that mattered most to her, that should have mattered to anyone else. Babe was not the only target. Reporters were also suspicious of Stella Walsh. Gaston Meyer, the editor of the French daily sports paper *L'Équipe*, wrote in an article, "This large brunette, of whom it is said that she shaves every day . . ."

DESPITE THESE BEING the second Games in which women could participate in track and field, many male athletes were still reluctant to accept them. A reporter named Westbook Pegler, who'd gone to Los Angeles to cover the athletes, and in particular Babe, agreed that their male counterparts were always complaining that "women's place in the Olympics meets is in the water and not on land, and [so they] urge that they be . . . prevented from cluttering up the lot with delicate parodies of the mighty feats that males perform." One paper acknowledged the men's team's gripes but noted that the crowds still appreciated the women: "Male athletes and most male coaches won't take the feminine side of the Olympic Games any too seriously, but you will find the girls will have a continued appeal to the crowds in the stands. They will provide a refreshing variety, even if they don't come close to male marks."

Among those watching from the stands was Dick Hyland, who

now worked as a journalist, though in the 1920s he had been an All-American football player at Stanford. He'd been assigned to cover the women's track-and-field events, which to him seemed only a bunch of "comical antics." He did not see the female athletes' participation as a demonstration of physical feats but merely as silly scrambling from a group of little girls who should have stayed home, particularly as they hurried to the finish line.

BETTY WAS NOT in attendance to defend her title, which opened the door to others who had always been defeated or overshadowed by her. The undisputed favorite was now Stella Walsh. Indeed, Stella crossed the finish line of the 100 meters in 11.9 seconds, well below the Olympic record, running down the cinder tracks "with a fury no other girl sprinter ever has known." Although she had accomplished what many thought impossible, her achievements were—in Americans' eyes—marred by the fact that she had not won for the United States. Even as she crossed the finish line, she did not feel the acceptance that she had always craved from the Americans. Her neighbors in Cleveland agreed. "We are glad to see Walsh win, of course," admitted the publisher of the *Polish Daily Monitor*, echoing not only Walsh's but also the rest of the immigrant community's sentiments. "But we would have been more glad if she had finished her naturalization and won as an American. We are Americans."

SEVERAL EVENTS WERE disputed. Unlike at the 1928 Olympics, where a handful of close finishes had been left to the judges' discretion to determine, in Los Angeles there was no possibility of such a controversy. The officials had thought of every detail, including the use of new technological innovations such as photo timing. In fact, the "Kirby two-eyed camera" was the latest in a string of apparatuses officials were trying to employ. The camera had been tested earlier that month at the US Championships and Olympic trials, where, found to be accurate to one-hundredth of a second, it was deemed reliable enough to include in the Olympics.

Within the US contingent, the relay team would go down in history for the choices Coach George Vreeland made in selecting its members: he picked only white athletes, though both Tidye Pickett and Louise Stokes had qualified. "Times were different," recalled Tidye years later. "Some people just didn't want to admit that we were both better runners." Tidye and Louise were relegated to the stands, where they watched as their teammates won the gold medal and set a new world record—without them.

Among the first results to be called into question was the 80-meter hurdles, in which Babe went head-to-head with fellow American Evelyne Hall. As the two reached the finish line, Babe had a nearly two-foot advantage between the fences, though Evelyne quickly caught up with her. By the end of the line, the two were matching strides, but Babe, being faster, managed to break the ribbon first, a mere two inches ahead of Evelyne, for the win. Aside from winning the gold, Babe also managed to set a new world record of 11.7 seconds.

A further dispute occurred in the high jump. Jean Shiley and Babe were tied for first place. Olympic rules did not allow for ties, and a winner had to be chosen by a jump-off. Babe went first, bringing up her legs and clearing the crossbar; Jean followed and also cleared the bar. But Babe was disqualified from the game, referees citing her technique. Her Texas hedge-jumping running style was a method she had developed, not as a way to cheat the system but out of necessity. Regulations dictated that the hurdles used in official competitions be about two inches thick. As a child, Babe had jumped over not competitive hurdles but garden hedges. The hedges were more than two feet wide, and the only way for her to clear them without ripping off her skin was to angle her right leg slightly inward as she jumped. She rightly pointed out that she had been doing so throughout the Games, including at the trials, up until the jump-off with Jean, and no one had complained. Her argument didn't stick. She was suspended, and Jean moved to a winning jump of 5 feet, 5¼ inches, a new Olympic, world, and US record. Jean's teammates cheered for her.

It did not matter. By the time the Olympics drew to a close, Babe's records were undeniable. In the opening heat of the 80-meter hurdles, she had equaled the world record of 11.8 seconds, eventually breaking that record with 11.7 seconds in the final heat, winning the gold. And she continued the gold streak in the javelin, with a record throw of 43.69 meters.

DESPITE THE COMMONLY held idea that women could not compete alongside men, it seemed that by the time the Games ended many reporters agreed that Babe had done much to cement her legacy not only in sports history for herself but also for women athletes as a whole. Not everybody was caught up in the buzz. A few sports writers questioned whether or not there was actually *any* value to her records; whether what she had accomplished, when compared to a male athlete, was indeed all that extraordinary. "When you get down to the elemental, she didn't do very much," Joe Williams, a columnist for the *New York World-Telegram*, later wrote. "All the records she made were ordinary. The same year she became the greatest woman athlete in history, a comparative chart shows that she had not equaled one record made by a masculine high school champion of the same period." To further undermine her accomplishments, he continued, "Instead of furthering admiration for her sex she had lowered it. By her championship and accomplishments, she had merely demonstrated that in athletics women didn't belong, and it would be much better if she and her ilk stayed at home, got themselves prettied up and waited for the phone to ring."

Babe did not wait for the Games to end but quickly returned to Texas, where she planned to make the most of her victories and propel herself not only to national stardom but also to a paycheck that reflected her accomplishments. It was not something that a female athlete had done before, but she had studied the market and noticed that parlaying athletic victories into financial success had worked out for several male athletes. Male swimmers, such as Johnny Weissmuller, boxers and sprinters, and even some basketball stars who had reaped success in their respective fields had moved forward to gain financial advantages after the Olympics. Why should it be different for a woman? She had no interest in marrying anyone, she told the reporters who asked her if now that she had gotten athletics out of her system, she was ready to settle down and have children; she had no intention of getting hitched or birthing a herd of kids; she could take care of herself. She wanted to run and make a lot of money. People did not think that unusual for a man, did they? Why did it seem so strange for a woman?

STELLA, ON THE other hand, kept the promise she had made to herself a few months earlier: she packed her medal and her bags, said good-bye to her parents and her sisters, and sailed to Poland on a hot August day. She was giddy as New York faded behind her; the typical insecurities of moving to a new place, though she had been born there, were nowhere to be found. She was eager to depart America, to leave behind all she had endured: the nicknames, the heartbreaks, the gossip and chatter that always seemed to follow her. In Poland, she had convinced herself, she would be known only as the Olympic great, not as Bull Montana.

Having received a full scholarship from the Polish Federation, she enrolled at Central University, an all-female institution in Warsaw, to study physical education and journalism for what would be a three-year stint. But the reality of a life in Poland soon became clear. In her native country, she felt like more of a foreigner than anywhere else she had ever been. She had fewer friends in her new home than she had made in Cleveland, and she found she was leading an even more solitary life than she had before. Everywhere she went, the pangs of loneliness accompanied her, and she came to realize that in the United States, though it was true that she had often been taunted, the reality was that she had also been admired and celebrated for her athletic abilities. People had looked up to her, and she had been accorded inches of space in the newspaper columns. In Poland, no one cared about her, either personally or as an athlete. It wasn't long before she began to lament her decision to move to her native land.

Her insignificance revealed itself to her in January 1933, when she stepped across a railroad track on her way home and caught her foot, falling facedown. Something tore in her ankle. The pain she felt in that moment was great, but the horror of possibly never running again struck even deeper. There was no one to help her, and as she slowly got up and hobbled to a doctor, her pain magnified. The physician on call indicated that her ankle had been severely sprained but was also bleeding internally. There was, indeed, a possibility that she would never run again. She sent word to the Polish Olympic Committee but never heard back from it. No one there, it seemed, cared that an accident had occurred or that it could very well end her career. Poland had gotten out of her what it had set out to get: an Olympic medal.

Left to fend for herself, Stella now understood her grave mistake. None of this would have happened in America, in Ohio, where she was relatively famous, even doted on, despite her retiring disposition. She wistfully consoled herself with the knowledge that in Cleveland people would have cared; if she returned, they would do so once again. She had betrayed them, she had been made fully aware of that, but she hoped she might be given a second chance.

She was done with Poland for good; as soon as she could manage, she decided, she would sail back to Cleveland, hoping to try for US citizenship once again (she would not gain it until 1947) and to begin physical therapy to heal her ankle. She was broken in so many ways. But after six months of intense treatments, she resumed her training and began running again, participating in a Chicago meet where she crushed her competitors in her first meet on US soil again. It was good to be back, even if only for the event.

PART THREE

BERLIN, 1936

CHAPTER FIFTEEN

THE NAZI GAMES

Now that the Los Angeles games were over, interest turned to Berlin, where Betty Robinson hoped to make her comeback. But as she read the newspapers outlining the upcoming events, she feared that these Olympics would never come to pass and she would never have a chance to return to the Games.

Berlin had been scheduled to host in 1916, but the outbreak of World War I had changed those plans. As time went by the city became anxious for a do-over, and in 1931 the IOC awarded the 1936 games to Germany again. Principally responsible for bringing the games to Berlin were Theodor Lewald, the president of the German Olympic Committee, and Carl Diem, whose post included a stint as the secretary of the Organizing Committee—both very well known in the German sports arena.

The Games signaled a sort of "welcome back" for Germany after the loss of World War I. By 1933, when Adolf Hitler and the Nazis came to power, the country's government had devolved from parliamentary democracy into a dictatorship. Despite the political upheaval, AOC president Avery Brundage did not see the situation as too worrisome. The Olympic Games were administered by a world-wide organization that fell under the IOC umbrella; they did not belong to Germany or any other country; they followed international guidelines and not nationalistic views. Or so he believed.

The Germans had a lot to prove. Since 1912, when Germany had garnered only a sixth-place overall standing at the Stockholm Olympics, German athletes had been undergoing rigorous training, Berlin dedicating many resources to their preparation. Physical education had been added to the curriculum of all German schools, which ran the classes with an injection of militarism that would become the Nazi regime's trademark. Hitler himself, in *Mein Kampf*, suggested that at least two hours of every school day should be devoted to physical education, regardless of its form. Now, with the Olympics ahead, there was such tremendous pressure on German athletes to do well—how far were they willing to go to secure their places on the podium?

When Hitler first took power, the Olympics did not align with his overall philosophy. They promoted ideals of fairness in sports regardless of religion, race, and politics (if not gender), so he was naturally against them. Soon thereafter, he informed the IOC that he didn't care whether or not the Olympic Games would ever be held in Berlin. He had always assumed that the games were "an invention of Jews and Freemasons," and his country would not be a host to such shenanigans. Right away, Theodor Lewald made a beeline for Joseph Goebbels's office, where he suggested that a Berlin Olympiad could provide a massive opportunity for propaganda. Goebbels, who had been in office for only three days at the time, pondered the possibility. It would be not only a chance to show off the city and the country's great power but also a means of fostering the myth of "Aryan" racial superiority that the regime was trying to spread.

The concept of Aryans as a master race was fiercely promoted by the Nazis, who believed in a white race that not only was mentally superior to the rest of the population but also looked markedly different. Aryans were tall, blond, and blue-eyed; they possessed boundless courage and energy and sharp intellect. Anyone who did not fit into that description was grouped into the small, black-haired, coal-eyed community, a collection of people one had to be disdainful of at best, exterminate at worse. But Goebbels, the strongest proponent of the master race theory, was the least likely to depict it physically. A small-framed, anemic-looking man lacking any outward physical superiority or attractiveness, he prized in others that which was not evidenced in him. The tartness of his character, some argued, was perhaps due to his own physical inadequacies. But in pondering the Olympian idea and what the Games would bring to the country, the manipulative Goebbels began to realize the opportunity they presented: What better way to show off Germany's glory than with a worldwide spectacle such as the Olympics? What a feat that would be!

Still, when first consulting with Hitler, Goebbels decided, as an initial course of action, not to allow competition between Jews and so-called Aryans. As a further shock to the sporting community, Hitler and Goebbels ousted Lewald, who they learned was part Jewish. Lewald was not observant, but he had a paternal grandmother who was Jewish. He was replaced by Hans von Tschammer und Osten. In April 1933, the Nazis promulgated an "Aryan only" policy regarding sports, stating that not only Jews and those of Jewish origins but also Gypsies, homosexuals, and the disabled would be banned from all sporting associations in Germany.

A growing number of people in the United States were alarmed by these new developments. Gustavus Town Kirby, AOC treasurer and former AAU president, called on the AOC and AAU members to hold off accepting the invitation to the Berlin Olympics until they received assurance from Germany that Jewish athletes would be allowed to participate and would be treated with fairness. Brundage, on the other hand, argued that the United States had no grounds for refusing to attend or for refusing to respond if they saw no indication on the part of the Germans that they were behaving unjustly toward athletes or disregarding IOC rules and regulations. Brundage's ideas of the Olympics were similar to Pierre de Coubertin's in many respects, and he nurtured close friendships with the Germans Lewald and Diem, as well as the IOC member Karl Ritter von Halt. Although he was besieged by demands for an American reaction to the Germans, Brundage felt that politics and sports did not mix. Nationalism, he thought, was not part of the Olympic Games, so it demanded no response from him. A more telling reason for his reluctance, though, was his private belief that this was a problem created by the Jewish population itself, not by the Nazis. The Jews, he said, were "clever enough to realize the publicity value of the sport," and he once described them as "wolves that appear in sheep's clothing," intent on doing the greatest harm to the Olympic cause.

Officials in Germany were aware that their movements were being scrutinized, particularly in the United States, and did not take the threats of a boycott quietly. The German Athletic Federation even issued a statement meant to appease those who still had doubts: "The German Committee stands squarely on the ground of the Olympic idea. There can be no question of any attempt of discrimination. On the contrary, all athletes coming to Germany in 1936 to participate in the Games can count upon being received with the heartiest hospitality, irrespective of nationality or race," further adding that "as a principle German Jews shall not be excluded from the German teams of the Eleventh Olympiad."

But not all were convinced that the Germans were going to play fair. William Dodd, the US ambassador to Germany, was convinced that his compatriots were being taken in by the glossy Hitler regime. President Roosevelt had chosen Dodd, a professor of history at the University of Chicago, to serve as ambassador to Germany. Teaching, reading, writing, and researching were his passions, particularly American history with a smattering of European lore thrown in. Born in Clayton, North Carolina, in 1869, he had earned a doctorate from the University of Leipzig, where he had defended a dissertation on the life of Thomas Jefferson. In 1901, he had married Martha Johns, an intelligent and educated woman from Auburn, North Carolina, and in 1934 he had risen to the position of president of the American Historical Association. Though most Americans had known little about Dodd prior to the 1930s, his record of distinction had caught the attention of President Roosevelt, who decided to appoint him ambassador to Germany.

On arriving in Berlin, Dodd had become convinced that Hitler and his henchmen were trying to fool the world into believing their intentions were not as harmful as perceived, and Dodd's words and warnings earning him a reputation as an "alarmist" in Washington. But very few other people seemed to grasp the gravity of the situation.

WASHINGTON HAD NO interest in becoming involved in the Olympic feud; President Roosevelt, who thought it a very unexpected situation, found himself caught between a rock and a hard place. He appreciated the point of the boycotters: one could not overlook the fact that Jewish athletes were being discriminated against and that American Jewish athletes would suffer the same injustice. But he also could not politicize the games; the argument did not rely on him. (Besides, there were economic issues to consider: if he took a stance against Germany, the Germans might take offense and spitefully refuse to repay World War I reparation bonds still owed to the United States.)

FDR often received correspondence from the public urging him to speak up against the Germans' blatant discrimination. But he managed to wiggle out of doing so. "The German authorities are treating the Jews shamefully and the Jews in this country are greatly excited," he wrote to Ambassador Dodd very early in the controversy. "But this is not a governmental affair. We can do nothing except for Americans who happen to be made victims. We must protect them and whatever we can do to moderate the general persecution by unofficial and personal influence ought to be done."

Judge Samuel I. Rosenman, one of FDR's Jewish advisers, was aware of the president's position. He even consulted with American IOC member General Charles H. Sherrill over what the response from the White House should be. Sherrill, of course, had been assured that the Germans would not stray from the rules the IOC had set up, and he was intent on the Americans participating in Berlin; he didn't believe the president should get involved in the controversy.

On August 24, 1935, Sherrill traveled to Munich to visit Adolf Hitler. He had a long history in the Foreign Service, with membership in the IOC being only one of his duties and the latest of his posts. In many ways, his views were not unlike those of Brundage: he was aware of the situation in Nazi Germany and felt he needed to try to smooth things over. It was not ethics that prompted him to get involved in the Berlin uproar but politics. ("It does not concern me one bit the way the Jews in Germany are being treated," Sherrill once stated nonchalantly, "any more than lynching in the South of our own country.") Which is not to say that his visit to Hitler was a friendly one. A Gallup poll had recently reported that 43 percent of Americans favored a boycott and that the number was growing steadily. Sherrill was on a mission to suggest including at least one Jewish athlete on the German Olympic team, as a "token" to show the world that the Germans were willing to make some allowances. If they did so, Sherrill argued, the Americans would not boycott the Games and the rest of the world would follow their example.

But Hitler was not a man to be easily dissuaded. Capriciously, he retorted that any country was free to boycott. And if the IOC decided to take the Olympics away from Berlin and give the hosting privileges

Betty Robinson running under the banner of the IWAC, after winning gold in the 100 meters in Amsterdam in 1928. *Courtesy of the Library of Congress*

Betty Robinson in Evanston, Illinois, 1936, training to earn a place on the U.S. Women's Olympic Team, and eager to get back on the track as fast as she could. *Courtesy of the Library of Congress*

Mildred Ella Didrikson, also known as Babe, as a child. *Courtesy of Lamar University*

Babe had five siblings, but she was closest with Lillie, featured in this photo (along with their younger brother, Arthur), who shared her love of running. *Courtesy of Lamar University*

Babe attended Beaumont High School, where she developed a reputation for being difficult. The only place she felt at home was on the basketball court, after joining the Miss Royal Purples—the sole girls' team at the school. *Courtesy of Lamar University*

In February of 1930, Colonel Melvirne McCombs, an insurance man from Dallas, discovered Babe during one of her high school games. Impressed, he offered her a position on his team, the Dallas Golden Cyclones. *Courtesy of Lamar University*

Babe, shortly after her wins at
the Los Angeles Games in 1932.
Courtesy of Lamar University

United States athletes traveled
to Berlin on the SS *Manhattan,*
which departed Pier 60 in New
York on July 15, 1936. Along
with the athletes were members
of the AOC, newspaper
reporters, and a handful of
family members. *Courtesy of
the State Historical Society of
Missouri*

Stella trained to recapture gold in the
1936 Olympics in Berlin but came up
just short—losing to the American
phenom Helen Stephens. Stella always
felt like an outsider and was forever
trying to find her place in the world:
Was she a man or a woman? Was she
Polish or American? *Courtesy of the
Western Reserve Historical Society,
Cleveland, Ohio*

Stella Walsh was born
Stanisława Walasiewicz in
Poland. She won gold in the
100 meter dash at the 1932 Los
Angeles games. Although she
had meant to run for the United
States, she received a job offer
from the Polish Consulate,
with the understanding that
she would compete for Poland.
*Courtesy of the Western Reserve
Historical Society, Cleveland,
Ohio*

Helen Stephens training with her first coach, W. Burton Moore. Moore was the track coach for the Fulton High School and a recent graduate of Westminster College. He was the first to notice Helen's running abilities and encourage them. *Courtesy of the State Historical Society of Missouri*

Helen Stephens at the starting line of the 100 meters. Although people still weren't sure what to make of female runners, the stadium was filled to capacity. *Courtesy of the State Historical Society of Missouri*

Helen Stephens at the 1936 Olympics. Helen participated in the infamous Nazi Olympics, winning gold in the 100 meters and gold in the relay team. Although she hoped these would be the first of many games she would participate in, they turned out to be the last. *Courtesy of the State Historical Society of Missouri*

Collage including Helen Stephens and several of her teammates preparing for the 1936 Berlin Olympics. The top middle photo includes Betty Robinson, while the top left features Dee Boeckmann, Betty's friend and cabinmate from Amsterdam. *Courtesy of the State Historical Society of Missouri*

Helen Stephens meets Adolf Hitler. Following Helen's win in the 100 meters at the 1936 Berlin Olympics, Hitler requested a meeting with her; her powerful athletic abilities and physique had impressed him. The invitation led to one of the most peculiar encounters in sports history, which Helen relished recounting. *Courtesy of the State Historical Society of Missouri*

to another nation, Germany would go ahead and carry out "purely German Olympic Games."

Sherrill's acquiescence infuriated Consul General George S. Messersmith, who was devoting far too much time to the issue. Messersmith agreed with Dodd that most of the US officials were either ignorant or working hard to appear so. Messersmith had entered the Foreign Service young, in 1913, and been appointed consul to Canada, Curaçao, and Belgium before becoming consul general of Belgium and Luxembourg and subsequently earning a post as consul general of Argentina.

In February 1934, he was given a position in the ministry of Uruguay. As it happened, just days prior to embarking on his new job, George H. Earle, who was then in the ministry of Austria, was reassigned, and Messersmith relocated to Vienna. It seemed ideal, and though the White House was pleased with its decision, the Germans were not, as even from Vienna Messersmith would be capable of keeping an eye on their doings.

Soon after beginning his assignment in Vienna, Messersmith believed that conditions brought up by the Nazis about the United States' handling of the "Berlin question" would have further repercussions throughout Europe once the Olympics ended. "There are many wise and well-informed observers in Europe who believe that the holding or non-holding of the Olympics in Berlin in 1936 will play an important part in determining political developments in Europe," he prophetically wrote. "I believe this view of the importance of the Olympic games held in Berlin in 1936 is not exaggerated."

An astute man, Messersmith saw the much darker underlying intentions of the Nazis and warned that they should be taken seriously, writing, "There is no longer any doubt that all persons with any strain of Jewish blood, no matter how attained, will not be permitted to compete for the Germans." And that, he feared, would only be the beginning.

Nonetheless, early in 1934, Germany sent out official invitations to the Olympics to fifty-three countries. Prior to accepting the invite and in order to placate those who threatened to boycott, Brundage announced that he would be traveling to Berlin to assess the situation himself. During the trip, he found that, despite reports trickling into the United States, all seemed well and in order; even before he finished the official visit he drafted an article for the *Olympic News*, declaring that Germany had more than fulfilled its obligations and that he was returning to the United States gratified by the experience. Later that month the AOC met and finally came to a decision: "In light of the report of Mr. Brundage and the attitudes and assurances of representatives of the German Government, we accept the invitation of the German Olympic committee to the 1936 Olympic Games."

Brundage was thrilled by his victory, and so were the Germans. By default, so were most of the athletes in America, especially Betty Robinson.

CHAPTER SIXTEEN

REBOUND

As the 1936 Olympics approached, women's participation finally seemed like a done deal, although there were still those who opposed their attendance and wanted to return to the days of the past. Oddly enough, some of the most vocal detractors were women. In December 1934, an article appeared in the *Women's Division* written by Annie Hodgen, who had witnessed the 1932 Games: "The more I saw of the Games . . . the more convinced I was that women had no place in them and that we must work with renewed enthusiasm to interpret our standards to all nations until we should be able to prevent the exploitation of women for such spectacles."

Betty read articles expressing the grievances she had been hearing since her early running days, as well as updates on German affairs, and wondered how they might influence her participation. Germany seemed so far away, the events so remote and bewildering, that she felt a sense of detachment, as if she were reading a book of fiction and the occurrences were not those of real human beings. She tried to pay the reports she read little mind, though if these events came to fruition, her dreams would be over.

She trained and competed in local meets in the hope of gaining enough strength to participate in the qualifying trials, to be held in Providence, Rhode Island. Since she couldn't crouch in the starting position, the only chance she had of returning to the Games was not as an individual sprinter but as part of a squad. In 1934, she volunteered for the AAU National Indoor Championships 4-by-100-meter relay team, becoming a member of a Brooklyn team as its third leg. Unlike her appearances in previous competitions, this one went unnoticed; her team finished dead last. But knowing she could compete again gave her confidence, a boost, a buoyancy she had never experienced before, though her team's dismal results troubled her.

She continued to volunteer for any relay competition that would accept her, each time—on reaching the finish line—finding herself visibly shaken. Her teams often lost their meets, which prompted other members to blame their losses on the former Olympic champion, who they said could no longer pull her own weight.

The accusations pained her, and while she struggled to regain some measure of strength, both physical and mental, she watched from the sidelines as other athletes—Stella Walsh in particular—received the accolades that had once been hers. Each time she attended a meet she found herself, by instinct, heading for the track where the 100-meter race was being run. Though she was grateful for the chance to participate at all, it was the 100 meters that tugged at her, the place where she wished to be. She'd sit in the bleachers, watching as the runners dug their holes, crouched down, and dashed off when the pistol fired. She felt her own body react as the gun went off, her hand automatically rubbing her sore leg, her mind flashing back to the finish-line tapes she had broken, the ribbons and medals she had received, the records she had demolished. But even though she privately grieved, no one ever saw her cry; she never allowed herself to.

Her goal had become the relay team bound for the 1936 Olympics in Berlin. It would bring her much-needed consolation, she thought, as well as a sense of closure. But as she trained with renewed determination, she realized that her chances were growing slimmer. A whole new generation of talented runners had blazed onto the scene, vying for the same spots, and, much as she herself had done years earlier, another young woman was lighting up the national landscape, a girl most people expected to dominate in Berlin.

HELEN STEPHENS WAS born in Fulton, Missouri, a small town deep in Callaway County, situated about 100 miles west of St. Louis and 150 miles east of Kansas City. The tiny rivulets traversing Fulton grew heavier and wider as they traveled down to join the Missouri River, which frequently flooded the banks of nearby Jefferson City. Fulton was a simple, rustic place, but its inhabitants were very proud of it, the few roads leading in and out of the town itself often congested with the latest Model Ts as soon as the cars came onto the market.

By the 1920s, Fulton was home to nearly six thousand people, while the county had grown to twenty-five thousand inhabitants. It boasted a handful of racially segregated schools, several veterinarians, two flower shops, a blacksmith, a theater, a doctor's office, an adjacent drugstore, and a scattering of shops that sold everything, yet nothing in particular.

Helen Stephens herself arrived in Fulton on February 3, 1918, in what was then a diverse neighborhood of Irish, English, French, and German immigrants, not to mention a good smattering of first-generation Americans. There were a few African American families living in Fulton, but they kept to themselves, residing on the other side of town and scarcely ever mingling with the white population. Helen's birth year was a calamitous one, not only for the country but also throughout the world. In Europe, World War I was ending, but its effects were felt at home; closer to Fulton, an influenza epidemic was sweeping the county, eventually moving through the country and killing more than half a million individuals, several hundred in Calloway County alone.

Helen did not spend a lot of time being a child. Her parents always spoke to her as if she were an adult, sharing their concerns about money or the lack of it, the farm that never returned its harvest, physical labor, and the economy. In this large extended family, everyone seemed to have strong opinions about how Helen should be raised, especially when it came to her appearance and behavior. She grew up tall like a beanstalk, with feet that grew to size 12 and flopped like wings when she walked. On her face, she bore a purple birthmark that did not fade with time. But her eyes were big and expressive, fringed by long eyelashes and thick eyebrows, and they lit up with a spontaneous, genuine smile.

Her hands seemed as large as her feet, though they were delicate on her harmonica, playing cowboy songs about the wide-open fields. She blew on the instrument in the way her idol, Babe Didrikson, had once done—in fact, she had learned to imitate the Babe when she was very young. She herded sheep and cows; cleaned the pigsty; and dragged bales of hay across acres of land, to the delight of her father, who always believed she should have been born a boy, her gender a cruel trick the heavens had played on him.

Shortly before Helen was born, her father, Frank Elmer Stephens, had worked as a brick master for several companies in Fulton and Mexico, both in Missouri. But he soon realized that he was not meant for that kind of work and turned to farming, as, having married Bertie Mae Herring in September 1916—a college graduate, no less—he felt she deserved a better life than the haphazard jobs he had been doing.

Most people who first met Frank and Bertie Stephens found them an odd pair. She was soft and rather quiet, whereas he was loud and rough. She was reserved; he wanted to be the center of attention. He brought to the marriage old farming skills that had long gone out of fashion, while she brought her own college education and a Wurlitzer piano, upon which she unleashed her nimble fingers. She was taller than he was by several inches, but he compensated with a big mouth that often got him into trouble.

Upon their marriage, Frank and Bertie moved to a rented farm west of the Illinois Central Gulf Railroad. It was a large farm, well over 150 acres, a place he hoped to fill with sons. Being one of seven children—five boys and two girls—he desired a large family more than anything.

Frank liked being a farmer; he liked the independence of it, an attitude he would pass on to his children. Unlike his neighbors, who relied on the latest technologies to plow their fields, he toiled away at the land in the old-fashioned way, believing that one day his sons would help him do the same. That dream kept him going at back-breaking work that would have destroyed the strongest of men.

When, in 1918, Bertie handed him a (nearly) ten-pound baby girl with a fine mop of wheat-colored hair, Frank stared at the child with suspicion. Immediately he noticed that the baby had been born with two horrific defects: there was no penis, and what was apparent more than anything else was a large, uneven purple blotch on her right cheek. But he told his wife not to worry too much; she would do better next time. As Bertie took the baby back into her arms, she asked her husband what they should name her. He shrugged, not having given any thought to girls' names, so his wife selected Helen. Helen Stephens had a strong ring to it—and strength was something Bertie had a feeling this child would need.

By the time Frank's boy, Robert, arrived, on April 16, 1923, Bertie had suffered several miscarriages and the family had moved to a new farm. Though Frank was pleased with his son, it was a short-lived happiness—he was already looking forward to the next. But there would be no next son. Bertie's insides were too scarred. The doctor told Bertie she could never have any more children.

Helen and Robert got along as well as siblings could, and they soon became best friends with the seven sons of a farm family who lived several miles down the road. The boys taught Helen how to smoke, use a BB gun, and eventually fire a real rifle. She unloaded that .22-caliber freely behind her father's farm, bringing down large birds and black crows that circled the midwestern sky—or, if chance would have it, aiming it at the rabbits that disturbed her garden.

Though Frank found happiness on the farm, Bertie did not. She knew there should be more for her and her children than a life tending unyielding fields, corn that never turned to gold, vegetables that never ripened—and she wished they had greater opportunities. She was a retiring type who never shared those hopes and dreams with her husband, who couldn't have understood. Frank presumed that Bertie's fondness for music and poetry, together with her college education, would be frivolities his own daughter would eventually fall victim to, and he noticed those tendencies in Helen from an early age. Helen loved reading so much that her schoolteachers eventually began to give her their advanced materials, which she gleefully accepted and often took to Fulton's Methodist church, where she secretly devoured them within its pews.

It wasn't difficult for Helen to see the differences between her mother's and father's characters and how those differences played out within the household. Inevitably, an invisible line was drawn, with Helen and her mother on one side and Robert and her father on the other. Frank doted on Robert, but Helen and her mother often took the brunt of Frank's anger, which sometimes involved the sting of his hands. He had become a bitter man, ill tempered due to the troubles on the farm, which did not produce at the level he had wanted and expected; the extra sons who had not come; and the women, neither of whom, according to him, seemed capable of fulfilling the duties a female was supposed to fulfill—Bertie with her poetry and piano, Helen with her reading and her awkwardness. During the few moments she had to herself, Helen hurried to her favorite hiding spot, an isolated depression that Frank never plowed called Salt Lick, which she had made into a sanctuary. From there she loved to imagine all that existed beyond the farm, and how she yearned to see it.

FRANK'S SIBLINGS INCLUDED Charles, Oliver, Ray, and a sole sister, Laura. But it was Oliver of whom he was jealous. Ollie, as he was known, was fond of reading literature and playing music, traits not unlike Bertie's, which did little good on a farm. He had a particular fondness for Helen, and Helen for him. She appreciated his company more than that of her own father, which did not go unnoticed by Frank. Even worse, it seemed that Bertie felt the same way. It would not have been implausible, he reasoned. After all, the two were very akin to each other, and the more he thought about that, the more it ate at his soul, and the more it nagged him, the angrier he became.

Despite the challenging politics at home, Helen benefited immensely from the fresh, wholesome, farm-grown food she ate and the exercise she got by performing the chores her father assigned to her. Her body changed, and she grew into a muscular girl, taller than her schoolmates and able to outrun anyone, even the boys. She attended Middle River School, a one-room schoolhouse filled with nearly thirty students, mostly daughters of farmers. The school educated pupils from first to eighth grades. Though most of the students rode their ponies to school, Helen walked or ran, regardless of the weather. Along the way were hilly lanes flanked by tall trees, mostly oaks and elms, that her father never visited but that Helen liked to explore.

That she was meant to travel and leave Fulton was further reinforced one summer afternoon in 1931, as she climbed a hill behind her house and found a quiet spot. Sprawled on her back, a blade of grass between her teeth and sunlight warming her face, she watched the movements of the clouds overhead and began drifting not quite into sleep but into a sort of reverie. On that occasion, she saw herself at a starting line inside a stadium, waiting to run a race on a cinder track. She heard the thunderous applause coming from the crowd and saw herself breaking a winner's ribbon and raising a medal to the sky. A multitude of flags flapped loudly in the breeze, and national anthems echoed in her ears.

She opened her eyes, convinced that she had experienced not a dream at all or even a hallucination brought on by the heat; it was an actual glimpse of the future. She had read of Babe Didrikson's accomplishments at the Olympics and beyond. Suddenly she saw no reason why such accomplishments couldn't be hers as well. Seeking her father's approval was out of the question; he was as unyielding as the land he plowed. But she could keep the vision close to her heart, just hers, at least for now.

In the fall of 1931, Helen was thirteen and a half years old and starting as a freshman at her new high school. Taking stock of herself, she became aware that she did not look like anybody else. Tall and long-limbed, an awkward girl who had adopted a boyish look by wearing hand-me-downs that weren't her mother's or aunts' but her uncles' (their dingy overalls and tennis shoes were the only things that fit her). An air of poverty clung to her. Though many of her schoolmates were also the sons and daughters of farmers, their parents thrived on their lands, thanks in part to the innovations they had implemented. Her father still refused to go along with the times, either out of lack of money or just out of sheer stubbornness.

She had entered a class of cliquish adolescents in which the contrast was even more striking. The girls wore silk blouses adorned with pins, long skirts of fine fabrics, nude hose, and shining pumps. Their eyebrows were plucked, but hers remained bushy arches; their hair, teased to a magnificent height, surprised and amused her as she touched her own limp strands; their gleaming fingernails glittered in the light. Those girls epitomized the standards of beauty and fashion that newspapers and magazines advertised. The blotch on her face would start to throb, as it always did on awkward occasions, as if a reminder of her unpolished manners, more fit for a farmhand than a lady.

COACH W. BURTON Moore was the track coach at Fulton High School when Helen enrolled. He was in his third year of teaching and had only recently been a student at Westminster College in Fulton, where Brutus Hamilton, the Olympic track star who had been a coach for Westminster before taking a higher-paying position at the University of California, had cemented his knowledge of track and field. Moore was twenty-six years old and very tall, with movie-star looks. He was soft-spoken but direct and had impeccable manners, all of this conspiring to make the physical education requirements more tolerable for the girls who had to endure them. (To their great sadness, he was already engaged to Mary Lou Schulte, a local girl who'd caught his eye and whom he planned on marrying.) At the high school, sports for girls were typical of the time: they fulfilled their physical education requirements by taking classes, while the boys became involved in any sports they desired, as the after-school programs offered many options.

Moore had spotted Helen at the end of the summer, just a few weeks before the fall term began, while she was playing in a women's basketball game at the local Methodist church. Her height and agility had impressed him, but not as much as her speed. She was rumored to be quite a runner, and he had a general suspicion of how fast she was, but nothing was certain.

On a day that seemed too warm for fall, Moore placed Helen and seven other girls on a cinder track with the pretense of fulfilling the class's educational obligations. In reality, he wanted to clock Helen's time. Clad in tattered pantaloons her mother had stitched together and a pair of worn-out tennis shoes, she took her place on the track and waited for the starting whistle. She was aware that the other girls were looking at her, ungainly as she was, which caused her to reflexively lift her hand toward her birthmark.

She was not excited about the prospect of running; lately she had not been excited about anything at all. She was still concerned about fitting in at her new high school, but there were other matters on her mind. The Depression had hit Fulton, and Frank, unable to keep up with the mortgage, had lost his property. Appraisers had shown up at their farmstead, setting a value on every object the family owned. The farm had eventually been bought by a local farmer for four thousand dollars. It was difficult, but not unlike the hardships facing other farmers in Fulton. Helen tried her best to bear her sufferings stoically, but in truth they pained her. Her worries also revealed a young woman who had never carried herself with pride, as her other schoolmates did, and who now was forced to stoop even lower. Although she continued her studies and fulfilled her school duties, she felt no joy in them. Coach Moore sensed all that.

The 50-yard dash was not a strenuous run. All of the girls Moore lined up should have been able to complete it. When Moore called its start time, Helen streaked down the track well ahead of the other girls. She felt the brief rush of wind in her face, her legs lifting off the ground, and then it was over. Moore pressed his thumb over the stopwatch. He asked her to run the course again, to be certain his time was accurate. It was. 5.8 seconds. Helen Stephens, a poor, untrained farm girl from Fulton, Missouri, had just tied the 50-yard outdoor world record time held by the nation's first female track-and-field gold medalist: Betty Robinson.

FOR VERY DIFFERENT reasons, her parents only grudgingly tolerated Helen's new passion. Her father suspected that her training would prevent her from finding a paying job, and Bertie saw it as further proof of her daughter's tomboyish inclinations, which were growing stronger each day. She would have preferred that Helen take a typewriting course, specifically at William Wood College, her own alma mater. Nonetheless, with their reluctant blessing, Helen's training began in earnest, with Moore christening her an "Amazonian" who could go all the way to the Olympics.

No one shared his faith in her; the school's officials even refused to pay the two-dollar entrance fee for the AAU National Championships in St. Louis, scheduled for March 1936. Moore was determined to see her compete, even if he had to pay the fee himself. He could not predict the color of the medal, but he was certain Helen would be wearing one around her neck when she returned home from Berlin, as he knew she would be attending those games. He felt it with the same certainty Helen had felt it in her waking dream on the farm.

IT WAS A long, rough ride to St. Louis, Moore's Ford plowing through a relentless rainstorm, the roads muddy and congested. Helen sat quietly in the backseat, listening to the pinging on the roof and to Coach Moore's rattling off the names of the participants in the race, along with their statistics: Stella Walsh, Betty Robinson—athletes she had heard of, along with many others she hadn't. As Moore ticked more competitors off his tongue, Helen could feel her body tingle with anticipation.

She was aware of those names; her room was a virtual shrine to female track-and-field athletes. On one side of the room was tacked a newspaper photograph of Babe Didrikson, flashing her crooked smile, her legs slim as a bird's, her nose thin and pointy, flanked by a crowd of spectators. Stella Walsh watched from another corner of the room, her smile awkward and sly, a gold medal slung around her neck. Betty and the others elbowed one another for space in the small room. There were no family portraits, no movie-star photographs ripped out of magazines, no matinee idols flashing bright smiles at her, no advertisements for beauty products. Just star athletes reminding her of possibilities.

Moore had warned her that few people expected her to make much of an impact. She was unknown and virtually untrained and had never participated in a meet; she would be running against national and Olympic champions. Still, she should not feel inadequate, for in the beginning they had also been unknowns. Besides, several times she had unofficially beaten Betty's time. He looked forward to testing that on a real track.

On arriving, they learned that Betty had not shown up for the competition. The woman to beat, then—Helen's only true competitor—was Stella Walsh. Helen had never met Stella, but she was hard to miss, strutting onto the track with reporters in tow, every rumor Helen had ever heard about her finally coalescing. Seven years older than Helen, Stella looked every inch the athlete, her body trim at the waist but muscled and unusually well built below it. She never smiled, never spoke to the others, never acknowledged them with a word or even a gesture. She stood apart, digging her holes at the starting line, awaiting the pop of the gun.

Everyone steadily watched Stella, though Helen was eye-catching in her blue running outfit. Despite her impressive physique and the fact that Coach Moore had told reporters that Helen had unofficially broken the world record several times, few of the spectators paid much attention to her. Helen was just fine with the lack of recognition—for now.

Her first event was the 50 meters. In the preliminary heat, she stumbled at the start, and though she recovered at the last second, she lost to Stella. However, by the final heat she was ready. The two made equally excellent starts and ran down the track almost neck and neck. Nearing the final stretch with the finish line in sight, Helen edged forward and took the lead, keeping the rhythm and smashing through the tape, Stella just behind her.

Nobody was more surprised by her victory than Helen. A *Missouri Express* reporter thrust a pen and notepad in front of the newly minted victor and asked her how she felt about beating Stella Walasie-wicz. Helen, arching her eyebrows in surprise at the foreign name, re-plied, "Stella who?" Reporters took her answer as youthful boasting and hurried toward Stella, who was quickly gathering her belongings.

This was Stella's first loss in years, journalists pointed out to her, and she had lost to a beginner. What did it feel like to lose to Helen? What did she attribute the loss to? Was she aware that Helen did not have a clue about who she was? They went on, attempting to tease out drama from the situation and start a feud between the two stars. But if Helen's win had left Stella rankled, she didn't show it. She chalked up her loss to Helen's good fortune, not the girl's talent. It was "just a fluke," she replied to reporters. "I can beat her anywhere," she boasted before leaving the arena.

Stella's words riled Helen, who knew her win had not been just a lucky break at all. In fact, she suspected this would only be the start of her streak, and the newspapers agreed. "From Farm to Fame on the Cinder Track," read one of the headlines. "Surprise Star of the Women's Track Meet: Olympic Sprint Hope." Even *Collier's*, a na-tional publication with a reputation for social reform, dedicated a long feature to her, crowning her the fastest runner in the world.

UPON RETURNING TO Fulton, Coach Moore built a training regi-men to take Helen through the summer, helping her condition and train for the various upcoming competitions he had planned for her. Only one thing stood in his way: Helen's father. Frank was strongly opposed to a sporting life; he had planned something different for Helen upon her high school graduation. He wanted her to find a job, any kind of job that would earn steady money, which she in turn would hand over to him to help the family. He didn't think there was any need for Helen to continue her education, nor did he think that there was any use in her sporting activities.

But Moore prevailed—as did Bertie, who urged her husband to allow Helen to attend college. Helen settled on William Wood College, to her mother's pleasure. Although Frank was unhappy about his daughter leaving home, William Wood was close enough for her to return on weekends and holidays to take care of her household duties. She also received an athletic scholarship, though the college was not really known for athletics. In fact, the institution did not believe in physical education as an appropriate course of study for young women at all. Female students did participate in tennis, archery, and golf, but those activities were pursued more for recreational purposes than anything else. Other schools were vying for Helen's attention—larger, better ones with an emphasis on athletics—but Coach Moore was hired to coach half-time for Westminster College, the boys' college affiliated with William Wood, where he could continue coaching Helen. Now it was time to strategize.

CHAPTER SEVENTEEN

OFF TO BERLIN

By early July 1936, the athletes had arrived in Providence from all over the country. "All were bent on one destination: the Olympic headquarters at Room 108 in the Crown Hotel, where the final details for the most novel meet that has ever been presented to the Rhode Island public are being arranged," stated the *Providence Journal*. Once again, July 4 was the date of the AAU National Championships, and once again they would also serve as the Olympic try-outs.

Only one anticipated athlete had not arrived yet, and she would never arrive: Babe Didrikson. Though she had seemed like the obvious favorite, she had violated the terms of her amateur status after her wins in Los Angeles, forfeiting her chance to participate in the next Olympics. A photograph of her had been used to advertise a car, which was against AAU rules. Olympians could not use their names or likenesses to advertise anything while remaining amateurs, and immediately after her photograph was published the infraction came to the attention of the AAU. It seemed to officials (particularly to Avery Brundage) that Babe was once again showing off her impertinence. Her violations of the Olympic principles, not only of the written rules but also of the moral laws that governed amateurism, went too far. This time something had to be done about her, and Brundage was happy to lead the way.

As the controversy over women's participation in track and field continued to play out in the courts and the newspapers, Brundage was asked how he felt about it. He replied, "You know, the ancient Greeks kept women out of their athletic games . . . they would not even let them in the sidelines. I'm not sure that they were right." On December 6, a *New York Times* headline blared, "Babe Didrikson Banned by AAU." Her career as an amateur runner was over.

BETTY HAD RIDDEN the train east to Providence and on arriving in the city had immediately felt the weight of this being her last shot at the Olympics. Unlike in Newark, she felt nervous, tense, fighting the anxious energy that filled her body. She recalled her youthful self of nearly eight years earlier, leaving Union Station brimming with excitement and naiveté at the adventure opening up before her. Back then, she had barely heard of the Olympics, her competitors, or the stakes ahead. All she had genuinely cared about was the prospect of an adventure abroad, which had culminated in a gold medal.

The meets began at 1:30, at the height of the afternoon heat, on the grounds at Brown University. Upon arriving, the athletes were not immediately allowed to visit the track, so they milled about the hotel lobby and corridors, reading the list of scheduled events, which included several dances and dinners. They would also be guests of honor at the Crescent Park Management team dinner on the shore of Rhode Island. But no one seemed particularly interested in any of that; they wanted to run. A reporter covering the story commented on the seriousness he saw plastered on the athletes' faces.

Dee Boeckmann, who would coach the US Women's Track and

Field Team, had arrived a few days earlier to survey the conditions of the track, check the forecasts, ensure that hotel arrangements had been set, analyze the physical condition of the athletes, and, most important, investigate the money situation. A slew of reporters also waited to speak to her.

There would be eleven events in the program, five of them Olympic qualifiers: the 80-meter hurdles, 100-meter dash, javelin, discus, and high jump. Only the winners of those events would go on to Berlin, and Dee had to make certain athletes could compete at their best. She found the track surface in excellent condition. Weather reports anticipated warmth, which she knew would be welcomed by the California and southern contingents. In such warm weather the muscles tended to relax more, allowing for easier and more pleasant runs. She was thrilled to see that the athletes had arrived even earlier than scheduled and that, despite their long journeys, they displayed pep, which she trusted would translate into excellent running days.

However, though Dee found the conditions of the grounds and the weather agreeable, she could not help but bemoan the economic circumstances they were facing, which—much like the rest of the country—had left a mark on their sport. "Much will depend on the funds available," she told the press when asked who would be going on to Berlin and how the women would manage to pay for the journey if they were not provided with financial assistance. "So for that reason we hope for a fine turnout on the part of Providence and Rhode Island tomorrow," she went on. "If the money to finance the team to Berlin does not come in at the gate, we will make an appeal for aid to the states from which the girls came, for we hope to have a full team in the Olympic meet."

SO MUCH HAD changed. Betty herself was teetering at the edge of a precipice: save for her smile, there was nothing in her demeanor to remind spectators of the girl she had been eight years earlier, the care-free, all-or-nothing sixteen-year-old who had stormed into Newark with a swagger in her stride. Those were the relics of a life that had long since passed. Here instead stood a jittery woman nervously flicking the bracelet General MacArthur had given her after her 1928 win, now trying to calm herself. She watched the other competitors, all younger with bounce in their steps. She always struggled when she recalled the plane accident, and she hoped that today would not be the day when any traumatic memories came flooding in. She no longer flew with her cousin Wil. He could barely walk, never mind pilot a plane. Years later, in the throes of middle age, his mother long dead, Wil would go on to amputate the leg that had so bothered him, wishing that his mother had agreed to do it earlier or that he had had enough courage to defy her.

Forced by her health and economic circumstances, Betty had dropped out of Northwestern, a fact that pained her as much as her wounded leg did. By the 1930s, the family's debts had grown, and neither she nor her father could continue to pay the tuition, which—coupled with the expenses of her rehabilitation—eliminated her dream of taking a degree in physical education. Regardless, they were luckier than many, and she knew it. Her father had lost his job at the bank but managed to keep afloat by working security for Acme Steel, and though it was unlike other jobs he had previously performed, he was glad to have steady work while others had none. And they had their home, which was paid in full. However, many were not so fortunate. Betty watched as caravans of people whose homes had been repossessed left Riverdale daily, a chair, a battered suitcase, or a dog—the remains of a once prosperous life—strapped alongside the children in the backseats of cars.

Betty had joined the rest of the unemployed in searching for work. It was not the most auspicious time, she knew, as tens of thousands of other people were also looking for employment. It was easy to become disheartened, to wallow in one's own misery. As she drove to and from Chicago and Riverdale, she could see the misery all around her, in the men and women waiting in breadlines or scavenging through refuse like rats; she could see it in the eyes of children, who sat alone on steps and stared into the distance as she had once stared down a cinder track. And she could see it in her own family, in the relatives whom the Depression had touched most deeply. There was no more attending dance classes, plays, recitals, or dinners with her groups, as she had done as a youngster and college student, because there were no more groups. And she no longer spoke with Bert. There were also no more college classes or jaunts across the quads from her sorority house to meet Frank Hill on the track. There was no more Frank; no more official training, just the meets she volunteered for. Eventually, unlikely as it seemed, she had found work as a secretary, a far cry from what she had set out to do, but work nonetheless.

Indeed, so much had changed, but running had stayed constant. She could always run.

HELEN STEPPED ONTO the hot track, looked around, and wiped her brow. She spotted Betty and walked over to her. They had already been introduced when nearly eighty of them had been escorted to the city's State House to meet Rhode Island governor Theodore Francis Green earlier in the day. He'd instructed the women to "uphold American ideals of democracy and freedom, not apologetically but proudly." But the athletes, especially Helen, were not keen on all the formality; they wanted to begin the heats.

By the time she arrived in Providence, Helen was no longer a local farm girl trying out her skills for the school coach. A college woman, with all the experiences an academic life provided, educational as well as the romantic, she felt confident, and with good reason. She was even in the newspapers, having become the type of person she had often read about, her picture now possibly plastered on someone else's wall. She had won several heats already, even beating the indomitable Stella Walsh.

Although Coach Moore kept her up to speed, Helen preferred to read the newspapers herself, to see what the reporters were writing about her. And preceding her arrival at the trials were headlines touting her not only as the best hope for a new Olympic title and record holder, but as "a New Didrikson," a comparison she enjoyed, having always admired the Babe, whose style evoked natural comparisons. As a tomboy, Helen knew that Babe had received a lot of jabs for her looks and attitude, but she had come out victorious on the track nearly every time.

Helen was not as boastful as Babe Didrikson, but they both wanted to be the best, and Helen knew that, just like her idol, she could back up the promises the newspaper writers predicted. She had a sense that the city itself would be fortunate—Providence, the name itself was a good omen.

JULY 4 WAS just as hot and suffocating as it had been eight years previously in Newark, the temperatures soaring as they were in the rest of the country. As the athletes awoke and read the papers, one of the headlines featured Helen Hull Jacobs and her win at Wimbledon, whose "elusive all-England tennis championship" had finally come true at last. There were also headlines that had nothing to do with sporting events but that still had an influence on their lives, particularly those from the Midwest. One read, "Heat Interferes, Drought Ravages in the Mid-West. Temperatures 100 to 110 Degrees Prevail in Most of Afflicted Areas."

The unseasonably hot weather had already been blanketing the middle of the country for much of the summer, and the Central Weather Bureau's forecast station predicted that the temperatures would top 100 degrees Fahrenheit for at least the next several weeks, forcing farmers to lose their crops to droughts and people to find whatever means of cooling they could. But in Rhode Island, at least for those who came to see the athletes, the economic shifts due to the weather conditions were set aside.

The ache in Betty's knee worsened as she made her way to the track. Her arrival had been hailed with articles of praise describing the usual "smiling Betty." One such story ran, "Little Betty Robinson, Chicago girl who set a world record in winning the Olympic 100-meters at Amsterdam in 1928, is another standout." But she didn't feel like a standout. So much more hung in the balance this time, and the thought of the stakes had made her feel uncharacteristically edgy. She wanted to prove that she was still an Olympic champion, as everyone was heralding—and there was only one way to do that.

Her misgivings settled in her stomach as she fiddled with her bracelet. She had never taken it off, even while flying. It had emerged from the crash much as she had, a little bent but still intact.

She took her starting position for the 100-meter race and sized up her fellow competitors; she was the oldest among them. It was hard not to make the comparison. In 1928, she had also been called "the Babe" for being one of the youngest competitors on the entire American delegation. Now some of the other athletes referred to her as a "senior member."

The firing of the pistol sent the competitors tearing down the track, Helen immediately setting the pace and taking a convincing lead. Betty, on the other hand, jumped in at an unexceptional pace. She felt her lungs expanding as she drew in the warm air around her; her knees were popping like firecrackers, and a burning sensation was spreading throughout the back of her legs, traveling upward along her spine, to the base of her neck, her fists balling at her sides and her face twisting with effort. Every breath she took seared her insides, and she could not help but notice runner after runner passing her, so fast she could smell their scent and feel the wind they kicked up behind them.

Helen finished first, while Betty crossed the finish line in a dismal fifth position, her legs buckling beneath her. She was timed at 12.5 seconds, exactly the same speed she had clocked during the final qualifying run at the trials of 1928. Then it had been good enough to win the qualifier. Now it put her in fifth place. It was one of her poorest showings in a competitive race, and her physical exhaustion showed on her face.

Only four thousand people sat in the stands. It was a discouraging turnout, but the journalists assumed female track and field was still a novelty in Rhode Island, and the fact that it was a national holiday once again didn't help. But those who attended were rewarded with Helen's performance.

She ran the preliminary track in the pole lane in 12 seconds flat, two-tenths of a second better than all of the other women, then returned in the same lane in the semifinal, to better her time and equal Stella's record of 11.8 seconds. During the final, Helen once again drew the lane next to the wall, to the delight of the rest of the competitors; that was considered the slowest lane, and they assumed she would be placed at a considerable disadvantage because of it. But it didn't seem to matter to her; she ran through the course in 11.7 seconds, breaking the world record. While the crowd erupted loudly on learning that they had just witnessed history, to her it seemed like nothing but routine. Twice already she had unofficially broken the record at 11.6 seconds.

THE FOLLOWING DAY, *The Providence Sunday Journal* ran several competing stories on its front pages, but by far the paper's longest featured the women's track-and-field race. A large photograph captured the last moments at the finish line with the headline "Helen Stephens Sets World Record for 100 Meters." Helen had entered the limit of three events allowed by the AAU and won all of them, including the 100 meters, the discus, and the shot put.

In years past, Betty had assumed that by the 1936 trials she would be one of the coaches, if not the main coach, for the Olympics. Instead, the coach was Dee Boeckmann—her former cabinmate on the SS *President Roosevelt* on their way to Amsterdam—who had followed the career trajectory Betty had originally set for herself. After Amsterdam, Dee had competed in Los Angeles and become involved in the operational and administrative side of track and field, a lucrative job further adding to her wealth. She had then been chosen to coach the team to Berlin. This was life as it should have evolved; how ironic that Betty's own dreams had been fulfilled by someone else. Did Dee know that she was living the life Betty had planned for herself?

It was up to Dee to select who would make up the team for Berlin, assisted by the chairman of the Women's Track and Field Committee, Fred Steers, who had also been watching the races. Though Betty had performed well, she had not been spectacular, and they all knew it. But what she had going for her was not only her performances in Providence but also her history and her gold medal. It would not be easy to discard her background—or so she hoped.

"The group of qualifying athletes is the very finest we have ever had for our Olympic bid," Dee told reporters, who were pestering her about her choice. She reiterated that her "only concern right now is that we will have enough funds to send over the three finishers in each event, and three extra girls for the 400 meters relay to be selected from the fourth, fifth, and sixth finishers in the 100 meters run. I hope that we can send a full team, for the leading contenders were all so good, that it would be almost a sacrifice to leave anyone of this list behind."

Unlike administrators, coaches, in particular female ones, were never well paid, but this time there wouldn't be any money for her at all—only the fame that went along with being the first female coach of a women's team. Dee had decided to settle for the glory.

It was late in the afternoon, back in the hotel, that Betty received the news: she would be part of another Olympic team, after all. She had not heard from Dee directly, but word spread through the hallways. It did not really matter to her how she learned of it, for the outcome was the same. She had earned her spot on the team and would be going to Berlin.

CHAPTER EIGHTEEN

PHENOMS

"Miss Robinson's comeback is the most remarkable of all," *The New York Times* wrote as Betty prepared to leave for her new transatlantic voyage. "Winner of the dash in 1928, she was so badly hurt in a subsequent airplane crash that it was feared she never would walk again, much less run."

Her triumphant return, however, was already in jeopardy. The cry to boycott the Berlin Olympics had grown stronger, gaining ground daily, even from those who several months earlier had supported the United States' participation in the games. And along with the outcry against Germany, there was also the question of economics that was still plaguing the country.

On July 13, 1936, the *Brandon Daily Sun* loudly declared, "Betty Robinson Unable to Go to Olympics Because of Cash Shortage." It continued, "There will be a broken heart . . . unless a full United States team is sent to Germany, but the bitterest heartache will probably tug within the chest of a great and courageous girl whose dramatic comeback seems destined to be halted by cold money." The paper rehashed her story; she knew it was trying to elicit sympathy for her, but at that point, she didn't much care.

Following the trials, US Olympic officials had brutally crushed the hopes of the many Olympians who had qualified, including Betty's: there was a deficit of almost $150,000, meaning that only four athletes would be fully financially supported in Berlin. The others would either have to be eliminated from the team or find a way to pay for the trips themselves. Such cuts were more significant on the women's team than the men's.

That fact did not go unnoticed, especially by Helen Stephens, who paid close attention to the way men and women were treated, or mistreated. "It is a terrible thing for the girls who qualified and now won't be able to make the trip. There is disappointment in sports enough, without this. I feel terrible to think that some who qualified for the team won't be able to go. It looks to me like a plain case of discrimination in favor of the men against the women in using the available money," she said bluntly. "There's been so much log-rolling that I'll believe I'm in the Olympics when I actually take the mark in Berlin."

Helen had not grown to be a retiring type, like her mother, and she had become even more outspoken in college. Exposed to new experiences and new people, to women who espoused fresh ideas, she was far more acutely aware of gender discrepancies, even within her own family, and she was not going to stand for them.

Due to backlash like Helen's, the AOC agreed to send five women athletes, which it thought was fair, given that several months earlier it had considered not sending a women's team at all. But it was still not enough of a concession. The women athletes were now waging public war, with such resilience and ferocity that eventually the AOC relented even further, announcing that it would back up—at least partly—all eighteen women athletes who had qualified, as long as they managed to come up with five hundred dollars each to augment their travel expenses to Berlin. That was the best it could do.

But few people possessed enough disposable income to support athletes sailing overseas in pursuit of their Olympic dream, despite the pride such wins would provide the country during the devastating economic slump. Female athletes, most especially, were not even fully supported by their families, let alone the AOC. Brundage made it clear that "unless we get money in the next 10 days, we can't sail." Helen Stephens, Annette Rogers, Anne Vrana, and Tidye Pickett would have their whole voyage paid for, but Betty Robinson—who had barely qualified—was not on the list. If she wanted to take part in the Games, she would have to come up with the five hundred dollars herself.

Betty did not know how she was going to scrape together that much money for the passage, but she knew she had to. After she had come perilously close to dying, her conviction had brought her to this point, allowing her to walk and to run again. She would not allow money to stand in her way, not now that she was so close to returning. She needed to go to Berlin. It was a visceral, urgent, persistent need, a demand she felt deep in her soul. Jim Rochfort, her brother-in-law, ever present to urge her forward, agreed that she had to finish what she had started, and the two of them began to solicit funds from anyone they could.

She scrounged up all she possessed and anything she could borrow from others; she sold Olympic pins and ribbons—even memorabilia that had seemed trivial when she originally collected it was now essential to her purpose.

JUST DAYS LATER, on July 15, 1936, tired but delighted, Betty Robinson stood on the deck of the SS *Manhattan*, along with more than 330 fellow Olympians, amid streamers and balloons, watching while the low-hanging clouds mingled with the soft plumes of smoke being exhaled by the ship as it slowly made its way out of Pier 60 toward Europe.

The *Manhattan* departed to the tune of blaring bands, accompanied by the encouraging shouts of spectators who had come to wish the athletes well. Nearly ten thousand of them had gathered to cheer the well-dressed athletes who were leaning over the rails, waving exuberantly back at their fans. Alongside Betty were two other former Olympians: Olive Hasenfus, who had been chosen again as an alternate for the track team (though for the second Olympics in a row, she would not get the chance to run), and Anne Vrana (now Anne Vrana O'Brien), who had given birth to a little girl and quickly found out that motherhood had a way of interfering with her training schedule.

The three veterans wistfully reminisced about the previous Games; they were no longer starry-eyed little girls on their maiden voyage. Life was different now. Hours that once had been happily dedicated to their training on the cinder track were now devoted to marriage, an unfulfilling day job, or a child who was left in the care of grandparents but who usually required full-time care. Their bodies were different as well. The realization was sobering and humbling.

THAT EVENING, THE athletes assembled to recite the Olympic Oath and meet with Avery Brundage, who to Helen seemed to have an "almost dictatorial power" as he spoke to the crowd. Following the conference, they had a chance to assess one another before retiring to their cabins. The athletes had been given accommodations in steerage; the first-class compartments were reserved for reporters, AOC officials, and other dignitaries traveling to Berlin.

When Betty saw her cabin number, cabin 35 on deck 6, she had a shiver of déjà vu. It was the same cabin number she had had during her previous Olympic voyage to Europe. And one of Betty's cabinmates, she soon learned, was Helen Stephens, the young woman from Missouri she had met during the tryouts in Providence.

· · ·

HELEN HAD AWAKENED early that morning, taking the bus at 8 a.m. after saying good-bye to Coach Moore and his fiancée. As she readied to leave, she had felt something shift subtly in her coach's hug: an ending and a beginning all at once. When she next saw him, she would no longer be the girl who had haphazardly run the 50-yard dash for her school physical education department; she would be an Olympian.

Arriving on the ship, Helen marveled at the sumptuous decorations and the ornate railings; the vessel was a virtual floating hotel. It thrilled her that she would be rooming with Betty. It didn't take long for Helen to become dazzled by Betty. More mature than most of the athletes on the ship, Betty was the personification of everything Helen felt she was not and would never be: at twenty-four, Betty was more worldly and sophisticated than anyone Helen had ever known, including her college friends and the ones she had romantically been linked to. Although obviously tired by her new secretarial job, her personal circumstances, and the demands of training, Betty managed to display a casual elegance, particularly while sitting cross-legged on the promenade with a cigarette dangling from her mouth. She was pretty and popular, and everywhere she went she caught people's attention; everyone loved her low and beguiling laughter. Her jovial, amiable personality allowed her to get away with infractions others would have been punished for, including drinking and smoking. Helen found her captivating. She began to follow Betty everywhere, overwhelmed by her, hungering for her affection. But she never revealed then what she had been afraid to reveal to anyone yet: that she was attracted to women.

Although the term "lesbian" was not commonly used in popular culture until the time Helen was already a middle-aged woman, the reality was that she had become aware of her sexuality as a young child—though she had been unable to articulate those feelings at that age. She recalled times when her schoolmates had become curious about the boys who surrounded them, yet Helen had felt no curiosity whatsoever about the opposite sex. Instead, it was the schoolgirls themselves who piqued her interest. Later in life she admitted that even as a young girl of six and seven, she had a sense that there was something different about her, something even more singular than people had already noted.

When Helen was nine, and in the fourth grade at the local elementary school, a fourteen-year-old cousin of hers who had always been taken with her height had invited her to visit a loft in the schoolyard, away from prying eyes. He had asked her if she wanted to see something unusual, so she was interested. She had no idea what was about to happen, and even later in life she seemed to remember the episode in a daze, recalling the sweat dripping from her cousin's body as he took her hand in his and led her to the loft, while outside recess continued undisturbed. Once there, he dropped his pants and underwear and proceeded to show Helen his penis.

She had been curious, to a certain extent, to watch as he fumbled in his own nakedness, until he instructed her to undo her underpants so that he could sneak a peek at her body, too. She had not been frightened by him or by his request, or even embarrassed; merely curious, a word she continued to use for decades. She had been privy to neighbors' conversations and those of her other cousins when they spoke of such things, but she had never felt any interest. Now, as she saw the real thing, her curiosity dimmed even further, his puny naked body unappealing to her.

Her cousin did not feel the same way. He proceeded to fondle her that day and for days afterward, the fondling turning into sexual assault and rape. Helen never told anyone about what happened in the loft, and it was only when a teacher accidentally discovered them that her parents were informed. Her mother cried uncontrollably, while her father arrived at the school armed with a shotgun, ready to unload it on his nephew. He didn't do it, but Helen was transferred to a nearby school, while her cousin remained where he was.

Two years later, she had another experience that further influenced her sexual awareness. A local teacher had begun to room at the Stephenses' farm when her permanent lodgings had not been ready by the start of the school year. It was not unusual; when out-of-state teachers arrived and their residences were not ready, they boarded with local families who had the space to host them. The teacher, a lovely young woman in her midtwenties, slept in Helen's room for several nights, and Helen distinctly recalled the woman's tendency to go to bed stark naked, with only a sheet covering her. Helen awoke one night to the sighs of the teacher stroking herself, which did not stop, even when she noticed Helen watching her. If anything, the idea that her future pupil was staring at her seemed to thrill the young woman, and she invited Helen to place her own hand beneath the sheet, too, and to continue what she had been doing herself. Helen agreed and never looked back.

Years later, Helen could still recall the moans ensuing from the young woman and the pleasurable sensations they had brought her. The experience had allowed her to realize something very fundamental about herself, and though she never came out in public, everybody knew that she was a lesbian.

THOSE ON BOARD the *Manhattan* knew as well. Helen clung to Betty consistently, almost intimately, in the indiscreet manner she had been noted for when attaching herself to others in college. There she had found like-minded people who shared her tendencies, albeit quietly or even secretly, but it seemed to her that nothing romantic could occur on the ship, least of all with Betty. Betty did not overtly repudiate Helen's advances, as some had done before, though she made it clear where her own interests and desires lay. Helen sometimes watched her as she sidled up next to men, coyly inclining her head and smiling just so before taking a drag on her cigarette. Betty seemed amused and flattered by Helen's affections but was otherwise remote. Betty could have turned Helen away, mocked her, or even thought her some kind of a freak, as some had; instead she befriended and respected her.

AS BETTY STOOD leaning against the rail of the *Manhattan*, watching the shifting colors of the day change while New York faded behind her, she learned of another former acquaintance who was also on the ship. The swimmer Eleanor Holm, also a gold medalist, who had been one of the youngest competitors in 1928, was also returning to the Games. She had captured the top spot in the 100-meter backstroke in Los Angeles and had further matured in the interim years, her strokes improving to such a degree that she hoped to repeat her feat in Berlin. Betty liked Eleanor; the two of them had been favorites of General MacArthur in 1928. Through the papers she had followed Eleanor's rise in the world of swimming, knew of her accomplishments and of her private ordeals.

Now known as Eleanor Holm Jarrett, she had already reached the pinnacle of her success, both professionally and personally. For the past seven years she had been almost unbeatable in the pool and was now only one of a handful of women to be participating in her third Olympics. Like others, Betty was impressed. Eleanor had recently married Art Jarrett, the well-known singer and bandleader at the Cocoanut Grove nightclub in Los Angeles, where she also performed on occasion. Now, at twenty-two, her marriage, money, and swimming accolades bestowed upon her a greater dose of self-confidence, and she felt superior to the rest of her teammates.

It was her beauty, she said, that had been the catalyst for her gradual drinking problems; men were always buying her drinks and chatting her up in the hope that it would lead to romance. Aside from her athletic abilities, soon after her win in 1932 she had entered the entertainment business. Hollywood had been irresistible, and she had consented to screen tests proposed by the movie studios. Unfortunately, drinking would be her downfall on the *Manhattan*.

Though liquor was not condoned for the athletes, first-class passengers were free to indulge in it. And although, financially, first-class and steerage passengers were worlds apart, in reality only a stairway and a corridor separated them on the ship. Booze traveled quickly from one compartment to the other, and athletes were often invited to parties hosted by reporters and rich guests heading off to Berlin. Frequenting those parties were also AOC officials, who gave free rein socially to the same behaviors they vilified in speeches and guidelines. Fun, gregarious Eleanor, stowed below with the rest of the Olympians, was frequently urged to make her way upstairs to sip champagne among the fashionable first-class crowd. Though she knew such mingling violated the Olympic code, she always greedily accepted the invitations. She was caught one night returning to her room; two officials were holding her by the armpits, and she was babbling uncontrollably, reeking of champagne.

Nothing had happened, she told Ada Taylor Sackett, the team chaperone, who had caught her, and later in an interview she made light of the situation. But Ada quickly hurried to complain to Avery Brundage, who, although often tipsy himself, expected sobriety from his athletes.

The reality was that Olympic team members had a standard to uphold. Eleanor had often been warned to be careful, lest she be discovered. When Ada had seen Eleanor unable to walk back to her room and fraternizing with two unmarried ship workers, she had called on Dr. Lawson, the ship's doctor, who upon inspection announced that she was suffering from "acute alcoholism." Several of her teammates were there. They had been shoved into the cabin to look at her, the drunk, disheveled Eleanor, held up as an example of a bad girl, exposed like a pet in a zoo, humiliated. This was not what Brundage had in mind for his athletes. Upon learning of the event, he immediately dismissed her from the team. The following morning, Eleanor learned she would not be participating in a third Olympics. But on hearing of the AOC's decision, she was hired by the Associated Press to cover the Games, only angering Brundage further.

BETTY, WHO WITNESSED the event, was astounded. She began a campaign to have Eleanor reinstated. Her efforts were futile; the AOC officials had no intention of rethinking their decision. Betty found that odd; she had seen other team members abusing alcohol, smoking, and carousing, and nothing of the sort had occurred. She had indulged in those things herself on several occasions, just a tad more sneakily. Brundage was also aware that most of the men trained while still in the throes of alcoholic stupor, but he chose not to punish them or to reprimand his own AOC members for the same infractions. Eleanor, perhaps because she was a woman, was the first athlete to be dismissed from the team.

BETTY AND HELEN soon got into a routine, becoming nearly inseparable. The blue mornings were delightfully free of anxiety as they performed calisthenics while swaying to the rhythm of the ship, ran laps on the promenade, or walked at a brisk pace, working up a sweat and inhaling the sweet scent of the ocean, while Tidye and Louise, who were suffering from seasickness, kept mostly to their cabin.

More often than not, Betty and Helen were distracted by the warm sunshine beating upon their backs, though the abundant meals always proved alluring. Their days began with a heavy breakfast, followed by a bountiful lunch, and then the athletes bided their time until a lavish dinner was presented, on which they gorged. Their mission had become to dodge Dee Boeckmann, who kept a watchful eye on her athletes. She was a stickler for the rules and was particularly fanatic about her charges' diets. She knew what the results of too little training and too much indulgence were and wanted to prevent a repeat of the 1928 debacle. She supervised everything that passed through her girls' lips, forbidding snacks between meals, as well as all forms of cakes, ice cream, pastries, and anything else that had sugar in it. As she struggled to keep them in line, she advised her athletes to fuel their bodies with chicken, vegetables, and loads of fruit washed down with water. She knew that she had a few renegades in her group, the water exchanged for liquor and champagne, but they would be the ones paying the price once they reached Germany.

Not a day after boarding the *Manhattan*, Dee had come across Helen, about to shove a piece of lemon chiffon cake into her mouth, and she had barreled down the buffet line in time to stop her with a quick slap on the hand, the cake falling limply from Helen's grip. The admonition, though perhaps warranted, struck Helen as uncalled for, and she felt her face burn with humiliation. How was Helen ever going to bring home a medal, Dee wanted to know, if she insisted on eating cake? Dee was certain that Stella Walsh wasn't gorging on lemon chiffon cake.

AS THE SHIP traversed the ocean and the start of the Games approached, there was one thing that Helen was *not* thinking about: college. She had enjoyed the social life and activities William Wood had provided but disliked her classes—a reality clearly reflected in her grades. Much like Babe, her idol, she fulfilled only as much of her school's academic requirements as necessary to play and continue to benefit from her scholarship. Though curious about the world at large, she saw sports as her only way of life and imagined that they would figure even more prominently upon her return home from Berlin, in some way or another.

Matters were different at home. Despite Helen's success on the track, her mother's frustrations escalated. She was worried that Helen would eventually leave college without any tangible skills and unsuited for a job. And Frank, rather than seeing his daughter's grades as a disappointment, regarded them as confirmation that he'd been right all along. He had always had his doubts about Helen's attending college; her modern history major had further infuriated him, as he considered the subject useless, much like the pursuits Bertie engaged in and that she often encouraged. If things had gone according to his plans, Helen would have remained on the new farm, her size and muscles put to better use lifting bales of hay, digging ditches, and even driving a tractor. Instead, she insisted on senselessly running up and down a track. Leave college and this running business *now*, he demanded every time she visited. He could use the help at home, he pointed out, burdening her with hopes that were his own and that she would not and could not fulfill.

ALTHOUGH DURING THE day the sea was calm, in the evening large waves pummeled the ship. A few hardy athletes braved the careening vessel and slick promenade, walking a little unsteadily to view Mother Nature's fury, despite having been instructed to the contrary. It was often at night when, unable to sleep, Helen stepped alone onto the boardwalk, feeling the wind bluster on her face, wondering if it was strong enough to unlatch the lifeboats rattling by the side of the ship. As she stared up at the sky, the stars looked as big as the ones back in Fulton. On one such nocturnal escapade, she noticed activity by the gangway, beneath one of the lifeboats. Something was moving under the tarpaulin spread out to cover it. She waited a few moments, and then an unknown girl sprang out, adjusted her clothing, and rushed away, passing Helen and uttering a soft good night. Moments later, Jesse Owens jumped out of the boat, smiled at her, and left in the opposite direction. Helen had no idea how to respond to the sudden encounter, so she just watched him go.

. . .

AS THE SHIP neared the mainland, an unexpected shot of pain coiled itself from the soles of Helen's feet all the way up the back of her legs. She described the stiffness and soreness to Dee; her calves felt like they were being ripped apart. They were the classic symptoms of a painful inflammation of the muscles and tendons. The doctors on board advised her to take a step back from her routine. So far, the training had not been strenuous but had included sprinting around the upper decks and some calisthenics, the coaches believing that that would be enough to keep the athletes in shape during the crossing. Yet whatever she was doing was provoking a dull ache that only the pounding of a masseuse could dissolve. Dee advised her to keep the news of her soreness to herself. She certainly didn't want nosy reporters finding out and badgering her with questions. Helen agreed; their stories should speak only of her winning streak.

Though Helen continued to walk on the deck, the lounge chairs became more inviting; there she sat, drinking in the warmth of the sun and playing her harmonica. She often called out to Betty, who'd join her without reserve, and together they whiled away the hours that were normally reserved for training. They also never talked about the "Berlin question," as it was often called. Until one day the question found them.

Helen had crossed paths with Dee early one morning on the promenade. She was surprised to notice a fine network of lines creasing Dee's forehead and bunching out from her eyes that hadn't been there before; the coach looked as if she had not slept well in days. She suddenly seemed tense and fidgety, lost in thought. Later that morning, Helen received a note instructing her to see Dee for a chat, and at 10:30 Helen made her way to Dee's cabin. She knew that Helen no longer paid attention to the boycott letters she received, Dee said, speaking in low tones behind closed doors; but she worried that the rest of the girls did. She asked Helen to discreetly keep an eye on her teammates, to listen for any hints of a boycott, to talks about Hitler and his henchmen, to anything that did not include track and field.

The sneakiness didn't sit well with Helen, and she wondered why Dee had picked her to observe her teammates. Was it because she had noticed that, much as she had done in high school, Helen preferred to observe rather than be observed? She assured Dee that German affairs were of no interest to most of the girls, unless they had to do with their spots on the team. It was talks of boys that engrossed the girls most of all, European boys and what they would be like, as well as the idea of having an exciting time abroad. They were already mapping out their itineraries for the places they wished to visit while in Berlin, some of them outside the city itself, if they could afford the train fare. But Dee ignored Helen. She knew that some of the girls were not as tough as Helen was, and were easily persuaded by men and their arguments. She counted on Helen to watch them. Helen had to wonder if Dee knew she was attracted to women; how else would she have known that men would not persuade her, too?

On returning to her cabin, Helen spoke to Betty about her conversation with Dee. They were alone, and Helen trusted that Betty would keep the conversation private. Betty was surprised, almost alarmed by the news. Although the athletes were about to gather in Berlin, there were still those who wished the United States would take a stand and refuse to participate. Betty and Helen understood what people feared would occur in Germany. Helen especially, who kept abreast of current events, was aware of the complexity of the Games being held in Hitler's Berlin. They spoke for a few minutes longer and agreed that, having come this far, they would not ruin their chances for anybody, much less because of a few letters they might occasionally receive. If Dee or Brundage insisted on seeing any correspondence pertaining to the issue, they would allow her or him to peruse it.

· · ·

ON JULY 18, the athletes were invited to the Captain's Ball, making up for the cool weather that had plagued them most of the day. The music was loud, the brilliant sparkling lights casting shadows on the giddy, buzzed competitors. Flasks filled with spirits made the rounds.

Three days later, as slivers of moonlight crept through the portholes, many of the athletes rushed onto the promenade, where, in the distance, they saw the hills of Ireland. The morning breeze was chilly as they watched the flickering lights of a new country sparkle like frost. Helen and Betty huddled deeper into a blanket they had brought along as morning broke, watching as pretty cottages glimmered in the distance. Small buildings were sprinkled haphazardly among the hills.

The ship docked in Hamburg on the morning of the twenty-fourth, and Helen found herself standing in line beside Dee to leave the ship. Several days had gone by since their little chat in Dee's cabin, but every time they bumped into each other, Dee took the opportunity to sidle up to Helen, smiling conspiratorially. Here she was again, drawing closer to Helen and, out of earshot, advising her to keep her eyes open, watching not only her teammates but people in general, especially reporters. Some, Dee told her, were spies hired by the Germans to tease out information from foreign athletes.

THE ATHLETES WERE loaded onto buses and transported to Hamburg's City Hall through streets decorated in flags and banners fluttering in the early-morning breeze. Following a short welcoming ceremony, they boarded a train to Berlin. Helen was whisked away to a different compartment from the rest of the team, along with Jesse Owens, NBC reporter Bill Henry, and Avery Brundage. There, for the first time in history, they would be broadcasting from a moving railroad car to radio stations in America.

The air at the Berlin train station was heavy and the streets crowded; all of Germany seemed to be there to welcome them. The city's monuments, offices, and churches were bedecked in German and Nazi flags, which quivered in the occasional breath of wind. Long rows of linden trees were broken by a succession of poles bearing Olympic flags and swastikas. Ecstatic spectators rested their backs on them as they waved national flags, drank beer, and munched pretzels. There was no sign anywhere that just days earlier, on July 16, some eight hundred Roma who had been living in Berlin and its surroundings had been rounded up and interned in a special camp in Marzahn, one of the city's suburbs. The Nazis camouflaged their real selves under the cover of Olympic glamour: beyond the swastikas, the athletes were privy to little of the darkness surrounding them.

THE FEMALE ATHLETES were housed in the austere Frauenheim, a dank dormitory not far from the train station. On the first night, their windows banged heavily, and the athletes woke early every morning to constant rain pinging on the rooftops, the walls soaking up the moisture and retaining it with a tight grip. As the athletes drew their curtains apart, the hundreds of Olympic flags interspersed with red banners bearing black swastikas greeted them. They breathed in the room's dampness, its chill, and its thin walls (which left no sound to the imagination). Each room was lit by a slender bulb hung from the ceiling, strung on a single wire, sparking to barely illuminate two twin beds, their thin mattresses covered with frayed blankets. There was a slight military feel to it; the temperature was kept below normal, chilling the athletes through their bones, as if to discipline or punish them. In the evening, beneath the windows, they saw shadows flitting about like rats, hiding and scurrying.

As if the rooming conditions were not bad enough, the breakfast of dry, dark rye bread and tart green apples added to the unyielding ambience. Helen eventually complained, her discontent so potent that officials were pushed to replace the bread and apples with the more familiar breakfast fare to which the team was accustomed: eggs, sausage, bacon, juice, and pancakes.

The men, on the other hand, were lodged in the Olympic Village. It was usually used as police barracks and would revert back as soon as the athletes departed. German officials had visited Los Angeles four years earlier and noted its Olympic Village. Taken by the idea, they had vowed to build bigger and better facilities when the 1936 games rolled around, repurposing what they had and adding more. In the village, the international male athletes were truly taken care of, offered all manner of food and comforts, along with the occasional smuggled cigarette, bottle of booze, or prostitute hired for the occasion by the German government.

Despite the discrepancies between the men's and women's quarters, the women appreciated the location of their sleeping quarters, for they were only two hundred yards away from the training facilities and the train station was nearby. In the late afternoon, following refreshments, groups of them visited the Olympic Stadium or strolled to the city proper, where efforts had been made to rejuvenate and modernize the city. Interpreters speaking dozens of languages had been hired to roam the streets near the stadium so that they could aid visitors and help the athletes navigate.

Just at the outskirts of the city, if one of the athletes ventured that far, the real Berlin was revealed, the dullness of the uncomely urban landscape that officials had tried to wipe away lingering. The buildings were drab and old, run-down, the squares full of tall concrete statues memorializing long-forgotten figures, framed by bloodred banners and swastikas, a few signs declaring "Kill the Jews" affixed on the sidewalks.

ON JULY 25, the rain struck with even more passion. It was slow at first, a drizzle splashing against the windows and keeping the athletes awake throughout the night before, further dampening their spirits.

In the morning, Betty and Helen did their laundry quietly, unable to shake the dreariness of their living arrangements or the weather.

After picking up their official badges and uniforms, which cheered them slightly, Helen and Betty strolled to the swimming pool, where the male athletes were training. Tidye and Louise joined them for a walk to church, then took the subway into Berlin proper. The sound of motorcars reverberated in the streets as they stepped off the train. The loud voices of German and international visitors thronging the avenues and crowding the cafés met them in the city. They walked behind a stand of linden trees, then followed the curve of the streets to quieter areas, until they tired and returned to Via Triumphalis, which led them from the Lustgarten down Unter den Linden, then all the way back to the stadium. The city's buildings did not seem particularly imposing, and the people appeared hospitable—though, since African Americans were not common in Berlin, they stared at Tidye and Louise as the group traipsed from street to street. Helen stared back at them, defiant.

ILL HEALTH SWEPT through the women's dormitories. Colds were rampant, and Helen's shin splints were worse than ever. When the sun occasionally made its appearance, Betty and Helen ditched their workouts in favor of walking outside or opted for an outdoor massage from a sturdy German masseuse. Radio interviews were also taking up a good portion of their day, which they didn't mind; the coverage would allow folks back in their hometowns to share in the immediacy of the Games.

The dark, sunless days continued, punctuated by excursions. Athletes were disembarking in Berlin daily, and Helen soon learned that Stella Walsh and her Polish contingent had just arrived, whispers already trickling in that she had been running the 100 meters in 11.6 seconds. That knowledge propelled Helen to discontinue her carousing around the city and begin her workouts in earnest.

. . .

THE GAMES WERE set to start on August 1. Clouds had gathered again that morning and promised a fresh round of showers. Helen woke early and spent the hours before the opening ceremony receiving treatments for her still-bothersome legs.

Around Unter den Linden, streets were swarming with cars and pedestrians heading toward the stadium. Despite the lack of sun, the avenues were a sea of colors, mostly red, as fifty-foot-tall stands had been erected on either side of the streets from which large flags displaying the swastika waved relentlessly. Spectators lined up to await the arrival of the torch as it made its way to the stadium.

On Via Olympia and toward the stadium, the chaos of people and crush of banners became more prominent, flanked by small patches of multicolored flower beds that would disappear the moment the Olympics ended. For those who did not hold tickets to the events, the loudspeakers installed along the street offered up-to-the-minute notices on the athletes' triumphs and disappointments. When the Games were not on schedule, music piped out to keep the crowds entertained.

Outwardly, Berlin gave no sign that anything sinister was happening behind the scenes. But rumors abounded within the women's dormitories, and even inside the men's Olympic Village a few issues had arisen. The athletes had heard of special camps where groups of people were being segregated, though on arrival in Berlin, neither Betty nor any of the other athletes had noticed any. On occasion they even came across members of Hitler's brownshirts "beating old men and women with their sticks," Helen recalled. They had stood apart, afraid yet unable to look away. The atrocities they had read about in the papers had coalesced before them.

Despite such occurrences, which Berlin officials made sure arose infrequently, it was hard not to be awed by the spectacle. And having just come from a country experiencing one of the world's worst national depressions, the glitz of Germany "looked pretty good" to some of the athletes. At night, Berliners and visitors strolled the busy streets, particularly the Lustgarten, admiring the display of flags and flickering lights. Café Kranzler on Unter den Linden had become a popular hangout, its back wall a large Olympic banner.

For those who had been to Berlin before and were there to report on the Games, the city appeared shielded by a coat of denial. The journalist William Shirer was one of the few who didn't seem taken by Berlin's facade or its "glittering appearance," aware that the elaborate preparations had been set into motion simply to camouflage the regime's much darker intentions. Even most Germans did not see the lengthening shadows ahead, or they pretended to ignore them. There was a feeling of exuberance in the air, and most people reveled in that. The country's economic depression appeared to be over, and its citizens looked with optimism toward the future under the Hitler regime.

THE ATHLETES PROUDLY emerged from the tunnel into the stadium, the thick humid air streaked with rain and laced with the shouts of thousands of spectators. They looked up to see the *Hindenburg* outlined against the gray sky. The crowd and the athletes were captivated, watching the dirigible soar like a bird, flaunting the swastikas painted on its tail fins along with the five-ringed Olympic insignia. Many of the attendees would recall the experience not a year later, when in May 1937 the *Hindenburg,* while attempting to land in Lakehurst, New Jersey, burst into flames, its glow visible from miles around.

Adolf Hitler and the IOC president, Henri de Baillet-Latour, strutted into the stadium side by side, followed by a flock of nearly two dozen IOC officials. A great chorus of cheers heralded Hitler's arrival as he made his way from the 243-foot-high bell tower into the stadium. He was greeted by a small girl in white, who bowed as she handed him a bouquet of flowers before he hiked up the stairway to his box. As soon as the officials took their spot, a band began to play the German national anthem, which was immediately followed by a rousing rendition of the "Horst-Wessel-Lied," a notorious Nazi Party anthem and coanthem of the German state.

More than a hundred thousand spectators awaited the torchbearer, also clad in white, as he made his way into the stadium and toward the Olympic cauldron. He dipped the torch to ignite the flame, and the athletes marveled at the spectacular blaze leaping in the kettle, burning as brightly as they had so often imagined. A bell rang, and doves soared over the stadium, sweeping up the spectators in the frenzy of excitement.

IN THEORY, THE torch relay was created to serve as a link between the ancient Games and the modern ones, yet—to strengthen the Nazi ideal of Aryanism—the athlete chosen to carry the torch was a very tall, blond, blue-eyed young man, the kind of specimen Germany was pushing as the embodiment of a "superior" race. As soon as the flame was lit, Hitler walked toward the microphone and with a rare economy of words announced in German, "I proclaim open the Olympic Games of Berlin, celebrating the Eleventh Olympiad of the modern era."

Milling about with the other team members, Helen opened the autograph book she had brought with her from Fulton to a blank page. She had chosen it specifically for Hitler's autograph. She didn't know how she was going to get it, but having read about him in school, she had made up her mind to meet him, out of sheer curiosity.

AS THE GAMES got under way, spectators and competitors learned that one athlete who would not be participating was the German Jewish high jumper Margaret "Gretel" Bergmann. Word had reached her two weeks prior to the start of the Games that she would not be allowed to attend. The news had disappointed—though not surprised—her. At the tryouts, she had obtained a record score of 5 feet, 5 inches in the high jump, more than enough for a spot on the team. Yet officials were now informing her that her scores were not high enough, casting her aside due to her "mediocre achievements."

Upon Gretel's removal, officials announced that the aloof Dora Ratjen would take her place. Dora had come to the Games harboring a shadowy reputation; her coarseness and perpetually surly disposition were off-putting to athletes, much as Stella's attitude had been. Some athletes suspected that she was a boy masquerading as a girl, but no one had investigated the allegations, as nobody wished to argue with the German officials. Two years later it was confirmed that Dora was indeed a man; Dora herself admitted as much. Conspiracy theorists assumed that German officials had been aware of it but had allowed Dora to be placed on the team in order to take Gretel Bergmann's place, as she was a Jew.

HELEN HAD DECIDED to initially hold back a little and allow other competitors to win the preliminary meets. Those watching wondered if all the hype about the American's physical abilities was just that: hype.

While the track was being prepared for the women's 100-meter dash, Helen stretched her legs at a nearby bench and watched the rest of the competitors perform their own prerace rituals. She still nursed her shin splints, a bothersome reminder of her time on the *Manhattan*, which, along with a cold, created a general feeling of discomfort to which she was unaccustomed. Her plans to defeat her nerves and treat the Olympics as just another race, similar to all the ones she had already run, had not worked. The pageantry of it all—the large stadium, the multitude of officials arriving from countries around the world, as well as the athletes who either were returning for another chance to take home a medal or were at the start of their careers— caused her apprehension to bloom. She had not imagined that the

Games would unnerve her as much as they did, that their size would be so disorienting. Suddenly the future she had imagined back in Fulton was materializing into her present.

At one point she spotted Stella, whose jaw was set in concentration. As the current Olympic gold medalist in the event, Stella was heavily favored to win again, but one would not think as much to look at her, given her hunched shoulders and anxious behavior. She paced back and forth like a caged animal. She had lost weight, Helen noticed, her new trim physique reinforcing her masculine look. Like other competitors, Helen had always thought that Stella bore a striking resemblance to a man. Slimmer than a woman at the hips, yet full of muscles and bones that should not have been there, she moved like a man, too. Helen had never caught a glimpse of the removed beard, but on the day the Polish team had arrived, she had noticed faint shadows on Stella's face. She mentioned it to no one.

The crowds began to chant, signaling that the races were about to begin. Helen and Stella walked to the starting line, where they stood side by side, unsmiling, a height disparity of only a few inches—Helen a hair under six feet tall, while Stella was precisely five feet, nine inches. Helen's stride, however, had recently lengthened to nearly that of Jesse Owens, almost nine feet. That was a crucial factor, of course, as the length of her stride coupled with the frequency of it would increase her velocity; it came down to simple mathematics, her trainers postulated, numbers that Stella had yet to hit. Stella often read the papers and memorized the statistics, but outwardly showed no stress as the numbers were revealed before her eyes.

Although she had vowed not to show her best during the first preliminary meet, Helen beat Stella with a run of 11.4 seconds, toppling Stella's world record of 11.9 seconds. But given the wind's direction, the record was not allowed to stand. Most of the spectators, and Stella herself, believed that it had to be the weather conditions—or perhaps sheer luck—that had helped Helen in her run.

But as the second heat began, no wind was reported. The two

stood side by side again, awaiting the pop of the pistol, and when it came, Helen bolted down the track in 11.5 seconds. Still, the ultimate test would be in tomorrow's final.

HELEN WAS STILL very achy when she awoke on Tuesday, the day of the 100-meter final. The previous night, a downpour had reduced the track to muck. Helen feared the conditions would hinder her running time.

The men's track events were leading the stories in the newspaper, while the women had been relegated to the sidelines at best, to virtual oblivion at worst. Still, as Helen inserted her arms into her Olympic jersey and pulled her running shorts on, she was happy: the track conditions, her painful shins, and obnoxious reporters became almost insignificant as she swaddled herself in a sweatshirt and left the locker room.

Outside, she stood apart and watched her competitors warm up. Aside from herself and Stella, twenty-nine athletes had been competing in the 100-meter sprint, and now only six remained. She feared, as some of the coaches were guessing, that Stella had allowed herself to be beaten in the previous two heats. This was when the runners would unleash their true competence, and Helen still felt brazen enough to trust that she could beat Stella again.

BETTY STOOD ON the sidelines, watching as competitors and friends lined up at the starting line for the 100 meters. She recalled the race she had run eight years earlier; how relaxed she had felt, without the butterflies that now fluttered within her. She looked toward Helen—as young, apprehensive, and inexperienced as she had been—and must have felt a tug for her old self. Helen was jogging in place, moving from foot to foot as the competitors found their spots, excitement and fear radiating off her body. Filled with pride and without resentment, Betty gave Helen a thumbs-up.

By the afternoon the rain had disappeared, but the ground remained a glob of muck, sticking to Helen's spikes. She removed as much of it as she could but abandoned the effort when she heard the "set" command being called. The runners settled into their places. As soon as she heard the official's gun pop, she hurled herself from the starting line, her spikes pulling up thick lumps of soil from the track as she left her competitors far behind her. Her speed never diminished as she made her way toward the finish line. The persistent drizzle didn't bog her down; neither did the wind. Even the mushy turf beneath her couldn't slow her down. Betty cheered wildly as Stella fell behind Helen, who was now several strides ahead. Helen lunged forward, flinging herself toward the finish line, breaking the ribbon at 11.5 seconds—and matching the record she had set the day before. She was a comfortable two meters ahead of Stella, who came in second at 11.7, while Germany's Käthe Krauß was clocked in third, at 11.9 seconds.

Pandemonium broke out. Stella reluctantly joined Helen on the tracks for a commemorative photograph. Amid the glare of flashbulbs the two shook hands, Stella's face as grim and tight as their handshake, a misunderstood gesture of graciousness that made the rounds of the world's newspapers.

THE EPISODE THAT followed soon after Helen's win became one of the most peculiar in sports history and one of the most uncomfortable moments ever in an athlete's early career. As with any story, each passing decade reshaped it, its time and meaning altered even by Helen herself. Reporters embellished it even further. The most accurate portrayal of the episode was jotted down in Helen's official Olympic diary, which she kept for the duration of the Games.

Like all the other athletes, Helen had known that Hitler would be present throughout the Games. Caught up in preparing for her run, she had not noticed that he was sitting in the stands during the 100-meter dash, nor was she aware that she had dazzled him with her astonishing speed and strikingly tall frame—not, that is, until shortly after she had received her medal and was making her way to an interview with an American radio broadcast in a small interior room reserved for journalists. On her way, in the corridor, a young uniformed Nazi officer invited her to accompany him to Hitler's private quarters. Dee was with her, and though Helen had initially wished to meet Hitler, she found the request unsavory. Helen and Dee argued with the officer, claiming that they were on their way to do an interview, but the official wouldn't leave. He'd been told to take Helen to Hitler and to do so by any means necessary. The officer escorted the two women down a hallway into a densely draped area, thick with black-shirted, heavily armed, ominous-looking men who did not even blink when the women came in.

Hitler entered, flanked by several guards. Helen was surprised by how small and pale he was—he looked nearly anemic. She surpassed his height by several inches, and her years on the farm had given her a healthy, vibrant complexion. His cold blue eyes stared directly into hers, and she fearlessly returned his gaze, which made him smile.

By many accounts, those who met Hitler thought his eyes mesmeric, but Helen saw nothing special in them. She had never heard him speak, aside from the few words at the opening ceremony, but she had read that his rhetorical skills were universally praised. His tiny mustache seemed a stain she wished to wipe off, and his ill-fitting suit needed ironing. She nearly laughed at his tall boots, which he obviously wore to add height. Without saying a word, she thrust her autograph book into his face. Taken aback, he jumped and refused to sign it. So she held her hand out to shake his.

He appeared momentarily stunned by her audacity, then finally grasped her hand. Rather than quickly releasing it, he gripped it, pulling Helen closer to him, hugging her, and pinching her round behind, caressing her in an intimate manner that made her squirm. Wriggling out of the embrace, she had not noticed the photographer hiding in a corner until the flash of a camera hit her face.

"A little guy wearing a uniform and press identification tried to snap a picture," she wrote in her diary that evening, her small penmanship clear and neat. "I never saw a man change his disposition so fast as Hitler did. And as the camera flashed, Hitler jumped about two feet in the air. When he landed fists flaying, he bellowed something like '*Was Fällt Ihnen ein?* Get him! Destroy the evidence!' Hitler's face turned red, and his eyes flashed hatred and rage."

She continued, "While the guards restrained the photographer, Hitler snapped his leather gloves across the man's face, then pinched him and kicked his shins, all the while screaming in German." Helen was stunned by the transformation.

Then, as if nothing had happened, Hitler turned to her and through his interpreter asked if she liked Berlin. Helen, still through the interpreter, responded that she did. They continued to engage in small talk until Hitler's interpreter mentioned that Hitler wished to invite her to spend the weekend with him in his villa in Berchtesgaden.

Throughout the exchange, Dee had not said a word. But at that request she jumped in, playing up her role as coach and taskmaster, announcing that Helen was training for the upcoming relay race and could not go to the villa but that they were grateful for Hitler's generosity. Perhaps Dee would like to spend the weekend with them as well, the interpreter asked, as Hitler smiled. It was not hard to understand what the men were implying. Dee declined again; she had lots of duties to attend to, she told him, much like the Führer himself.

Hitler nodded, appearing none too pleased with the outcome of the visit, and stomped out of the room. By then both Helen and Dee had become uncomfortable, instinctual fear spreading through both of them. They wanted to leave. The young Nazi officer led the way out of the room to the stadium, where both were relieved to see the light of day.

HELEN KNEW IT was odd that she had attracted Adolf Hitler. Most people were less than charmed by her looks, and the press made no secret of it, as one journalist wrote in an article in the *British Olympic Reporter*: "Miss Stephens' style was certainly not attractive, judged from the point of the charm of Jesse Owens. She possessed a phenomenal stride and the power of a quarter-miler. From the aesthetic point of view the palm should be awarded to [the German runner] Miss Dollinger, who finished fourth." Helen was not surprised by that, and she remained determined not to let it hurt her. Yet the following morning a vicious rumor spread throughout the athletic village that would cause her more hurt than she could ever have imagined.

THE ATHLETES CELEBRATED Helen's victory well into the night. German dignitaries were hosting parties across Berlin, and the team was invited to attend all of them. The athletes were mesmerized by the German homes, their dangling chandeliers and plush carpets, the numerous glasses of champagne and liquor that were offered, the loud music that greeted them, and the tall blond officials who entertained them. They feasted from evening until early morning, Betty and the rest of the girls swaying to the rhythm of the music in the middle of the ballroom while inhaling numerous glasses of champagne. Helen watched her teammate Harriet Bland, in particular, as she "stepped into the dance floor with any chap who invited her—an athlete, an officer, an attendant." There was something irksome about the redhead, Helen complained to Betty, something she thought was tainting all the athletes who so far had participated with such dignity. She was also aware that Harriet could potentially make the relay team, which did not please her at all. Mindless and conniving, Harriet was not, to Helen's mind, a good addition to the group.

In a corner, Avery Brundage swallowed tall glasses of champagne and mingled with German officers. At one point he joined Gretl Braun in toasting her sister Eva and Eva's lover, Adolf Hitler.

NOT EVERYONE WAS happy with Helen's win. As she awoke the following morning, she learned that she had become the talk of Berlin, as a rumor put forth by the Polish Federation began to circulate contending that Helen was not being truthful about her identity: she was a man and she won the competition while masquerading as a woman. Shocked, she did her best to deny the accusations. But the Polish Federation went on to allude to such a possibility not only to the press but to the IOC, going so far as to lodge a complaint with the organization.

The insinuation stung; Helen couldn't even breathe. She knew she was not beautiful, had never thought of herself as such, but being compared to a man was mortifying. The accusations followed the logic that no one that tall, with a stride that long, nearly six feet, with a form so graceless, could be anything other than a man.

The press gobbled up the gossip and regurgitated it for readers around the world to feast on. Looking at Helen, they reported, there had been clues scattered throughout her life: her career, a repository of masculine gestures, postures, and attitudes no one had dared to mention before. Just look at the size of her hands and feet, they suggested. To some readers, the arguments smelled suspiciously like the ones Paul Gallico had flung against Babe Didrikson four years earlier, during the Los Angeles Olympics.

The support Helen received from her teammates and other Olympic officials did little to dispel the fabrication. The Associated Press got in on the act, as did the *New York Mirror*, alleging that Stella had started the rumor by speaking to the officials of the Polish Federation. Helen's teammates supported her and tried to amuse her by calling her "Stevie," but she couldn't laugh. She knew that such a serious accusation would have to be investigated. To compound Helen's indignity, the IOC acted swiftly and requested a physical genital examination to confirm her sex.

Helen was aware that some of the athletes were catty, but as she lay on the cold examination table, her legs spread wide apart while an IOC physician prodded her, she realized that this was no longer petty jealousy; it had turned into something more insidious. She looked up at the white ceiling, the lines running across it appearing like creases on a map that she mentally traced, the movement allowing her, at least momentarily, to ignore what was happening below her waist. The experience not only traumatized and humiliated her; it angered her. Still, the results of the exam put an end to the malicious rumors, and her gold was upheld.

KEEPING AN EYE from the sidelines was Coach Lawson Robertson, who found the whole ordeal deplorable, not only because of Helen's dreadful experience but also because of the attention it was taking away from the athletic competitions. "These games are for world champions, not sex appeal," he said, agreeing that the Greeks had had the right idea when it came to women in the Olympics. "The world's record established by Helen Stephens, the best woman sprinter, is at least 18 years back of Owens. It makes women in comparison look like children. They are not in the same class with men."

Helen heard his comments and did not know what angered her most: the intrusive physical exam she had undergone and the questions about her gender and sexuality, or the words of Robertson and the others, denigrating her achievements and those of the other women.

· · ·

THE RELAY RACE took place the following Monday. It was crucial for all the athletes to know how to execute their roles. Being fast was not enough; there had to be a strategy. Dee knew what each of her runners brought to the team. Looking over the charts, she made her choices based on proven principles: the first athlete had to have terrific speed and be capable of tightly hugging the curve; the second had to possess strong legs and also be adept at surges of momentum in case she needed to come from behind; the third had to have steady control of her speed around the curve, but she also had to be the best out of the four at receiving and passing the baton; and the fourth runner, who would anchor the team, had to be the most reliable and skilled overall.

Helen's win in the 100 meters made that part of the decision easy: she would anchor the team, running the last leg of the race. Dee also chose Annette Rogers and Betty Robinson as team members, not only because they had prior Olympic experience but also because their qualifying times had earned them a spot.

There was only one spot left, and it could go to either Tidye Pickett or Harriet Bland, the ginger-haired firecracker Helen wasn't particularly fond of. Harriet and Tidye had both had some success at the Games, but both had suffered disappointment, too, and neither had truly distinguished herself. Back home Harriet had trained under Dee's guidance and been one of the coach's favorites, but Helen, for one, hoped Dee would overlook that and instead grant the spot to the athlete who deserved it most.

Tidye had made history earlier in the week. The 80-meter hurdles she had run had been the first time an African American woman had represented the United States at the Olympics. But her glory had ended there; during the qualifiers she had tripped on a hurdle and injured her shoulder, the damage eliminating her from the final race. The team had rallied around her, Betty doing her best to alleviate Tidye's disappointment by speaking of future opportunities; on the sidelines Harriet smirked.

Based on scores alone, Harriet should not have even been considered. She had been eliminated in the early qualifying for the 100-meter dash, and her overall times were several seconds slower than Tidye's. But she was healthy if slow. She pleaded her case to Dee, who did what most of the athletes had expected her to do: given their special relationship, Dee handed Harriet the spot that should have been Tidye's.

Comforting Tidye became Helen's duty. She was already a winner, she insisted. Participating in the Olympics made her a champion regardless of anything else. But her attempt at consolation missed the mark. "That's easy for you to say," Tidye shot back. "You've got your medal."

Betty and Helen were both unhappy with the choice. Betty, in particular, found Harriet's scheming unbecoming; more than that, she felt Tidye deserved to be on the relay. Helen also supported Tidye, agreeing with the others that Dee had simply given the spot "to her pet." Unlike Tidye, Harriet had never participated in the Olympics, and they knew the hoopla would unsettle her. She was the slowest and most excitable, and she had an attitude that had garnered her the nickname "the brat."

But Harriet had become very popular in certain Berlin circles, particularly with the German guards and bureaucrats who insisted on taking her out to see the city or, predictably, on romantic dates. Helen had warned her to be careful, but Harriet rebuffed her; she thought Helen was jealous of her romantic rendezvous. It was not jealousy, Helen persisted, but concern for her and the entire team. What did a girl like Helen know about the excitement of being in a foreign city? Harriet snapped. Truthfully, she didn't know, either. So, even though the athletes had a curfew, she'd sneak out and spend the night with the Germans, despite Helen's best efforts.

THE NEWLY FORMED relay team quickly made its way to the training grounds. Coaches from the opposing teams were watching to determine their weaker points. Although that was common practice, Dee soon decided to shake things up. Two days prior to the preliminary heats, with the team still tweaking their runs in full view of the German coaches, Dee had them switch positions on every other practice, even adding several members who had not made the team, just to confuse the Germans.

THE FOLLOWING MONDAY, the team entered the arena. They were nervous, and physical soreness hampered them. Helen's legs were still aching, and the previous day Betty had tripped during practice, bruising her hip. She had seen many other athletes knocked out of races after what seemed at first to be innocuous falls; she feared becoming one of them.

Large crowds of German spectators were waving flags and chanting approval as the German team warmed up in the infield. The German team—Emmy Albus, Käthe Krauß, Marie Dollinger, and Ilse Dörffeldt—were the favorites. They had easily won their preliminary heats, beating the Americans with a world-record-setting 46.4 seconds, which topped the previous record of 47.1 seconds. During the preliminaries, the Germans' baton-passing skills had been flawless, every handoff down to a science: they passed the rod not only smoothly but without slowing down—a feat almost impossible for most teams. The American team's dejection was already palpable.

THE MORNING OF the final day, August 9, dawned as all the others had since the athletes had arrived in Berlin: gray and damp despite being early August, the bleak morning foreseeing a bleak ending. The stadium filled quickly, a good portion of the spectators German fans eager to witness their women sweep to another grand victory. Their shouts were deafening, almost maniacal, as the athletes took to the grounds.

As the day wore on, the clouds that had plagued the Games disappeared. A warm sun spread over the fields, the air becoming thick with humidity and buzzing insects. Helen wondered if the light and soothing warmth suddenly greeting them were a precursor of good luck. Betty, too, was in fair humor, although feeling sore. Her much-anticipated return had finally come, and she looked down at her leg, remembering the doctors who had told her that she would never walk again.

As the teams got ready, the women took their places on the track and began to prepare for what would turn out to be the last Olympics any of them would participate in. Betty walked the line, stretching her muscles, her knee stiffening. She tried to untangle the knots in her lower back by running in place. A massage the previous night had done nothing to relieve either her soreness or her nerves. She hadn't slept well, and the chilliness of their room had only added to the discomfort.

The race was about to begin. Harriet would be first, followed by Annette, Betty on third, and Helen to end it. The cheering crowd stretched toward the track, unnerving the athletes further as they gathered at the starting line. Hitler had also arrived and sat in his box.

Having positioned herself, at the sound of the pistol Harriet flung herself off the starting line, running ahead of Emmy Albus and quickly passing the baton to Annette, with Betty and Helen screaming along with the crowd. Although Harriet had led in the opening moments of the race, the Germans quickly found their groove, flying down the track to snatch the lead. Just behind them, Annette soon reached Betty and sleekly handed her the baton.

Betty held the baton tightly, running down the track with every ounce of effort she could muster; she felt the ground beneath her moving as she ran faster and faster toward Helen. Her arms pumped wildly, and her body leaned forward just slightly as she hugged the curve and bowed to the wind. The spectators could barely feel it, but the runners were facing a headwind and had to adjust, which was just what Betty did. As she rounded the corner, she lifted her head to see Helen waiting for her in the distance.

Helen positioned herself, ready to receive the baton from Betty, as did Ilse Dörffeldt, awaiting the baton coming from Marie Dollinger. Helen's eyes darted quickly between Betty and Marie. From afar, the two seemed to be running neck and neck, although Marie really held the lead over Betty by several inches. Marie, too, was conscious of her formidable opponent. Although currently in the lead, she was still worried; Betty could, perhaps, propel herself ahead.

But Marie reached her teammate before Betty caught up with Helen and passed the baton to Ilse, whose hand was stretched out as she started running down the track. Helen saw Ilse take off just as Betty handed her the baton. Helen dashed down the track, looking ahead, but from the corner of her eye saw something happen, just as everyone else in the stadium did.

Dee had instructed her runners to keep the baton in the hand in which they take it from the previous runner. The baton is never supposed to be switched from one hand to the other in the middle of a race. Ilse, however, crooked her elbow and brought her arm up, angled the baton across her chest, and tried to switch it to the opposite hand. In so doing, she lost control, dropping it.

It was a critical mistake, one that seemed to happen in slow motion: the baton slipping from her sweaty grasp, falling, and bouncing off the ground; Ilse making a desperate attempt to grab it but unable to do so, for the baton rebounded away from her; the sudden look of despair blanketing her face and twisting her features.

A collective gasp rippled through the stadium. Helen took note of the fumble and was tempted to look sideways to see if the baton had been retrieved, but she knew better. She kept her eyes fixed forward, pumping her arms and expertly increasing the tempo of her strides as she gathered momentum, coasting to victory with relative ease, breaking through the ribbon first as cheers, mingled with murmurs of dismay from the German supporters, rose from the crowd.

Ilse was sobbing as she fruitlessly searched for the baton, her teammates coming to her rescue and ushering her off the track. Ilse could not help herself, and neither could her teammates: they stared toward Hitler's box. He simply nodded.

"She received it all right," Helen wrote later in her diary of Ilse's accident. "But then dropped it when she exchanged it from one hand to the other. You don't have to do that if you were running last, but she was used to running first." Had the Germans not dropped the baton, one could only speculate what would have happened, although of course Germany, and even journalists from the United States, believed that the team had practically handed the Americans their win.

Jesse Abramson, of the *New York Herald Tribune,* agreed. "It is doubtful if the Americans could have won," Abramson wrote, attributing their success to luck as much as talent. But many begged to differ: Arthur Daley of *The New York Times* opined that "the chances were that the Reich would not have triumphed [as] Miss Dorrfeldt [*sic*] could not have beaten Miss Stephens even with an eight-yard lead in the getaway." (Conveniently, he neglected to mention that the Germans had done so before, winning all of their preliminary heats.) Helen put it more bluntly. "I could have chewed her up."

The New York Times speculated that the German women had found themselves "stage-struck" by Hitler, causing them to botch the pass. Regardless of that, the article continued, "Stephens, the wonder runner from Missouri who probably could have won anyway for the United States, was able to take things a bit more easily." Fred Steers added his two cents: "The German team had a lead at the finish of the third leg when they dropped the baton. However, judging from her race in the final of the one hundred meters, Helen Stephens could have overcome the lead easily had the German girls not met with this misfortune." And that's how it resonated into posterity.

·   ·   ·

AS THE CROWD stared in stunned silence, the four American athletes were guided to the podium, feted with the traditional laurel wreaths and their gold medals. Even more shocking was the sight of the American flag being raised on the German flagpole as "The Star-Spangled Banner" boomed throughout the stadium.

Betty clutched hold of her medal as she watched the American flag rising before her, the national anthem echoing throughout the field, and took it all in: the thousands of spectators clad in flashes of color; the enormity of the stadium around her; and, most of all, her teammates standing by her side, the women toward whom she felt the most immense gratitude swelling within her. She nodded, as if to answer the applause they were receiving but also in response to an internal question she had been asking herself and to which she had just received the answer. She knew as certainly as she had known that she would walk and run again that this was the last race she would ever participate in. She had proven herself and was ready to leave. She was officially done with running.

BETTY WOULD LOOK back on 1928 and 1936 as being in two different lifetimes. The individual medal in the 100 meters in Amsterdam had essentially fallen into the lap of a talented but cocky, lucky sixteen-year-old who believed that only her merits had brought her to that point. (Later she had come to admit that luck had also played a role.) Berlin was different. There had been no luck involved, she felt, and she dared anyone to tell her otherwise. She had *earned* her medal, just as her teammates had, proving that although she had been given a push into the limelight in 1928, in 1936 she had been the catalyst of her own good fortune as part of a team.

EPILOGUE

Shortly after the 1936 Olympic Games, Betty Robinson's story became the model of an athlete who had done well: a young woman with natural athletic talent, accidentally discovered by a tenacious coach with unfulfilled Olympic dreams; a young woman who, in short order, had been groomed to participate in the Olympics, where, in the first track-and-field games ever to be run, had captured gold. With much more expected from her in the future, a terrible accident had left her at death's door, nearly paralyzing her and leaving her unable to walk, let alone run. Her unflagging spirit had allowed her to become, twice and against all odds, a gold medalist. It was true grit that had propelled her to restore the strength she needed to win the second, in the company of excellent teammates, during the infamous Nazi Olympics, her story the stuff of legends.

Not surprisingly, following the Games, Hollywood came after her. By then she was twenty-four, and her beauty had grown irresistible, her family comparing her to the film legend Barbara Stanwyck. She had a batch of professional photographs taken to shop around as calling cards but then realized she had no passion for a movie career, despite the desire for notoriety she'd had early in her life.

She dated a lot, and soon after the Olympics she married a young man named Eddie Napolilli, who passed himself off as an entertainment agent intent on booking her work in Hollywood. When Betty changed her mind about the trajectory of her life, she also changed her mind about the marriage, which was annulled two weeks later. She continued to date, her suitors including a boxer named Tom Neal, who went on to lead a scandalous life as an actor. (He later shot and killed his last wife, for which he was sentenced to prison.)

Betty could have chosen to marry any man, which was why the family was surprised when in 1939 she decided to wed Richard Schwartz, a Jewish businessman originally from Hyde Park, Illinois, whom she had met in a diner lounge, where a mutual friend had introduced them. Things progressed quickly, and they married soon thereafter. They went on to have two children, a boy and a girl.

Betty and Richard moved often, landing in Colorado as well as in Florida, where she reconnected with her old coach Charles Price on the occasion of his one-hundredth birthday. Though their faces showed time having passed, their smiles revealed a fondness for each other that never wavered and a coach's pride in the accomplishments of his pupil.

In 1984, a reporter covering the Los Angeles Games reached out to Betty. Aside from wanting to know a little about her life for a human interest piece he was writing, he asked her about the 1936 Games and the ending of the relay race. She told him, "I wish they hadn't dropped the baton. . . . Helen was faster. We would have won anyway," displaying some of the arrogance that had been her signature as a young woman.

In 1977, the US Olympic Committee inducted Betty Robinson into its Hall of Fame as "the first woman from the US to win a Track and Field gold medal in the Olympic Games." In reality, she had been the first woman from *anywhere* to win an Olympic track-and-field gold medal.

FOR HELEN STEPHENS, whose hopes were to repeat her win in 1940, the Berlin Olympics proved to be her only chance at glory. The rise of Hitler led to a cancellation of the games until 1948, when the London Games took place. By then Helen had turned professional, her amateur career short, explosive, and victorious.

In 1936, she was named Sportswoman of the Year by the Associated Press. As time went by, she started the Helen Stephens Olympic Coeds, an all-female basketball team and a force to be reckoned with.

Throughout her life, questions about her sexuality and her gender continued to haunt her. Eventually, she shifted her attention to golf, truly following the life of Babe Didrikson, but she never deviated from the Olympic life, taking part in senior-sponsored Olympics well into her seventies.

STELLA WALSH PASSED away at the age of sixty-nine in a drive-by shooting in Cleveland. She had gone to a store to buy ribbons for visiting athletes from Poland, when two men robbed a nearby establishment. A shoot-out occurred in the parking lot where she had left her car, a stray bullet hitting her.

That was when the confusion about her gender became more public. The county coroner who performed the autopsy, Samuel Gerber, was the first to reveal to reporters about the male genitalia he had discovered while examining her body. In the report he wrote and released to the press, he stated that Stella "had a mixture of male and female chromosomes. She had no internal female reproductive organs, and possessed an underdeveloped and non-functioning penis, 'masculine' breasts and an abnormal urinary opening." Gerber concluded that her sex would have been ambiguous at birth, and that her parents could have raised her as either a girl or a boy. When the news broke, reporters clung to the lewder parts of the story, nearly forgetting her athletic career and denigrating her Olympic triumphs. Though many argued that it was no longer correct to call Stella a woman, doctors also agreed that it would not have been correct to call her a man, either.

Those who had harbored suspicions about her during her career and those who had lost races to her felt vindicated. But there were other questions to deal with: Had she somehow cheated by withholding her gender? And what was the IOC to do about it, now that so many years had passed? The answer: nothing.

BABE DIDRIKSON NEVER again participated in Olympic competition, due to her expulsion by the AAU. In 1933, she took up golf, which she had also played while in high school, and was a top performer in that sport as well. But much as it had with track and field, controversy followed her. In 1935, she won the Texas Women's Amateur Competition, but complaints by other players caused the US Golf Association to rule that "for the best interest of the game," she be banned from amateur golf, too, given that she had played professionally in other sports. It was nearly a decade later, in 1943, that her amateur status was reinstated.

Babe passed away on September 27, 1956, in Texas at the age of forty-five, following a long battle with colon cancer. That, it turned out, was the only opponent she could not beat.

ACKNOWLEDGMENTS

Writing *Fire on the Track* required the assistance of librarians and ar-chivists located throughout the country and even abroad. Thus, my first thank-you will go to them. Those librarians and archivists in-clude Elizabeth Levkoff Derouchie and Charlotte Holliman, Mary and John Gray Library, Lamar University; Penny Clark, Lamar Uni-versity; Jameatris Yvette Rimkus, University Library, University of Illinois at Urbana–Champaign; Paul K. Gjenivick, archivist and curator, United States Lines; Peter Mackie, Edward North Robin-son Collection of Brown Athletics; Tim Christ, president, Newark Historical Society; Stephen C. Nedell, Malden Public Library; Anna Sklar, Los Angeles City Historical Society; Michael Holland, Los Angeles City Archives; Kevin B. Leonard, Northwestern University Archives, Evanston, Illinois; Vicki Catozza, Western Reserve Histor-ical Society Library Research Center, Cleveland, Ohio; Barb Diehl, Riverdale Public Library; Claryn Spies, Manuscript and Archives, Yale University Library; Laura Street, Vassar College, Poughkeepsie, New York; April Anderson, Illinois State Archivist; Sharon J. Van Der Laan, Illinois State Library, Normal, Illinois; Kevin George, the State Historical Society of Missouri, Columbia, Missouri; Linda Stahnke Stepp, University of Illinois at Urbana–Champaign; Joan Gosnell, Southern Methodist University, Dallas, Texas; Beth Zak-Cohen, Newark Public Library, Newark, New Jersey; the reference staff at the Rhode Island Historical Society, Providence, Rhode Island; Lydia Uhlir, Forest Preserves of Cook County, River Forest, Illinois; Ellen Keith, Chicago History Museum Research Center; Lori Osborne, Evanston History Center, Evanston, Illinois; Janet Olson, Northwestern University Library, Evanston, Illinois; Bridget Lavalle, Cuyahoga County Library, Fairview Public Library.

I am thankful for the assistance of the athletes' families, friends, and biographers who shared their stories and were willing to answer questions, including John Pulaski, who gave me information on Stella Walsh; Rob Lucas, who worked on a short documentary on Stella Walsh; Sharon Hanson, Helen Stephens's biographer; Dick Riel, who is related to Bert Riel, Betty Robinson's college boyfriend; Carol Boatright, Bert Riel's niece; Richard Schwartz, Betty Robinson's son; Harlyn Mlynek, Richard Schwartz's cousin; and Jean Rochfort, also one of Richard Schwartz's cousins, who remembered Betty Robinson very well.

Having found a home at Crown, I am grateful *Fire on the Track* landed in the hands of the capable and enthusiastic editor Domenica Alioto. Her skills are unsurpassed. In the same vein, associate editor Claire Potter gave her time, energy, and boundless good humor on many occasions. I am grateful for them, and for their whole team.

I am certain that this book would not have come to fruition without my agent and friend Rob Weisbach. From the very first day, when he heard about Betty Robinson and the rest of the group, his enthusiasm for the project was boundless and has not abated yet, nor has his trust that this could be a great book. I believe him to be the greatest champion of this book. For his keen eye, sense of humor, and professionalism, not to mention patience, I am always grateful.

And finally, to my family, the unsung heroes, especially my sister, Francesca, and mother, Celeste, who had to listen to stories not only about these women but also about everything related to running nearly to the point of exhaustion, never complaining, eventually knowing everyone in the book almost as well as I did. Thank you for your love, support, and optimism, which keeps me going every day.

NOTES AND SOURCES

Prologue

Lee Newland: his life, job, physical description, likes and dislikes

Lee Newland's physical information and life details, including his work, come from an email correspondence with Betty Robinson's son, Richard Schwartz, Jr., on June 20, 2015, and an extensive phone interview with Schwartz's cousin Jean Rochfort, who knew Newland, in June 2015.

The Great Depression hits Chicago

Information on the Great Depression hitting Illinois was found in the Federal Reserve Bank of St. Louis archives; see also David A. Shannon, ed., *The Great Depression* (Englewood Cliffs, NJ: Prentice-Hall, 1960).

Chicago and Riverdale

Robert Cromie, *A Short History of Chicago* (San Francisco: Lexicos, 1984); David Lindsey, "The Founding of Chicago," *American History Illustrated* 8 (December 1978): 28; Donald L. Miller, *City of the Century: The Epic of Chicago and the Making of America* (New York: Simon & Schuster, 1996).

The Waco 10 biplane and the accident

Information on the plane and the accident comes from various sources: email correspondence with Betty's son, Richard Schwartz, on April 23, 2006; March 16, 2015; April 5, 2015; June 6, 2015; June 16, 2015; June 20, 2015; June 26, 2015; July 5, 2015; July 8, 2015; July 13, 2015; July 15, 2015; July 17, 2015; July 21, 2015; November 20, 2015; January 23, 2016; February 9, 2016; March 8, 2016;

and March 10, 2016. Additional information gathered from Harvey resident and historian Carl Durnavich. Also, *The Harvey Tribune* of July 3 and 10, 1931, covered the accident extensively.

Harvey, Illinois

Historical and physical descriptions of Harvey can be found in the files of the Harvey Public Library and the Harvey Historical Society.

Physical description of the victims

This information comes from email correspondence with Richard Schwartz on June 26, 2015; see also *The Harvey Tribune* of July 3 and 10, 1931, for extensive physical details, injuries, interviews with witnesses, and the aftermath of the accident.

The funeral home

The Harvey Tribune, July 3 and 10, 1931, covered Betty's initial ride to the funeral home.

Chapter One: ON TRACK

Coach Charles Price and his family

The personal life of Coach Price was researched and studied by Harvey resident and historian Carl Durnavich. He was kind enough to share his knowledge with me in a number of emails from 2015 to 2016.

Thornton Township High School

Extensive files on the high school, its history, and its description can be found in the Harvey Public Library Archives and the Harvey Historical Society.

Charles Price's college life, history of running, and teaching for the high school

See Thornton High School yearbooks for 1926, 1927, 1928, 1929, 1930, 1931, and 1932; also see Harvey Public Library Archives and Harvey Historical Society.

Betty Robinson's physical description, likes, and dislikes

Particulars about how Betty looked, what she liked, and her everyday preferences come from an email exchange with her son, Richard Schwartz, on June 26, 2015.

Charles Price sees Betty run; their conversation on the train

This was detailed in numerous emails from Betty's son, Richard Schwartz, from 2015 to 2016.

Chapter Two: A NEW ARRIVAL

Harry Robinson and Elizabeth Wilson Robinson

Mrs. Robinson was a tough, independent woman, unlike most women of her generation. Information about her life comes from email correspondence with her grandson Richard Schwartz on November 20, 2015. Also, more detailed genealogical information on Harry Robinson was made available by his great-grandson Andy Mills on July 17, 2015.

Life in Nebraska; moving to Chicago

Extensive phone interviews with Richard Schwartz on January 13, 2016, as well as email correspondence with him on July 17, 2015. See also Oscar Handlin, *The Uprooted: The Epic Story of the Great Migrations That Made the American People* (New York: Grosset and Dunlap, 1951).

History of Riverdale and the Chicago area, including their industrial revolution

Historic City: The Settlement of Chicago (Chicago: Chicago Department of Development and Planning, 1976); Donald L. Miller, *City of the Century: The Epic of Chicago and the Making of America* (New York: Simon & Schuster, 1996).

Jean and Evelyn are born

Richard Schwartz provided information on the birth of his aunts, along with birth records, in emails on July 17, 2015.

The birth of Betty Robinson

Betty's son, Richard Schwartz, detailed her birth in various emails throughout 2015 and 2016; Carl Durnavich, resident and historian, also provided birth records. The State Historical Society of Missouri, Columbia, Missouri, holds extensive files on her; of particular interest are folders 63, 109, 120–122, 128, 184, 221, 232, 234–240, 242, 245–249, 254, and 263–267.

Jean and Evelyn's husbands and children

Information about Jean and Evelyn, their husbands, their children, and their likes and dislikes, as well as their roles in the household, comes from email correspondence with Richard Schwartz on July 8 and November 20, 2015.

Betty's relationship with her sisters and the rest of the family

Richard Schwartz, in emails throughout 2015 and 2016, provided the dynamics of Betty's relationship with her family.

Betty's schooling, hobbies, activities, and accomplishments

The Riverdale Public Library and Harvey Public Library hold extensive material on Betty Robinson's younger days, spanning from her elementary education all the way up to the 1936 Olympic Games. In addition, her son, Richard Schwartz, detailed his mother's early days in extensive emails, as did historian Carl Durnavich and Jean Rochfort.

Chapter Three: A NEW PAIR OF SHOES

Physical description of the Thornton Township High School

A physical description of the high school, as well as the classes and afternoon programs it provided, can be found at the Harvey Public Library Research Center.

Betty's introduction to track and field

Women's Track and Field (Chicago: Athletic Institute, 1973); Tom Ecker, *Track and Field Dynamics* (Los Altos, CA: Tafnews Press, 1974); Dorothy S. Ainsworth, *A History of Physical Education in Colleges for Women* (New York: A. S. Barnes, 1930).

Robert "Bob" Wilson

Information on Bob Wilson can be found in the Thornton Township High School yearbook for 1928.

Chapter Four: THE DEBUT

Betty begins training with Coach Price

Women's Track and Field (Chicago: Athletic Institute, 1973); Tom Ecker, *Track and Field Dynamics* (Los Altos, CA: Tafnews Press, 1974); Vern Gambetta, *Track and Field Coaching Manual* (West Point, NY: Leisure Press, 1981).

Technical aspects of track and field

Dorothy S. Ainsworth, *A History of Physical Education in Colleges for Women* (New York: A. S. Barnes, 1930); Ecker, *Track and Field Dynamics*; *Women's Track and Field*; Gambetta, *Track and Field Coaching Manual*; T. R. Collingwood, "The Effects of Physical Training Upon Behavior and Self-Attitudes," *Journal of Clinical Psychology* 28, no. 4 (October 1972): 583–585; James F. Fixx, *The Complete Book of Running* (New York: Random House, 1977).

Coach Price's life beyond track

Information on Coach Price's personal life comes from email correspondence with Harvey resident and historian Carl Durnavich, on July 6, 2015; July 9, 2015; July 10, 2015; July 14, 2015; and July 20, 2015.

Track meet sponsored by the Institute Banking Society; Helen Filkey; meet of March 30, 1928; its outcome

See collection of articles at the State Historical Society of Missouri, folders 63, 109, 120–122, 128, 184, 221, 232, 234–240, 242, 245–249, 254, and 263–267.

Chapter Five: OFF TO THE RACES

Illinois Women's Athletic Club (IWAC)

The IWAC was an important institution in the lives of young female athletes. Information on the IWAC and its mission can be found in the Chicago History Museum Research Center, as well as *Women's Athletic,* vol. 12, no. 3; vol. 15, nos. 4–5; vol. 15, nos. 7–8; and vol. 15, no. 11.

Chicago's trains and automobiles

Bessie Louise Pierce, *A History of Chicago,* vol. 1: *The Beginning of a City, 1673–1848* (Chicago: University of Chicago Press, 1937); *Historic City: The Settlement of Chicago* (Chicago: Chicago Department of Development and Planning, 1976); Donald L. Miller, *City of the Century: The Epic of Chicago and the Making of America* (New York: Simon & Schuster, 1996); Bessie Louise Pierce, *A History of Chicago,* vol. 3: *The Rise of a Modern City, 1871–1893* (Chicago: University of Chicago Press, 1957).

Chicago, the Windy City

Pierce, *A History of Chicago,* vol. 1; *Historic City: The Settlement of Chicago*; Miller, *City of the Century.*

Betty's life versus that of her sisters and friends

Details of Betty's life at home with her sisters and friends were provided by her son, Richard Schwartz, in extensive emails and phone conversations throughout 2015 and 2016.

Glenna Collett Vare and Gertrude Ederle

Information on early female athletes can be found in the Manuscript and Archives Collections of Yale University.

IWAC's building

Miller, *City of the Century*; Jon C. Teaford, *The Twentieth-Century American City: Problem, Promise, and Reality,* 2d ed. (Baltimore: Johns Hopkins University Press, 1993).

Soldier Field

Robert Cromie, *A Short History of Chicago* (San Francisco: Lexicos, 1984); Teaford, *The Twentieth-Century American City.*

The DeVry family; Jim Rochfort

Information on this meeting was provided in a phone interview with Jean Rochfort in June 2015.

Chapter Six: OFF TO THE GAMES

Pierre de Coubertin and the first modern Olympics

See M. I. Finley and H. W. Pleket, *The Olympic Games: The First Thousand Years* (London: Chatto & Windus, 1976); E. Norman Gardiner, *Greek Athletic Sports and Festivals* (London: Macmillan, 1910); Allen Guttmann, *The Olympics: A History of the Modern Games* (Urbana: University of Illinois Press, 1992); John A. Lucas, *The Modern Olympic Games* (New York: A. S. Barnes & Co., 1980); John MacAloon, *This Great Symbol: Pierre de Coubertin and the Origins of the Modern Olympic Games* (Chicago: University of Chicago Press, 1981); Burton Holmes, *The Olympic Games in Athens, 1896: The First Modern Olympics* (New York: Grove Press, 1984).

William Penny Brookes; Evangelis Zappas

Finley and Pleket, *The Olympic Games*; Gardiner, *Greek Athletic Sports and Festivals*; Guttmann, *The Olympics*.

Alice Milliat and Femina Sport

Finley and Pleket, *The Olympic Games*; Guttmann, *Women's Sports*; Leigh and Bonin, "The Pioneering Role of Madame Alice Milliat."

Women's Olympics

Allen Guttmann, *Women's Sports: A History* (New York: Columbia University Press, 1991); Mary Hanson Leigh and Thérèse M. Bonin, "The Pioneering Role of Madame Alice Milliat and the FSFI in Establishing International Track and Field Competition for Women," *Journal of Sport History* 4, no. 1 (Spring 1977): 72.

Betty's vacations at Stone Lake

Jean Rochfort provided details on the Stone Lake cabin and the summer vacations the family took there on June 20, 2015.

Learning about the Amsterdam Olympics

Paul Arblaster, *A History of the Low Countries* (New York: Palgrave Macmillan, 2006); Fred Feddes, *A Millennium of Amsterdam: Spatial History of a Marvelous City* (Bussum: Thoth, 2012); Geert Mak, *Amsterdam: A Brief Life of the City* (Amsterdam: Olympus, 1994).

Newark Olympic tryouts

The *Newark Evening News* covered the Olympic trials in Newark. The articles from July 3, 1928 (the day before the tryouts), included "Olympic Try-On Tomorrow," "Girl Athletes Are Ready for National Track Meet," and "Snapped in Stadium as the Girls Fought for National Championship."

Elta Cartwright and the northern California track-and-field team

Articles on the Newark trials and detailed information on each of the athletes are available in the Newark Public Library. The *Newark Evening News* dedicated quite a lot of space to the trials, including coverage on July 2, 3, 4, and 5, 1928.

Mel Sheppard

The life of Mel Sheppard was extensively detailed in articles published in the *Newark Evening News* on July 4, 5, and 6, 1928. His previous accomplishments, records, jobs, desires, and upcoming responsibilities were detailed there.

Betty comes in second

Betty's finish was recorded in the *Newark Evening News* of July 4 and 5, 1928.

Stella Walsh

Stella Walsh's life has always been somewhat of an enigma, her immediate family refusing to grant interviews for fear of misunderstandings. Still, information does exist. I engaged in email correspondence with John Pulaski, who knew the family, on June 25, 2015. Also, the Research Center Reference Division at the Western Reserve Historical Society Library in Cleveland, Ohio, holds material. Of particular interest is Box 1, folders 2, 6, 7, 10, 12, 14, 15, and 16.

Chapter Seven: THE SS *PRESIDENT ROOSEVELT*

The SS *President Roosevelt*

Historical Brochures/United States Lines/1920s Gjenvick-Gjønvik Archives made historical information on the SS *President Roosevelt* available.

Stella Walsh

Information on Stella Walsh can be found in the Research Center Reference Division at the Western Reserve Historical Society Library in Cleveland, Ohio. Of particular interest is Box 1, folders 2, 6, 7, 10, 14, 15, and 16.

Amelia Earhart

Medford Historical Society, Medford, Massachusetts; Medford Public Library, Medford, Massachusetts.

General Douglas MacArthur

The life of Douglas MacArthur is detailed in the MacArthur Papers in the Clements Library at the University of Michigan, Ann Arbor, Michigan.

Athletes exercising

Report of the American Olympic Committee, Ninth Olympic Games, Amsterdam, 1928 (New York: American Olympic Committee, 1928).

Dolores "Dee" Boeckmann

Extensive information on Dee's life can be found in the Helen Stephens Life and Times Collection, State Historical Society of Missouri, folders 20, 37, 63, 109, 112, 114–123, 127, 128, 183, 185, 229, 232–234, 236, 240, 245, 258, 261, 265, and 266.

Betty's life on board

Betty enjoyed her life on board the SS *President Roosevelt* and took advantage of every opportunity afforded her, as described by Richard Schwartz in an email on June 16, 2015.

Parties on the ship

Parties were also very frequent on the ship, as detailed by Richard Schwartz in an email on June 16, 2015.

Johnny Weissmuller

Betty took a liking to Weissmuller from the very beginning, and he felt warmly toward her, too. Her liking for him remained for the rest of her life, as detailed by Richard Schwartz in an email on June 20, 2015.

Bud Houser; reports of Dutch lack of preparation; arriving in Amsterdam; description of Olympic stadium

See *Report of the American Olympic Committee, Ninth Olympic Games, Amsterdam, 1928.*

Difference between American and British athletes

The snide remarks between the teams were detailed in *Report of the American Olympic Committee, Ninth Olympic Games, 1928.*

Female athletes in Paris; opening ceremonies; and competition begins; men's trouble on the track

Report of the American Olympic Committee, Ninth Olympic Games, 1928.

Chapter Eight: QUEEN OF THE TRACK

Women athletes; Canadians Fanny "Bobbie" Rosenfeld and Myrtle Cook; Betty's win

Report of the American Olympic Committee, Ninth Olympic Games, 1928 (New York: American Olympic Committee, 1928).

Dee Boeckmann's preparation for the 800 meters; newspapers' response to the outcome of the race

State Historical Society of Missouri, folders 20, 37, 63, 112, 114–123, 125, 127, 128, 183, 229, 232–234, 236, 240, 245, 258, 261, 265, and 266.

Description of women's bodies versus men's

Michael A. Messner and Donald F. Saho, eds., *Sport, Men and the Gender Order: Critical Feminist Perspectives* (Champaign, IL: Humane Kinetics Books, 1990); Susan K. Cahn, *Coming on Strong: Gender and Sexuality in Twentieth-Century Women's Sport* (New York: Free Press, 1994).

Chapter Nine: A NEW BABE IN TOWN

Beaumont, Texas

Babe Didrikson Zaharias Collection, Special Collection and University Archives, Mary and John Gray Library, Lamar University, Beaumont, Texas; see also Susan E. Cayleff, *Babe: The Life and Legend of Babe Didrikson Zaharias* (Urbana: University of Illinois Press, 1995).

Babe Didrikson

Extensive and intimate information on the life of Babe Didrikson can be found in the Babe Didrikson Zaharias Collection, Special Collection and University Archives, Mary and John Gray Library, Lamar University, Beaumont, Texas; see also Jon Hendershott, *Track's Greatest Women* (Los Altos, CA: Tafnews Press, 1987).

Ole Didriksen and Hannah Marie Olsen Didriksen; Colonel Melvirne Johnson McCombs

Babe Didrikson Zaharias Collection, Special Collection and University Archives, Mary and John Gray Library, Lamar University, Beaumont, Texas.

The Golden Cyclones

Information on Babe's formative years and her life with the Golden Cyclones are available in the Babe Didrikson Zaharias Collection, Special Collection and University Archives, Mary and John Gray Library, Lamar University, Beaumont, Texas.

Introduction to track and field

See Cayleff, *Babe*; also see files in the Babe Didrikson Zaharias Collection, Special Collection and University Archives, Mary and John Gray Library, Lamar University, Beaumont, Texas.

The Los Angeles Games

Information on the Los Angeles Games is extensively reported in the *The Games of the Xth Olympiad, Los Angeles, 1932: Official Report* (Los Angeles: Xth Olympiade Committee, 1933).

Chapter Ten: WELCOME HOME

Return to New York from Amsterdam and MacArthur's refusal to acknowledge defeat

See *Report of the American Olympic Committee, Ninth Olympic Games, Amsterdam, 1928* (New York: American Olympic Committee, 1928).

Riverdale's preparations for the parade; Betty's arrival and participation in the parade

Historical files, Harvey Public Library, as well as the Riverdale Public Library. Additionally, the files in the State Historical Society of Missouri, folders 63, 109, 120–122, 128, and 184, were of assistance.

Betty's very expensive gifts

In an email correspondence on July 13, 2015, Richard Schwartz, Betty's son, wrote at length about the gifts she received after her return home and the parade.

Betty's return to high school and normalcy

The Thornton Township High School yearbooks for 1928 and 1929 detail Betty's classes, after-school programs, and extracurricular activities. Her son, Richard Schwartz, complemented these finds with extensive emails during 2015.

College days at Thornton Township Junior College

Information on Betty's college life, including the classes she was taking and the grades she received, comes from email correspondence with Richard Schwartz on April 23, 2016.

Moving to Northwestern University; Evanston, Illinois

Information on Betty being a sorority sister and on the sorority house itself comes from email correspondence with Richard Schwartz on July 21, 2015. Also, information on the university and the city itself was made available by the Evanston Historic Center, Evanston, Illinois.

Bert "Ball Hawk" Riel

Information on Bert Riel was made available through an email correspondence with Betty's niece Carol Boatright on September 28, 2015.

The Los Angeles Games

See *The Games of the Xth Olympiad, Los Angeles, 1932: Official Report* (Los Angeles: Xth Olympiade Committee, 1933).

Coach Frank Hill

Betty's relationship with Frank Hill is detailed in the files of the State Historical Society of Missouri, folders 63, 109, 120–122, 128, 184, 221, 234, 240, 242, 245–249, 254, and 263–267.

The 1930 Outdoor National Championships, Southern Methodist University

State Historical Society of Missouri, folders 120–122 and 128.

Tidye Pickett

Information on the life of Tidye Pickett comes from the Illinois State University Archives.

Louise Stokes

Information on Louise Stokes can be found in the Malden Public Library, Malden, Massachusetts.

Paul Gallico

See Paul Gallico, *Farewell to Sport* (New York: International Polygonics, 1990); Paul Gallico, *The Golden People* (New York: Doubleday, 1965).

Chapter Eleven: FLYING HIGH

President Hoover and the economy

David A. Shannon, ed., *The Great Depression* (Englewood Cliffs, NJ: Prentice-Hall, 1960).

Wilson Palmer

Wilson Palmer was one of Betty's favorite cousins, and he felt just as warmly about her as she did about him. A mischievous boy, he was as gregarious as she was. Some of the information about his life comes from email correspondence with Harvey resident and historian Carl Durnavich on September 27, 2015. Information also comes from the Thornton High School yearbook for 1931, p. 83; also email correspondence with Richard Schwartz on July 5, 2015, and Harlyn Myek (cousin of Richard Schwartz) on July 21 and 22, 2015.

Harold Brown

Harold Brown spoke about his role in the plane, when he had bought a third of the plane, how he had managed it, and what he thought of the accident in extensive interviews published in *The Harvey Tribune* on July 3 and 10, 1931.

Plane accident

Some of the information about the accident comes from email correspondence with Harvey resident and historian Carl Durnavich on September 27, 2015. *The Harvey Tribune* of July 3 and 10, 1931, also covered the accident widely. Also, Richard Schwartz, Betty's son, wrote at length about the accident in an email on July 13, 2015.

The aftermath and Jacob Minke

Betty's accident and its repercussions, along with updates from her doctors, were detailed in *The Harvey Tribune* of July 3, 4, 5, and 10.

Wil's leg troubles

The Harvey Tribune of November 20, 1931, wrote extensively of Wil's issue with his leg and of the doctors' desire to amputate.

Chapter Twelve: SUMMER WOES

Stella Walsh; the "Miss Stadium" competition; Pershing Stadium and accident on the track; "Queen of Cleveland"

Information on Stella Walsh can be found at the Research Center Reference Division, Western Reserve Historical Society Library, Cleveland, Ohio, Box 1, folders 2, 6, 7, 10, 12, 14, 15, 16, and at the State Historical Society of Missouri, folders 63, 77, 120, 124, 125, 190, 217, 233–236, 240–242, 253, 258–261, 263, 266, and 267,

Stella's sexuality

Helen Lenskyj, *Out of Bounds: Women, Sport and Sexuality* (Toronto: Women's Press, 1986); also, State Historical Society of Missouri, Sex-roles, folders 258, 266, and 267.

Betty awakens in Oak Forest Infirmary

Betty's stay at the infirmary is detailed in email correspondence with Richard Schwartz on June 6, 2015.

Betty returns home

See T. R. Collingwood, "The Effects of Physical Training Upon Behavior and Self-Attitudes," *Journal of Clinical Psychology* 28, no. 4 (October 1972): 583–585.

Betty and Jim's runs

Detailed information on Jim comes from email correspondence with Richard Schwartz on July 4, 2015. See also Collingwood, "The Effects of Physical Training Upon Behavior and Self-Attitudes."

Betty returns to Northwestern to train

Extensive conversations with Richard Schwartz throughout 2015 and 2016 highlighted the journey Betty took in returning to school.

Chapter Thirteen: CALIFORNIA DREAMING

AAU

See Robert Korsgaard, *A History of the Amateur Athletic Union of the United States*, EdD diss., Teacher's College, Columbia University, 1953; *The AAU Official Track and Field Handbook: Rules and Records* (New York: Amateur Athletic Union, 1953).

1932 Los Angeles Olympics

"Official Program, Xth Olympiad, 30 July through 14 August 1932"; Mary Hanson Leigh, *The Evolution of Women's Participation in the Summer Olympic Games, 1900–1948*, PhD diss., Ohio State University, 1974.

The Depression

David A. Shannon, ed., *The Great Depression* (Englewood Cliffs, NJ: Prentice-Hall, 1960).

Stella, her job for the Polish Consulate, and running for Poland

State Historical Society of Missouri, folders 63, 77, 120, 124, 125, 190, 217, 233–236, 240–242, 253, 258–261, 263, and 267; Research Center Reference Division Western Research Historical Society, Library Research Center, Cleveland, Ohio, Box 1, folders 2, 6, 7, 10, 12, 14, 15, 16.

Babe Didrikson and the Olympic tryouts

See Gene Schoor, *Babe Didrikson: The World's Greatest Woman Athlete* (New York: Doubleday, 1978).

Avery Brundage

See Allen Guttmann, *The Games Must Go On: Avery Brundage and the Olympic Movement* (New York: Columbia University Press, 1984); the Avery Brundage Collection (Ann Arbor, Michigan) holds material on his life and involvement in the 1936 Olympic Games, as well as on the Olympics themselves. Of particular interest are Box 1: The Amateur Athletic Union Correspondance and documents; Box 68: Volumes Summarizing Brundage and any connection with the 1936 Olympics; Box 93: The International Olympic Minutes; Box 260: United States Olympic Association and Committee Correspondence; Box 273: Avery Brundage speeches. The State Historical Society of Missouri also holds information under the Helen Stephens Life and Times Collection. This can be found in folders 223, 229, and 264.

Babe's arrival in Chicago and the start of the tryouts

Susan E. Cayleff, *Babe: The Life and Legend of Babe Didrikson Zaharias* (Urbana: University of Illinois Press, 1995); Babe Didrikson Zaharias, *This Life I've Led: My Autobiography* (New York: A. S. Barnes, 1955).

Chapter Fourteen: GO WEST, YOUNG WOMEN, GO WEST

Los Angeles Games

Extensive information on the 1932 Los Angeles Games can be found in *The Games of the Xth Olympiad, Los Angeles, 1932: Official Report* (Los Angeles: Xth Olympiade Committee, 1933); see also "Official Program, Xth Olympiad, 30 July through 14 August 1932"; Paul B. Zimmerman, *Los Angeles, the Olympic City, 1932, 1984* (Hollywood: Delmar Watson, 1984).

Harry Chandler and the *Los Angeles Times*

See Kevin Starr, *Material Dreams: Southern California Through the 1920s* (New York: Oxford University Press, 1990); Zimmerman, *Los Angeles, the Olympic City.*

Description of Southern California

The Games of the Xth Olympiad, Los Angeles, 1932; Starr, *Material Dreams*; Zimmerman, *Los Angeles, the Olympic City.*

Community Development Association (CDA)

The Games of the Xth Olympiad, Los Angeles, 1932; Zimmerman, *Los Angeles, the Olympic City.*

The Depression and the outrage over the Olympics

Zimmerman, *Los Angeles, the Olympic City.*

Southern California Committee for the Olympic Games

The Games of the Xth Olympiad, Los Angeles, 1932.

Athletes' train ride to from Evanston to Los Angeles; Denver and the Brown Palace Hotel; the incident involving Babe Didrikson, Tidye Pickett, and Louise Stokes

Babe Didrikson Zaharias, *This Life I've Led: My Autobiography* (New York: A. S. Barnes, 1995); Susan E. Cayleff, *Babe: The Life and Legend of Babe Didrikson Zaharias* (Urbana: University of Illinois Press, 1995).

Men's Olympic Village

The Games of the Xth Olympiad, Los Angeles, 1932; Lois Bryso, "Challenges in Male Hegemony in Sport," in *Sport, Men and the Gender Order: Critical Feminist Perspectives*, ed. Michael A. Messner and Donald F. Saho (Champaign, IL: Human Kinetics Books, 1990).

Women's Chapman Park Hotel

The Games of the Xth Olympiad, Los Angeles, 1932; Paula D. Welch, *The Emergence of American Women in the Summer Olympic Games, 1900–1972*, EdD diss., University of North Carolina, Greensboro, 1975.

Mary Carew

Historical Archives, Medford Public Library, Medford, Massachusetts; Medford Historical Society, Medford, Massachusetts.

Opening Ceremonies; Stella Walsh's win

The Games of the Xth Olympiad, Los Angeles, 1932.

Jean Shiley and Babe's jump-off; Babe's return to Texas

Zaharias, *This Life I've Led.*

Stella moves to Poland, then returns to the United States

The Stella Walsh files, State Historical Society of Missouri, are essential, particularly folders 63, 77, 120, 125, 190, 217, 233–236, 240–242, 253, 258–262, 263,

266, and 267; also, Western Reserve Historical Society Library, Research Center, Cleveland, Ohio, Box 1, folders 2, 6, 7, 10, 12, 14, 15, and 16.

Chapter Fifteen: THE NAZI GAMES

The Berlin Games

Duff Hart-Davis, *Hitler's Games: The 1936 Olympics* (London: Century, 1986); Susan D. Bachrach, United States Holocaust Memorial Museum, *The Nazi Olympics: Berlin, 1936* (Boston: Little, Brown, 2000); *The Olympic Games, Berlin, Official Report*, 2 vols. (Berlin, 1936).

Nazis

Hart-Davis, *Hitler's Games*; Bachrach, *The Nazi Olympics*; William Shirer, *The Rise and Fall of the Third Reich: A History of Nazi Germany* (New York: Simon & Schuster, 1960).

Adolf Hitler

Hart-Davis, *Hitler's Games*; Bachrach, *The Nazi Olympics*; Robert Cecil, *The Myth of the Master Race: Alfred Rosenberg and Nazi Ideology* (London: Dodd, Mead, 1972); Adolf Hitler, *Mein Kampf*, trans. Ralph Manheim (New York: Houghton Mifflin, 1998).

Joseph Goebbels

Hart-Davis, *Hitler's Games*; Bachrach, *The Nazi Olympics*; Cecil, *The Myth of the Master Race*.

Theodor Lewald and Carl Diem

Hart-Davis, *Hitler's Games*; Bachrach, *The Nazi Olympics*.

Gustavus Town Kirby, the US boycott of the Games, and President Roosevelt's unwillingness to become involved in the discussion

Avery Brundage Collection, 1908–82, the 1936 Olympic Games and Its Controversies: Box 1: The Amateur Athletic Union Correspondence and documents; Box 68: Volumes Summarizing Brundage and connection with the 1936 Olympiads; Box 93: The International Olympic Minutes; Box 260: United States Olympic Association and Committee Correspondence. See also Richard Mandell, *The Nazi Olympics* (New York: Macmillan, 1971); Allen Guttmann, *The Games Must Go On: Avery Brundage and the Olympic Movement* (New York: Columbia University Press, 1984).

Avery Brundage and female Olympians

Mary Hanson Leigh, "The Enigma of Avery Brundage and Women's Athletes," *Arena Review* 4 (May 1980): 11–12.

Chapter Sixteen: REBOUND

Backlash against women's participation in the games

Some of this information can be found in the State Historical Society of Missouri, folder 63, Diaries—Women, 1936.

Betty's personal struggles and rebounds

Extensive emails with Richard Schwartz throughout 2015 and 2016 provided a thorough background on Betty's private struggles during this time. Material is also available at the State Historical Society of Missouri, folders 63, 109, 120–122, 128, 184, 221, 232, 234–240, 242, 245–249, 254, and 263–267.

Appearance of Helen Stephens at the Providence tryouts

Some of Helen Stephens's background information comes from a telephone interview with her biographer, Sharon Kinney Hanson, on September 4, 2015; see also Sharon Kinney Hanson, *The Life of Helen Stephens: The Fulton Flash* (Carbondale: Southern Illinois University Press, 2004); Jon Hendershott, *Track's Greatest Women* (Los Altos, CA: Tafnews Press, 1987); Helen Stephens Archives, William Woods University.

Fulton, Missouri

The history of Fulton is detailed extensively in the Helen Stephens Collection, State Historical Society of Missouri, folder 257; see also "The City of Fulton," *Fulton Gazette*, September 3, 1935, reprinted October 13, 1984.

Frank Elmer Stephens and Bertie Stephens

Telephone conversation with Helen Stephens's biographer, Sharon Kinney Hanson, September 4, 2015; Hanson, *The Life of Helen Stephens*; Helen Stephens Archives, William Wood University.

Frank's farm

David A. Shannon, ed., *The Great Depression* (Englewood Cliffs, NJ: Prentice-Hall, 1960).

The birth of Helen's brother; life on the farm; Helen's school

Hanson, *The Life of Helen Stephens*; Helen Stephens Archives, William Woods University.

Coach W. Burton Moore

Helen Stephens Archives, William Woods University.

Helen on the track; Helen and the AAU National Championships; beating Stella Walsh

Helen Stephens Archives, William Woods University; "Stella Walsh and Helen Stephens Will Likely Meet Again," *St. Louis Globe-Democrat*, March 25, 1935; "Fulton Girl Becomes Famous Overnight," *Fulton Daily Sun-Gazette*, March 23 and 25, 1935.

Helen's new training regimen; Helen in college

Helen Stephens Archives, William Woods University.

Chapter Seventeen: OFF TO BERLIN

Providence

Historical information on Providence can be found at the Rhode Island Historical Society, Providence, Rhode Island.

Dee Boeckmann becomes coach

Dee Boeckmann's career is highlighted in the extensive files at the State Historical Society of Missouri, folders 20, 37, 63, 112, 114–123, 125, 127, 128, 183, 185, 229, 232–234, 236, 240, 245, 258, 261, 261, and 266.

Losing Babe

Babe's expulsion from track and field is highlighted in several books. A particularly good one is Susan E. Cayleff, *Babe: The Life and Legend of Babe Didrikson Zaharias* (Urbana: University of Illinois Press, 1995); Babe also talks about it in *This Life I've Led: My Autobiography* (New York: A. S. Barnes, 1955).

Betty arrives in Providence

Betty's arrival was heralded as the comeback of the century. *The Providence Journal* of July 2, 1936, wrote, "Smiling Betty, Hurt in Plane Cash, Who They Said, Could Not Live, Here for Olympic Trials."

Meets begin at Brown University

Upon the athletes' arrival, *The Providence Journal* began its reportage. On July 2, 1936, it wrote, "Headed for the Berlin Olympics with a Brief Stop-over in Providence." On July 3, it went on, "Girls Hopeful of Olympic Berths Flock into the City." And on July 4, it continued, "Women Track and Field Stars Who Will Compete in Olympic Trials Today," with a long description of the athletes.

Economic circumstances

David A. Shannon, ed., *The Great Depression* (Englewood Cliffs, NJ: Prentice-Hall, 1960).

Betty's bracelet

Betty wore a bracelet given to her by Douglas MacArthur soon after she won the gold medal in 1928. She never took it off and had it with her during the plane crash. It was a source of comfort and strength. Information on this most precious piece of jewelry comes from an email correspondence with her son, Richard Schwartz, on February 9, 2016.

Betty dropping out of college, unemployment, and looking for work

Shannon, *The Great Depression*.

Helen arrives in Providence; the heats

The Olympic tryouts are extensively detailed in the files of the State Historical Society of Missouri, folders 64 and 65.

Betty's new role with the athletes; Betty crosses the finish line

State Historical Society of Missouri, folders 62, 63, 66, 109, 120–128, 184, 221, 232, 234, 240, 242, 245–249, 247, 250, 254, and 263–267.

Helen is victorious

Helen's victory was written up in *The Providence Journal* on July 6, 1936, with the headline "Helen Stephens Sets World Mark for 100 Meters."

Betty makes the team

Betty making the team and detailed information on the rest of the athletes were displayed in *The Providence Sunday Journal*, July 5, 1936, with the headline "Striking Down the Road That Leads All the Way to Berlin." The same day, the newspaper ran several other articles, including "Helen Stephens Wins Top Honors at Brown Field" and "US Entries Will Be Chosen in 6 Events at Brown Field."

Chapter Eighteen: PHENOMS

No money to sail

David A. Shannon, ed., *The Great Depression* (Englewood Cliffs, NJ: Prentice-Hall, 1960).

Betty on the deck with old teammates

Historical Brochures/United States Lines/1920s GG Archives provided information on the SS *Manhattan*.

Betty rooms with Helen Stephens

When Betty became Helen Stephens's roommate, the two also became great friends, a relationship that would last for the rest of their lives. Richard Schwartz detailed that friendship on June 16, 2015, in an email. See also Helen Stephens, Olympic Diary (unpublished), July 15–September 16, 1936.

Helen's crush on Betty

A lot of information on Betty's involvement in the 1936 Olympics, her friendship with Helen, and her participation in the Olympics can be found in the Helen Stephens Collection, State Historical Society of Missouri, folders 63, 109 120–122, 128, 184, 221, 234–240, 242, 245–249, 254, and 263–267.

Helen's lesbianism

Helen's sex life is detailed in her diary, and also in the Helen Stephens Collection, State Historical Society of Missouri, folders 258, 266, and 267; see also Susan K. Cahn, *Coming on Strong: Gender and Sexuality in Twentieth-Century Women's Sport* (New York: Free Press, 1994).

Helen's past rape and childhood experience with her teacher

These are detailed in the Helen Stephens Collection, State Historical Society of Missouri, folders 64 and 65.

Fraternizing on the *Manhattan*; whiling away the hours; Jesse Owens; shin splints

Helen Stephens, Olympic Diary, July 15–September 16, 1936.

The "Berlin question"

The "Berlin question" came into play while the athletes were on the *Manhattan*. Helen Stephens's involvement is detailed not only in her diary but also in the Helen Stephens Collection, State Historical Society of Missouri, folder 63.

Arriving in Germany and Berlin

Helen Stephens Collection, State Historical Society of Missouri, Germany—Description and travels, folder 63; see also Richard D. Mandell, *The Nazi Olympics* (New York: Macmillan, 1971).

Female dormitories

Helen Stephens, Olympic Diary, July 15–September 16, 1936.

Male Olympic Village

Helen Stephens, Olympic Diary, July 15–September 16, 1936; Susan D. Bachrach, United States Holocaust Memorial Museum, *The Nazi Olympics, Berlin, 1936* (Boston: Little, Brown, 2000); Mandell, *The Nazi Olympics*.

Walking through the city

William Shirer, *The Rise and Fall of the Third Reich: A History of Nazi Germany* (New York: Simon & Schuster, 1960).

Opening ceremonies

Extensive information on the opening ceremonies can be found in the Helen Stephens Collection, State Historical Society of Missouri, folder 65, Programs, 1936; see also folders 62, 66, 247, 250, and 267.

Adolf Hitler

Information on Hitler can be found in the Helen Stephens Collection, State Historical Society of Missouri, folders 63, 258, 261–264, and 267.

Helen wins the 100 meters

Helen's win was detailed in a collection of newspaper clippings; these can be found in the Helen Stephens Collection, State Historical Society of Missouri, folder 64, Newspaper Clippings, 1936.

Stella Walsh

Information on Stella Walsh's involvement during the 1936 Olympics is available in the Helen Stephens Collection, State Historical Society of Missouri; the most relevant folders are 63, 77, 120, 124, 125, 190, 217, 233–236, 240–242, 253, 258–262, 263, 266, and 267.

Helen meets Hitler

Helen's meeting with Hitler is detailed fully in Helen Stephens, Olympic Diary, July 15–September 16, 1936.

Festivities after the win

Helen Stephens, Olympic Diary, July 15–September 16, 1936.

Harriet Bland

Helen felt an unusual dislike for Harriet, an athlete she found brash, annoying, and unlikable. Oddly enough, some of the traits she found annoying in Harriet were the same ones she adored in Betty Robinson, but there was a difference between how Harriet and Betty went about their lives, showing their likes and dislikes, their athleticism, and life all around. Information on Harriet can be found in the Helen Stephens Collection, State Historical Society of Missouri, folders 63, 115–118, 121, 122, 128, 218, 229, 245, 258, 262, and 263.

Helen's gender rumors and physical exam

Helen Stephens, Olympic Diary, July 15–September 16, 1936.

Women's relay race; picks for the race; Betty's role in the race; Tidye's dismissal from the race

Helen Stephens, Olympic Diary, July 15–September 16, 1936; Helen Stephens Collection, State Historical Society of Missouri, folders 64 and 65; also folders 20, 37, 63, 114, 123, 125, 127, 128, 183, 185, 220, 232, 234, 236, 240, 245, 258, 261, 265, and 266; also folders related to Betty Robinson: 63, 109, 120, 128, 184, 221, 232, 234, 240, 242, 245–249, 254, and 263–267.

Ilse Dörffeldt's blunder

Helen Stephens, Olympic Diary, July 15–September 16, 1936; Helen Stephens Collection, State Historical Society of Missouri, folders 64 and 65.

EPILOGUE

Betty returns home; Hollywood comes calling

Information on Betty's short-lived Hollywood dreams comes from email correspondence with her son, Richard Schwartz, on March 10, 2016.

Betty marries and divorces, remarries

Betty had a two-week marriage with the glamour agent Eddie Napolilli, who was intent on making her famous in the movies. Information on this marriage and the subsequent annulment comes from email correspondence with her son, Richard Schwartz, on March 10, 2016. Betty met her second husband in a diner lounge. Their courtship was quick, and their marriage soon followed. Information on this private side of her life comes from email correspondence with Richard Schwartz on March 8, 2016.

Helen Stephens

Sharon Kinney Hanson, *The Life of Helen Stephens: The Fulton Flash* (Carbondale: Southern Illinois University Press, 2004); Helen Stephens Archives, William Woods University.

Stella Walsh

Information on Stella Walsh can be found in the Helen Stephens Collection, State Historical Society of Missouri, folders 63, 77, 120, 124, 125, 190, 217, 233–236, 240–242, 253, 258–261, 263, 266, and 267; also see the Western Reserve Historical Society Library, Research Center, Cleveland Ohio, Box 1, folders 2, 6, 7, 10, 12, 14, 15, and 16.

Babe Didrikson

On Babe's life after the 1932 Olympics, her expulsion from the Games, and plans afterward, see Babe Didrikson Zaharias Collection, Special Collections and University Archives, Mary and John Gray Library, Lamar University; also Susan E. Cayleff, *Babe: The Life and Legend of Babe Didrikson Zaharias* (Urbana: University of Illinois Press, 1995).

INDEX

ABOUT THE AUTHOR

ROSEANNE MONTILLO is the author of two other works of nonfiction, *The Lady and Her Monsters* and *The Wilderness of Ruin*. She holds an MFA in creative writing from Emerson College, where she taught courses on the intersection of literature and history. She lives outside of Boston.